THE WAR ON GENDER

POSTMODERNISM AND TRANS IDENTITY

For Caroline and Ursula
and John Blundell.

THE WAR ON GENDER

POSTMODERNISM AND TRANS IDENTITY

CLAIRE RAE RANDALL

ARKTOS
LONDON 2022

ISBN   978-1-914208-81-2 (Paperback)
                    978-1-914208-82-9 (Hardback)
                    978-1-914208-83-6 (Ebook)

EDITING   Constantin von Hoffmeister

COVER & LAYOUT Tor Westman

🌐 Arktos.com   ❑ fb.com/Arktos   ◐ @arktosmedia   ⊙ arktosmedia

CONTENTS

Sections in Appendices included for reference used with kind permission of Hansard, Economic and Social Research Council and Dr Sally Hines.

ACKNOWLEDGEMENTS

I SHOULD LIKE TO express my gratitude to all of those who have given me so much support and encouragement during the long process of completing this book and who have waited so patiently for me to do so.

Most especially Carol Downing of Leeds Combined Arts who was so understanding and sympathetic in the face of the numerous interruptions and delays caused by, amongst other things, the circumstances of my two family bereavements during the process of writing, and who had waited so patiently for me to be able to launch it at an LCA book event. Carol herself sadly passed away suddenly only a month after I signed with Arktos and I am extremely glad that she saw her patience and support had finally been rewarded before she left us.

I should also like to extend my gratitude to my proofreader Rosemary O'Dea and the several others who have read drafts of the text and given me invaluable feedback, especially the lady who gave me a very close proofreading but wished to remain anonymous.

I am most grateful to Dr Jay Hayes-Light, Director of the UK Intersex Association (UKIA) for helping me to identify the extremely unusual intersex condition known as 5 α-Reductase Deficiency. Also to Richard Smith and Mark Griffiths for their helpful suggestions.

I am indebted to the Literary Estate of C. S. Lewis to whom I extend my gratitude for permission to quote short extracts from his *Perelandra* in illustration of the metaphysical concepts of gender.

I am extremely grateful to Professor Dr Sally Hines formerly of Leeds University School of Social Sciences for granting permission to include the until now unpublished paper of her research into the outcomes of the 2004 GRA in which I participated as a subject.

In particular I must thank Dr John E. Blundell for so graciously allowing me to dedicate this book to him, as well as my old friends Caroline and Ursula without whom I might never have begun this journey.

GLOSSARY OF TERMS

aetiology	The study of causation
afab	Assigned female at birth
AIS	Androgen Insensitivity Syndrome
amab	Assigned male at birth
CAIS	Complete Androgen Insensitivity Syndrome
CD	Cross Dresser
Chaos Magic(k)	A belief system which holds that the ground of existence is chaos and that there is no such thing as objective truth. Conceptually related to postmodernism
cisgender	Normative physical and social gender characteristics
FtM	Female to Male (Transsexual)
gender fluid	The claimed property of having a variable gender identity
gender fuck	Purposely presenting conflicting gender cues so as to shock and confuse people's conventional expectations
gender queer	Deliberately presenting ambiguous gender cues
Hermaphrodite	An individual having reproductive organs of both sexes
IS	Intersex: the quality of having interme-diate sexual characteristics
LGBT	Lesbian, Gay, Bi-sexual and Trans
Logos	Reason, cosmic law, the guiding principle of existence

MtF	Male to Female (Transsexual)
non-binary	Someone who claims or believes that they do not to fit into the gender binary of nature
PAIS	Partial Androgen Insensitivity Syndrome
queer	A term used by sexual or gender non-conforming individuals to apply to themselves, deriving from the use previously as a term of abuse
radfem	Radical Feminist
stealth	Term used by transsexuals to describe passing unnoticed in the desired gender
teedar	My own adaptation of *Gaydar* applied to reading trans people
TG	Transgender: general umbrella term used to describe all gender non-conformists
trans	My preferred colloquial term for transsexuals
trans trender	A person who engages in trans like behaviour for amusement or virtue signalling
trans*	The all-inclusive term used by those who wish to conflate all gender atypical conditions under one term, now apparently out of favour
trap	A transgender person who has not had medical reassignment but passes successfully in the female gender and engages in seducing heterosexual men
TS	Transsexual
TV	Transvestite
TV/TS group	Social group for Transvestites and Transsexuals

FOREWORD

'M TRANSSEXUAL and I went through my transition from male to female in the eighties.

Things have changed a lot since then and I'm grateful for the greater acceptance that people such as myself have won over the years.

Yet the *genderqueer* and *radical trans activists* who are currently seeking to destroy the model of gender which suits and satisfies over 99.5% of the population worldwide do not represent my views, or to my knowledge the views of many successfully transitioned transsexuals whose only desire was to pass in their preferred gender and disappear into society.

The idea of changing societal norms about what gender *is* or how it should be expressed was never an intention of mine and indeed to seek to do so would be entirely antithetical to my own path of trying to find a means of being which both minimised my own stress and at the same time allowed me to interface with society in as frictionless a manner as possible.

The changes in social attitudes around these issues which are being pushed through and even put into law at a rate of knots at this present time are disturbing to many people because they seek to enforce ideas which seem to have come from nowhere suddenly to become entirely dominant.

Where such radical changes are involved we should always employ the precautionary principle as a matter of course. A way of seeing gender, a map of reality which has served us since the earliest times and which we see omnipresent in nature, should not be discarded wholesale without good reason, and before we have a tried and tested replacement ready to put in its place.

Postmodern Gender Theory claims to do this, but I believe it is a sham. All it has is *critique* which fails ultimately to address the evolutionary and survival adaptive nature of the phenomenon which is being interrogated, but instead sees everything in terms of social power, moral blame, privilege and oppression, things inappropriate to the requirements of biology and evolution from which we sprang.

The strict binary of male and female, where never the twain shall overlap, is a model which has become a little creaky with age, but only because of those who seek to maintain it as a digital rather than an analogue system. The postmodernists argue destructively that anomalies destroy this model, while my position is that these anomalies can be fitted into an expanded version of the existing model with a little adjustment and open-mindedness.

We should seek to see gender as archetype, as fractal expression of universal energy propagation, not as a mere ideational construct or even a fixed and rigid division in nature. It is a dynamic, an essential function of existence.

The implications of this are profound. Either we seek to rewrite and override our instincts with the political enforcement of assumed moral imperatives, or we readjust our focus and allow that there is a little bit of indeterminacy around some fuzzy edges which might involve cognitive engagement, but that this doesn't abolish the basic model of gender we have inherited. It revises and enlarges it, as Copernicus revised and enlarged on Ptolemy. But the world was still a globe, the heavens still looked and behaved the same, the Moon still orbited the Earth; our understanding had grown of how we fitted into it all, and our context in the Universe; however, nothing in our immediate experience of it had changed.

This is what I seek to do here, in the face of the wildfires that are occurring all around in which suggestible people are being led into dangerous territory by the Pied Pipers of Gender Studies and radical trans activism, who wish to destroy traditional notions of gender.

Gender reassignment is a serious business and should be treated as such. The exploitation of the phenomenon for the political ends that it seems is being done at this present time is something which I never signed up for as part of my transition or life plan. Rather it seems to me that this is a cynical exploitation of the situations of people like myself for political ends, which extend beyond gender itself, to which I do not wish to lend my support.

On the contrary, I see it as my bounden duty to call this out and to challenge it.

As to a proper Gender Theory itself, all I believe we need, and which I propose, is a slightly enlarged and more nuanced understanding rooted in developmental biology and philosophy that encompasses the anomalies and reaches toward an *archetypal* understanding of gender, and the dominance of *Social* Gender Theory will be broken.

INTRODUCTION

And he that breaks a thing to find out what it is has left the path of wisdom.[1]

— Gandalf in *The Fellowship of the Ring* by J. R. R. Tolkien

IT IS WITH SOME reluctance that I find myself putting pen to paper and finger to keyboard on this vexed subject of gender.

To 'out' myself as a person with a past which includes gender reassignment over three decades ago is to a large degree contradictory to the position I develop here in this book, namely that transsexuals really should maintain their invisibility in society for the numerous reasons I detail. Not least sustaining the social perceptions of one's identity with one's peers and personal privacy.

For most of the thirty years and more since I established my revised identity I have endeavoured, with reasonable success it would appear, to be 'stealth' as the now probably out of date, and doubtless out of favour, slang used to go.

And I was quite happy to do so. It was fairly obvious to me at the time that most people didn't want to know too much about it. This phenomenon, in which I partook, was definitely on the edge, and scared people with their own misunderstandings, unconscious projections and fantasies.

Much better to be *stealth* and simply get on with your life.

---

1   Tolkien, J. R. R. *The Fellowship of the Ring*, p. 272. George Allen & Unwin (Publishers) Ltd, 1954.

I had art therapy clients, I worked as a nurse and then as a lecturer in further education and no client, no patient or student challenged me in an era when such a thing was quite possible. Even on the street I only recall one occasion of the mildest of bother, and that, in my early days, lasted only a few seconds.

But as someone once observed to me, it seemed likely to him that due to evolutionary recognition templates, one tends to intuitively categorise faces, people, as male or female, and then once this near instant judgement has been made, the gestalt of the person falls into place. This is akin to *figure/ground* illusions in which once one has seen one interpretation, it is hard to see the other, and vice versa. The brain likes to make perceptual judgements, and these judgements must be survival adaptive to threat or opportunity, and they must be fast, pre-rational.

So declaring myself as transsexual at the start of this book doesn't do me any good in that it allows, almost encourages, people to *not* perceive me as I would like to be perceived.

However, in that thirty-year period the presentation by the media of this phenomenon, and the social engineering around it that has attempted to exploit it for the purposes of *social justice* and *gender neutrality*, has made it into something that I do not recognise as being representative of my own lifelong experience.

Even the term *Transsexual* has been abandoned and attacked as *problematic* by many, despite the fact that many thousands of people around the world with experiences close to mine have been happy with the term since it was popularised by Harry Benjamin back in the 1950s, because it is supposed to imply some claimed superiority, rather than a taxonomic distinction between those who have, or desire to, become morphologically congruent with their desired sex and those who haven't. It seems that the only ones who are not bothered by people seeking to pass as women in female spaces while still retaining what they claim to be *female penises* are those still retaining them, and their political allies who seek to use this as a means of dismantling the entire conventional understanding of gender that has existed since time immemorial.

Transsexuals like myself believe that we have experienced developmental anomalies which gave us a nervous system more akin to the opposite sex of our bodies and wish to change the characteristics of those bodies to the sexed characteristics we feel should be the case. We know that we cannot change our chromosomes, but there is more to the expression of sex and gender than chromosomes alone, it is the neurological result that matters, and the desired congruency with one's body. Thus, transsexual.

It is remarkable how quickly the move from *transsexual* to *transgender* has been achieved, largely through the work of what I would term *Cultural Marxists* in places such as the Centre for Interdisciplinary Gender Studies at Leeds University (CIGS), to which I briefly entertained the idea of applying for the purpose of gaining a Master's or possibly even a PhD in the subject. *Cultural Marxism* is the practice of applying Marxist critique to culture rather than economics, seeking to break it down in ways summarised by Saul Alinsky in his *Rules for Radicals*, critiquing marriage, heterosexuality, families and so on in order to make it more vulnerable to infiltration, undermining and attack.

Fortunately I spent a year or two associating with some of their lecturers and post-graduate students, which gave me the understanding that this was not what I was looking for.

When I told Dr Sally Hines, then Director of CIGS that, having looked at the subject and her department, I had come to the conclusion that should I enter it, I would be constantly faced by the opposition of an entirely different mindset in nigh on every member of staff or student I might encounter, she replied that I could 'fight my corner'; but by then I had read Sun Tzu's *The Art of War*, and knew that not only should I pick my battles, but that the only way to win a battle that is unwinnable is not to fight it in the first place, if it is an impossible situation.

And it clearly *was* an impossible situation.

Gender Studies considered it axiomatic that gender was simply a social construction, that people such as myself had *acquired* our gender identities through some kind of social influences, modelling or reinforcement and choice, that there were no fundamental differences between the genders, that the use of the term *sex* was now out of date, and that we were heading towards a *gender neutral* world.

But what surprised me even more was that there were a couple of transsexuals in the department who went along with this.

I, on the other hand, had considered it axiomatic that there were differences between the sexes and their evolutionary psychologies, and that these differences were largely encoded in the nervous system. Thus the old term *'a woman's mind in a man's body'* really could be true, especially as there was evidence that the nervous system gained its sexual imprint at a different stage of foetal development to the genitals.

I considered this axiomatic because there is a large body of evidence that has been garnered over the decades indicating that this, the traditional view of gender, is basically correct.

Gender Studies, on the other hand, not only ignores but dismisses the evidence and arguments of evolutionary psychology, and instead studies social differences between cultures so as to demonstrate that all gender differences are merely socially constructed.

The axioms of Gender Studies are not based on the hard evidence of the examination of physiology, developmental neurology or comparative psychology. Rather they are posited on the basis of linguistic deconstruction of traditional concepts, the use of anomalies to argue to generalities, and politically applied moral judgements of social justice.

If this had been all that had been at stake I would have simply ditched my application and moved on.

However, in the decade or so since this went behind me I have seen the rising tide of its influence throughout society.

Transgender had already largely replaced *Transsexual* as the term in common parlance early in the new century, but now we began to see the assertion of *non-binary, gender neutral* and *multiple genders.*

These have been promoted by the left-leaning media and played on notions of *transphobia* to police those who wish to critique this absolute deconstruction of gender into something that allows anyone to be anything simply by declaring it to be so, as if being a *goth* or a *punk* were legal genders.

Simultaneously we have seen a massive increase in the number of people coming forward for transsexual treatments, a concomitant rise in the number of those regretting irreversible surgeries, and the introduction of gender treatments for ever younger minors.

There was a time when I might have been sympathetic to some aspects of this. People suffering with a variety of gender difficulties and confusions can be helped by being allowed the social space to explore their feelings and identities. Gender dysphoria and atypical behaviour in children can be monitored in order to assess the long-term probabilities of whether they might be persistently *gender dysphoric*, or whether they will experience remission of these feelings and adapt comfortably to who they are, as often occurs.

But we have now already gone far beyond taking a more sensitive approach, which can be helpful to those experiencing gender identity issues in their youth.

A recent piece of insanity around this was the proposal for a *Gender Declaration Bill,* whereby people would be empowered to be recognised in their desired gender simply by declaring it to be so. Fortunately this has been abandoned, at least for the present, by the British government for a mixture of reasons including public resistance, but we cannot be complacent and assume this is all over. The ideological war is far from won and we must kill this thing dead before we can rest or it will regrow heads like the Hydra of legend and continue to predate on our culture.

I heard many voices in the then online trans communities I inhabited back in 2004 or so raised in concern that the Gender Recognition Act of that year allowed for the possibility that people who had had no actual medical treatment to make them morphologically congruent with their desired gender could gain recognition in such.

I recall Andrew Selous, MP, raising the issue of such people, 'male to female' *transgenders*, who might go to communal women's changing rooms and cause offence whilst disrobing. This was dismissed by David Lammy, the Labour MP steering the Bill through the Commons, who said that no one would do such a thing, a statement we all thought absurd at the time. It was claimed that Gender Recognition Certificates would only be given to those who had not undergone morphology-changing surgeries in cases where the individual had sought to have them but had been rejected on strictly medical grounds, and that this would not become a commonplace. There is no provision for this in the actual Act which was passed by Parliament, and persistent pressure by lobbyists, especially since the 2010 Equalities Act, has effectively empowered even non-socially transitioned transgenders to claim social categorisation and the use of toilet facilities of their choice. In some instances on college campuses in both Europe and America student unions have lobbied their own women students to not be *transphobic* — not to question anyone who doesn't fit *gender stereotypes* whom they might find in their women's toilets.

But numerous amongst our number were the voices who warned that before long this would *indeed* become commonplace.

I recall an online discussion I was having on a website about challenging transphobia back in about 2006 or 2007, which I had initially thought seemed like a good place to be. It rapidly became not such a good place when I was attacked and vilified for suggesting that a degree of morphological congruence in the case of male to female transsexuals really was desirable if one expected to be taken seriously in one's presumed gender. I remember one response in particular which read: '*I'm perfectly happy with my female penis.*' This was probably the moment of inception when I realised I would one day have to write this book which you now have before you.

Policing how people choose to live their lives is not my principal concern in writing this book.

Rather I hope to help people who are experiencing forms of gender dysphoria and atypical gender identities to cut through the confusion of snake oil ideas with which they are currently being fed, and which are leading some into confused identities, while it is leading others to make permanent mistakes on a whim. It is also my hope that I will do something to help rebuild the normative concepts of sex and gender which trans people would, I believe, benefit from fitting into.

By this I do not mean to suggest that people with strong gender dysphoria should be socially pressured to conform to their birth sex, but rather that finding a niche in the existing gender structure is a more satisfactory result for all concerned, because the general population is also part of this *negotiation*, as the Gender Theorists would probably say, and reorganising the whole of society for the benefit of a tiny minority will not do; especially when this minority fragments into a multitude of totally diverse groups who often have very little in common other than the fact that they feel, or are perceived as, anomalous. The war on gender wants not only to eradicate all social concepts of gender but biological sex itself, abolishing all structure as inherently *oppressive*.

Perhaps I should say at this stage that I would very much have preferred to have been born as a normal boy or a normal girl. But that was not the case. And as I commented to an internet radio host once, I think I probably made some kind of pre-life choice, agreement, or commitment to do this in an arrangement when I was preparing for this incarnation. I shall not labour my spiritual and metaphysical beliefs here, as I know there are many out there who would like to tie me to purely material evidence and linguistic analysis, but there is more to reality than mere matter and the psychological constructs we may make around our experience of it, and I shall spend some time with that later. But for now, let me just say that for me an understanding of my own gender identity has more to do with Kant's *Thing In Itself* and Heidegger's *Dasein* or *Being* than it does with ideas of social constructs and oppression. While there are clearly likely to be material causes involved in this thing, in the end it is an existential question, a question on the path of individuation, a Jungian point in the psyche that must be at least brought to light and examined.

> If you bring forth what is within you, what you bring forth will save you. If you do not bring forth what is within you, what you do not bring forth will destroy you.
>
> — Gospel of Thomas, v 70

By quoting this apocryphal text I do not seek to authorise any and all impulses that might emerge from the Unconscious, but mean rather that these impulses should be brought out and dealt with in whatever way works best. The Jungian bringing to Consciousness of contents of the Unconscious which otherwise would remain in the Shadow. I believe that anyone who says that all this gender confusion and transition is perfectly normal and good and that anyone could choose to do it without serious questioning is running on the edge of crazy, to be frank.

We have numerous parties participating in all this. There is the seeming promotion of transgenderism by certain elements for ever earlier medical treatments for people too young to have adequately tested and understood the impulses, motivations and ideas which are emerging into consciousness as they grow and individuate, as well as the Gender Lobby, who argue that this is all a matter of social constructs and choice while dismissing people who have actually had personal experience of it which doesn't conform to their theories. In opposition to these we have the *TERFs* — *Trans Exclusionary Radical*

Feminists who want to take all this down. I am somewhere in there, not agreeing with most of it.

I should also make it clear at this early stage that I have the firm conviction that transsexualism is a real thing, a syndrome if you will, and that for some people reassignment can be a last resort to relieve the awful burden of strong 'gender', or perhaps we should say 'physical sex', dysphoria. The phenomenon has existed in various cultures at various epochs, and it has been socially managed in various ways. I shall explore this as we go and give my own understanding of it, but this is principally for the purpose of contrasting it with postmodern views and Gender Theory which hold that there is no objective condition or value and which I believe has exploited the genuine condition of *transsexualism* in order to spread it as some kind of new gospel which will free the world from gender tyranny under the revised form of *Transgender*.

This exploitation takes a variety of forms, as a means of undermining traditional concepts of gender as *oppressive conformity* imposed by the patriarchy, of psychologically policing the population with concepts I personally would identify as *Newspeak* and of socially engineering the more malleable members of our society into identities they would otherwise never have claimed on their own.

It seems likely that taking such a position I will be taken to task by those who will say or who have already said in private correspondence or on comment threads online, 'Why is it all right for you to be a transsexual and not for others? Why are you so special?'

To which my reply is that I do not hold such a position. As I have already posited, transsexualism is a fairly ubiquitous phenomenon to most cultures, and has been dealt with in different ways. It is not my purpose to police how people live their lives, but rather to expose and take down the false message with which Gender Theory and its advocates presume to infect the minds of our young people; namely that gender is an arbitrary construct, that it is oppressive, and that all ideas to the contrary must be brought down.

When I took the momentous decision to act on my life-long and enduring sense that I should have been a girl, that the body I inhabited felt alien to me, and pursue medical gender reassignment, the world was a very different place.

Today, I frequently read comments in message threads on social media in which people condemn those who loosely encourage gender reassignment as if it were the latest fashion, which is what it seems to be to some.

I am often reticent in these online discussions, though I agree with much that is said, since those I would be addressing do not have properly elaborated knowledge or understanding of the phenomenon, a recognition that there are competing factions, and so on. They might already have strong views that are resistant to being challenged with evidence which doesn't entirely fit their world view.

Often in such cases I might get severely attacked, perhaps by some who mistakenly misread me to be promoting transgenderism when I out myself, or just for the fact of identifying myself as *transsexual* at all. Then I am attacked as mentally ill, a gender deconstructionist, a sexual pervert, a sinner, and the rest, regardless of the fact that I agree with these people on the poisonous nature of the modern Gender Lobby, the social engineering around and associated with it, and on a wider collection of not obviously connected social and political issues; the principal connecting factor being that I am coming from a socially conservative (with a small c) position.

And I will acknowledge that they may have some reason to imagine that I possibly hold the views of the far-left gender deconstructionists, or at least that I would be generally of the Left, simply because most trans people are, at least the visible ones. It is my firm conviction that this is largely because they have been seduced by the promotion of Gender Theory, indeed that there is some sort of unholy alliance between Gender Theorists and the Left. Gender Dysphoria is seen as the result of oppression and victimhood, not as being an atypical neurodevelopmental condition (which would leave no one to blame). It has become one of the principal tools of the resurgent Left, along with a number of other mass social factors, which I shall leave aside for now.

But having gone through the *Slough of Gender Deconstruction* and found it wanting, found that it did not account for my own experience, that it tried to explain away that experience in its own terms, terms that were designed not around a real examination of the evidence of experience, but to couch that experience as an expression of their political stance on the world, I reject it.

Certainly I will allow that science cannot be entirely free of social context and influence, but to purposely seek your results and interpretations to not only fit the preferred political paradigm, but to use the phenomenon you are examining as an outlet and tool of it, is not only bad science, it is corrupt.

I denounce postmodern Gender Theory and most of the cultural lobby that is associated with it, and here it is my task to explain things more fully than I have been able to do in online discussions or even the podcast interviews that I have kindly been invited to engage in.

Achieving completed medical gender reassignment in the eighties was an entirely different thing from today. The social stigma was still fairly acute, the standard of transition expected by the Gender Identity Clinic I attended was high, and indeed to even see the consultant was a fairly major achievement. It took me almost a year to get past the various gatekeepers once I had set to it.

The resistance from all sides that had to be overcome was severe. And I will make my first comment that is likely to get a hyper triggered reaction from the LGBT lobby — *it should be.*

Why? You may ask why I would say that severe resistance to going through with transition should be necessary when the internal conflict of strong gender dysphoria is already so unpleasant.

I would reply that it must be tested.

Even as potentially objective neurological, and possibly genetic, tests are being developed with which to evaluate and diagnose transsexual patients, they still need to experience their own *self-evaluation*, and understand the implications, such as being unable to have children and how this may affect their prospects for relationships.

This is the basis of the so called *RLE — Real Life Experience,* which is still theoretically required by most Gender Identity Clinics. The difference today is that social attitudes have become so constrained by political correctness and the influence of *Gender Theory* that someone presenting to a GIC could pretty much appear as they liked and claim that they are *in gender,* and anyone disagreeing could be accused of *transphobia* and *hate speech.*

I can imagine a situation fairly soon, if it hasn't already happened, in which patients at GICs might demand treatments, including permanent surgeries, claiming that it is in their human rights, and sue if they are refused, regardless of their progress in transition.

The whole field has fallen into a conceptual confusion, in which competing, even disagreeing, theories are conflated and served up as a kind of intoxicating melange intended to separate us all from our innate instincts and traditional sense of identity.

The testing of the motivation, the drive, the desire to be something that, on the face of it, you are not is surely a reasonable thing. As the saying goes, extraordinary claims require extraordinary evidence. Nature has made male and female as they are for a reason, and if you feel you are anomalous and have the need to readjust how you fit into that framework of nature, then you should do it in such a way that it works, that you fit into the niche you feel you were meant for, that you are *seen* to fit in.

To do this effectively will surely involve overcoming obstacles and difficulties, mostly within oneself, unless Political Correctness removes those difficulties for you, in which case you will never go through the learning curve that would otherwise have been involved. I have known several *trans* people, one might call them *pseudo-transsexuals,* who in facing these challenges realised either that they could not cope with the demands that this path imposed upon them, or indeed that they were not really transsexual at all.

Okay, wait a minute, 'What exactly is this *transsexual* thing that you keep being so specific about?' you ask.

It has in the new century come to be renamed by some as *Harry Benjamin Syndrome (HBS)* after the clinician who did most to formalise the diagnosis of the condition in the 1950s and who described it in his 1966 book *The Transsexual Phenomenon*,[2] 'True transsexuals feel that they belong to the other sex, they want to be and function as members of the opposite sex, not only to appear as such. For them, their sex organs, the primary (testes) as well as the secondary (penis and others) are disgusting deformities that must be changed by the surgeon's knife.'[3] This has come to be controversial in some circles because he developed the hypothesis that those with this syndrome were what might be described as *psychic intersex* having intersex or cross sex brains from their sexual anatomy — those who experience no *dysphoria* and seek no physical reassignment surgeries to be congruent in their desired gender claim that this was an artificial division. We shall consider this at length.

Firstly, let me briefly describe the syndrome, and then present you with a pair of simple, logical syllogisms in order to test the propositions that men and women are the same apart from physical characteristics (drives, motivations, skill tendencies, social tropisms and other behaviours), or else men and women are not only different in their physical characteristics, but also in the area of thought and behaviour (as previously listed) and how these might relate to trans identities.

---

2   Harry Benjamin. *The Transsexual Phenomenon*. The Julian Press, Inc. Publisher, New York (1966).

3   Harry Benjamin *The Transsexual Phenomenon* online PDF version (2020) http://www.mut23.de/texte/Harry%20Benjamin%20-%20The%20 Transsexual%20Phenomenon.pdf.

Transsexualism is a persistent, lifelong sense of oneself that one should have been a member of the opposite sex to the one you apparently belong to, not just as a social being, but in all ways physically too. Gender, or sex, dysphoria includes a sense of physical disgust with the sexual characteristics of one's own body and a concomitant desire to be of the opposite sex. It seems that it may be on the rise due to endocrine-disrupting chemicals messing with people's hormone levels, especially *in utero*. Benjamin described six degrees of cross gender identification in his *Sex and Gender Role Disorientation and Indecision (Males)* from stage 1 *Pseudo-transvestite* to stage 6 *High Intensity Transsexual*. His association with Kinsey's *Sexual Orientation Scale* has since been dropped as inappropriate and misleading; some consider his classifications to be outdated, but in simple taxonomic terms they still apply to some degree, without the associations of sexual orientation, although the lower-end classifications may in some cases possibly correlate with acquired sexual fetishism and paraphilias which aren't related to neurological factors. Only these should today probably be recognised as not fitting Benjamin's otherwise sage statement that '[i]t must be emphasized again that the remaining six types are not and never can be sharply separated.'

Now let us present the syllogisms.

Major Proposition:
Men and women are the same in all but the obvious physical differences.
Minor proposition:
Transsexuals think they should be in the opposite gendered body to the one they find themselves in, explaining this as feeling as if they are 'a woman in a man's body'.
Ergo: *Transsexuals must be deluded since there is no difference between men's and women's brains and therefore minds.*
Or: *The state of having a transsexual identity is one of choice, social construction or conditioning.*

The Major Proposition above is one that the Gender Lobby would agree with; the Minor one they would disagree with in any objective sense, holding that such a feeling of one's identity could not be inherent or innate. That it is merely subjective, and must in some way have been acquired, through learning, through association, through trauma or some other mechanism.

They would then disagree with the conclusion that transsexuals are deluded, not for what I would consider a good reason, but rather because they think it is a perfectly reasonable thing for anyone to choose to do, in effect, which is the alternate conclusion. They ignore the evidence of discoveries which show sex differences in the brain.[4]

Clearly this is unsatisfactory. Or at least it is to me.

So let us try the second syllogism.

Major Proposition:

Men and women are not only different in the obvious physical differences, but in other less obvious ways to do with thought, feeling and behaviour, which are the result of differing developmental pathways in utero and childhood which affect neurological and endocrine development so as to cause these and perhaps other differences.

Minor Proposition:

Sexual differentiation of the nervous system and the genitals in utero take place at different stages of pregnancy; the hormones triggering these developments can be interrupted, causing there to be incomplete development of one or both, and thus potentially a mismatch between the brain and the body in one or more of morphological mapping, sexual orientation or emotionality; or in the event of a genetic influence, which inclines the brain to one gendered phenotype or the other.

---

4   Sherry Marts, Ph.D., et al. *Sex Differences in the Brain: From Genes to Behavior.* Oxford University Press, https://global.oup.com/academic/product/sex-differences-in-the-brain-9780195311587?cc=gb&lang=en&# (2020).

Ergo: *It is at least a logical possibility that some transsexuals have brain-body mismatches.*

This is a conclusion for which there is some evidence, which I shall allude to, but which is also anathema to the equalities brigade, who ignore all psychometric data on gender differences with the claim that it is socially conditioned, in favour of pushing their agenda to eradicate all gender differences, whether inherent or acquired. In 2017 a Google employee, James Damore, was sacked for internally circulating a document,[5] citing much objective evidence, discussing how gender differences in interests and skills influenced the low numbers of women in technical fields.

Should this be the case, then transsexualism could be a neurological syndrome, in which case it would be a legitimate 'thing', even if there are discernible degrees of intensity. But, for instance, someone who had what might in an earlier time have been considered a mismatch in emotional functioning and sexual orientation might be able to function perfectly well in society as a feminine homosexual or butch lesbian and not have any bodily dysphoria. The first of these is largely a matter of degree anyway and homosexuality is now accepted by many societies as just a variation within normal parameters, since it appears to have existed since the beginning of time in all societies and is even found in animals. Humans are extremely adaptable with a large overlap of redundancy between the sexes despite the statistical predominance of certain traits in each population.

I would suggest that the only populations which have real problems in adapting to life in their natal sex are those for whom there is a neurological mismatch with bodily morphology: this is the basis of the syndrome that is the *Transsexual Phenomenon*. The most important differences in gender are physical. We can all adapt to, or ignore,

---

5   https://www.scribd.com/document/355823379/Google-s-Ideological-Echo-Chamber.

the emotions or orientations of others, but at the most basic level our bodies are as they are.

We should perhaps allow that there may be what I would call *alchemical fusions* or *synergies* in the way that the various factors (of which those I have mentioned are probably not an exhaustive list) interact and combine. In the end it is a matter of what goes on in consciousness that matters, but if this is based in some organic reality, then it is a firmer foundation than some socially acquired habit, meme or behavioural adaptation.

I have barely even touched on the group who want to present socially as the gender opposite to that in which they were born but are apparently not bothered about their bodily sex.

It seems clear to me that this is an entirely different group from that in which I found myself, and used to be known as *transvestites* but now *transgender* since it is considered less pejorative. I won't seek to generalise too widely about this group, but some seem more motivated by their sexual orientation towards others than by their sense of personal physical identity, in my experience, and the presentation can morph from that of a feminine homosexual to apparent female through a route of social reinforcement. It is something I still struggle to understand that someone can present as female and yet be *quite happy with their female penis* as some say.

The Benjamin 6 stage scale has been abandoned these days because it associated *transsexual* or *transvestite* [sic] thoughts and behaviour with sexual orientations at a primary level. But while he acknowledged that it was a pragmatic tool and invited clinicians to improve it, the scale of severity is a useful one nonetheless. There does seem to be a divide between those who are only socially motivated and those who have a more full spectrum motivation, who feel they are unable to be able to properly express themselves socially without being morphologically congruent.

Gender Studies seeks to conflate these because of its pre-set assumption that these differences are of no consequence, even though there is simple *prima facie* evidence of taxonomic differences. However, it is my own experience that such people are more likely to be simply homosexual rather than actually female identified. Even the term *identification* is somewhat problematic, as I see it, because it suggests some sort of mental choice or judgement. As a child, however much I desired, aspired or yearned to be a girl, I could not *identify myself* as one because, simply put, I was not — at least physically.

Seeking to clarify the differences between what I term *transgenders* and *transsexuals* is one of my other aims since the obfuscation between them is a major tool of the *Queer Lobby* in their war on gender.

Transsexualism, as opposed to *transgender* or *transvestism*, is a difficult enough phenomenon, considering how to deal with it in relation to traditional mores. Some regard it as a mental illness, others a sexual perversion or paraphilia.

It doesn't properly fit either of these two categories, because in the first case the individual seems in many instances to otherwise be perfectly sane and able to carry on a functional life, except for the irrational dysphoria and longing they feel, and in the second case because it is reported from the earliest childhood memories of those suffering this particularly grievous obsession, long before any sexual development and the possible advent of unhealthy sexual attachments.

There are varying degrees of intensity of this feeling which probably arises from inadequately or overdeveloped brain structures during gestation due to irregular hormonal influences.

My own experience of this, which existed since my very earliest memories of becoming aware of myself, was unshakable, despite the considerable guilt I felt about it and the endless quest to rid myself of it. At no point in my life had I found myself not desiring this, not thinking about it on a daily, an hourly basis.

My motivation was absolute when it came to it, when I accepted that this would be with me to old age and that I had a narrow window of time left to me in which it might be possible to at least try to achieve my spectral goal, and that should I fail ignominiously, then at least I had tested my desire. I might be found wanting, but at least I would have tried. Perhaps I would learn something that would help free me from these chains.

So it was with some concern that I read recently that a diagnosis can be considered if a person has had feelings of gender dysphoria for as little as six months or more.[6] It may well be that hormonal changes at different life stages can intensify or lessen certain feelings that one may have about oneself, but I would argue that feelings that have only existed for six months or so out of a life of decades are a transient thing which can hopefully be integrated into the larger whole of one's existing and established life. As Heidegger might say, if I have understood correctly the reading of him given by Dr Jason Reza Jorjani,[7] the *monument* of one's past life is something that should be built on, developed and evolved, not critiqued to death because of a temporary fluctuation in feelings. Continuity is surely essential to finding meaning?

Something as extreme as a desire to have one's body changed, and concomitantly one's entire social persona, should be so persistent that it is a core part of that person's inner sense of themselves from the earliest of times. If not, then they must at the beginning have been not unhappy with what nature had made of them. In which case such a state must be retrievable, reaccessible in some way, I would suggest. If I had for one moment of my life actually liked the sexing of my body as it was given to me, then perhaps there could have been a path for me, a chink of light in the cavern leading to the freedom and air of the surface, a memory to cling onto that I could use as leverage to regain my freedom. But I had no such moment on which to rely.

I might still have been deterred if I had failed to pass the test socially, had not been able to fit within the margins of acceptable social parameters, having lived too long in my former state, had felt my own

---

6   https://en.wikipedia.org/wiki/Gender_dysphoria.

7   Jorjani, Jason Reza Ph.D.. *Prometheus and Atlas* (2016). Arktos, Arktos Media Ltd, London.

incongruity to be worse than that with which I had started, but I was fortunate that nature had been kind enough to me in my *prima materia*, perhaps it was meant to be.

I was surprised at how soon and how easily I achieved a satisfactory social presentation. Fitting in was something I had always sought, having felt so much of an outsider. Perhaps it was my determination and extreme motivation which enabled me to achieve this.

It was certainly not the kind of demands we see being made today under provisions such as the Equalities Act of 2010 that got me through. I would suggest that forcing yourself on people with threats of suing under the law, as has happened, is not the way to go about it, since this will only cause resentment. I myself only began to use women's toilets when it became apparent that I was being perceived as female on a sufficiently reliable basis that to use the gents' facilities would draw significantly more notice than I would in the ladies'.

I develop the whole issue of the practicalities of the use of toilets for transitioners and their responsibilities to society later on.

However, it is a miracle that the thing which Mr Andrew Selous MP[8] warned of in the Gender Recognition Bill debates in 2004 didn't become much of an issue until after the 2010 Equalities Act in the UK, or until 2016 in the USA when former President Obama declared that human rights equalities legislation should be allowed to apply to public 'restrooms', as they are known in the States, thus allowing men to enter these women's spaces simply on the basis of claiming that they *identified* as women. This is what would be allowed if a Gender Declaration Bill is put into law in the UK. I understand that some examples of this have already been enforced in this country under the 2010 Act by formal legal prosecution, but the newly proposed Bill could obviate such clunky methods and allow all and sundry to claim

---

8   Hansard 25 May 2004 column 1497 — 1502 which can be found way down on the
     following page online https://hansard.parliament.uk/commons/2004-05-25/
     debates/36c03d5e-4aa1-42ea-860f-877bc85d9ca7/OrdersOfTheDay (2020).

whatever identity they like without even any form of supporting evidence, such as their appearance, for example.

The chorus of virtue-signalling luvvies, such as Bruce Springsteen, added their voices in defence of *trans rights*, supporting anyone who chose to enter a female bathroom regardless of appearance but who claimed to *identify* as female.[9] An ironic cartoon had people pointing at a little girl in a restroom with the speech balloon having all in unison screech 'Transphobe!' when she said of an apparent man in the corner, 'Why is that man in here, Mummy?'

Clearly there are issues here, and they need to be dealt with in as rational a manner as possible, respecting the personal spaces of as many people as possible. However, we seem to have gone over an edge where the supposed rights of a very few atypical people are expected to outweigh those of the vast bulk of the general population, who simply have traditional expectations of gender, but end up being vilified as *transphobes* if they dare to express these in any way.

This has gone way past far enough.

I am willing to *out* myself for the greater good, and use my position as a long-term transitioned transsexual, who has some knowledge of Physiological Psychology and experience of working in the mental health field to critique this deconstruction, which is not simply applied to a small number of transsexuals and other transgenders.

At the same time, the deconstruction of the family, the social attack on men and masculinity and on all traditional, established values in our larger society is happening apace.

This is the *War on Gender,* and the *Trans phenomenon* has been enchained to its service.

Let them call me a self-hating *Transphobe.* All they have are words. I have the testament of my life and experience.

At the same time as refuting postmodern Gender Theory for its inadequate recourse to scientific evidence and concurrent use of

9   https://www.mirror.co.uk/3am/celebrity-news/bruce-springsteen-cancels-us-concert-7720439 (2020).

political ideologies, such as *Oppression* and *Privilege Theory* as the basis for their ideas of gender, it is my intention to propose a *New Paradigm* of gender in riposte.

The idea of *Paradigm Shifts* is elaborated by Thomas Kuhn in his philosophic work *The Structure of Scientific Revolutions.*[10]

He describes how old paradigms of understanding give way in time to new ones when the weight of inconsistencies and errors arising from the old becomes too great to sustain and a new model is required.

The replacement of the Earth-centred Ptolemaic system of cosmology by the Copernican is one of the best known examples of this. The *retrogression,* or apparently random reverse movement of the planets in their courses, had long puzzled astronomers who were accustomed to the former system, and who gave a variety of mostly metaphysical reasons for it. When Copernicus proposed the heliocentric model, many people were shocked. Kepler advanced the system with observations supporting the explanation of retrogression and discovered elliptical orbits, while Galileo added to the foundations with his observations of the planets and their moons.

The Church could rail against this, they could excommunicate its proponents, but in the end the new system prevailed, and within a very few generations we had the likes of Newton producing exact laws of motion, and civilisation had opened up a whole new pathway for exploration of its destiny.

And yet the sky looked the same by both night and day, the world continued to revolve, and to be imperceptible in its doing so. People did not spin off into space through the centrifugal force of the rotation because there were other laws at work which were not yet understood.

Existence continued in very much the same way as it always had done, except that this new, deeper understanding opened new possibilities previously undreamed of.

---

10   https://www.uky.edu/—eushe2/Pajares/Kuhn.html (2020).

A similar situation pertains with the upgrading of Newtonian physics to Einsteinian, or even Quantum. We understand better now why things in the macroverse or the microverse deviate from common expectation, but they do not contradict those things we already experience; they expand upon them.

To use Einsteinian relativist mathematics to work out the trajectory of an arrow, or the flight of an aeroplane will render correct results, but it is unnecessarily complicated, since the practical, local differences between Einsteinian relativism and Newtonian mechanics are so small as to be irrelevant.

So it is that I seek to lay the groundwork for a revised paradigmatic understanding of gender, based on natural law, but taking account of its anomalies, and, where necessary, ideas from social gender theory.

Like Relativity, it will not replace the already extant system in practical terms. Men will still be men, and women, women. But those anomalous folk who otherwise would have no place than to fall through the cracks can find a place which has more foundation than a mere *declaration of identification*, which it seems is what we are heading towards if we do not change course. And those whose identity is merely based on *claims* should be required to provide evidence for those claims before being able to change what would otherwise be considered the default state of affairs.

But in large part I must seek to demolish the false image of this postmodern Deconstructionism because it has sought to destroy scientific understanding and replace it with moralising Utopianism about how they think genders *should be*, rather than how *they are*.

My theory will only be new in its detail and presentation, however, for it is intended as a revivification and slight revision of traditional gender models from the past, models which have receded in their cultural influence and prevalence recently under attack from the postmodern and *Queer Theory* versions, and thus need bringing up to date so as to include the now available evidence.

The simple logic of all sex and gender being encoded in the genes, that we are absolutely determined by these things, has been broken down partly by the material evidence of intersex and other anomalies of gene expression, and partly by the sophistry of linguistic and social deconstruction.

The Palaeo-Conservative who rages that someone must be a man because they have a Y-chromosome, or insists that someone should always and automatically identify with their genital sex regardless of the state of their nervous system, that they are mentally ill to even have such feelings, is the Neanderthal of our time. We may wish to preserve some of his genes or genetic memory that have use or function, but to remain a Neanderthal is to become obsolete. He has some good stuff, but to refuse to modify it, to fine tune it and bring it up to the present is non-adaptive.

The opposite is true of the postmodern Gender Theorist, who has already thrown the baby out with the bathwater on the basis of an assumed politically correct morality, which claims that the baby is *oppressive* and a *tool of the patriarchy*. To them, there is no *essential nature* of gender, not even a polarity of types, but mere random characteristics, and power. An invention.

The Neanderthal is in the larger scheme more adaptive, and that is why traditional gender is retained by so many. It is only the superficially educated classes who are deceived by Gender Theory, an idea which believes that bodies are secondary, burdensome things, and that its own Utopian ideals should replace them and their material hegemony over our existence. And it is only through political correctness and its associated social signalling that this is ever able to spread and infiltrate its influence more widely.

Postmodern attitudes are based on ideas of *power* as being the basis of all relations, rather than *function* as I would propose is more proper. In so doing, it gives away that in itself it is only interested in power. It proposes to do away with all existing structures, many of which have grown up over generations, centuries, millennia and the depths of evolutionary time, in order to replace them with supposedly *non-oppressive* systems, untried as they might be and which only exist in theory. It is a form of anarchism.

I would suggest that an analytic interpretation of this might involve looking at their tantrum-like behaviour in trying to destroy something that has stood the test of time, rather than seeking to better it, to iron out anomalies, to adapt it to the present.

What is now needed is a two-pronged approach which will use their own deconstructionist tools against such schools of thought, while at the same time *enlarging our own models* so as to adequately include the anomalies which have become evident in the last century or so, and thereby expand our general understanding, the way that the Copernicans did, or post-Einsteinian scientists. They may have changed our views of the larger universe, but our daily lives are much the same.

While I wish to somewhat enlarge our conception of gender, I do not seek to fundamentally change what it is, or how we experience it in the world. I contrast this with the postmodern concept of gender, which intends to *radically alter it,* and make it politically correct, in order to replace it with one they consider more *equal*, one based on a Utopian fantasy which seeks to contradict nature because they see the latter as *oppressive*. To force equality, of human value and before the law, into *sameness*.

But an apple can never be the same as an orange, however much you want it to be, and men and women can never be *the same* in the sense that they want them to be, because they are fundamentally different. Equality under the law is good, and equality of opportunity; but to impose equality of outcome is to force nature against itself.

There are only two genders or sexes, and some anomalies. I don't mind being in that category of anomalous gender, for that is what I am. But while those of us in anomalous categories should, I would argue, be allowed the opportunity to present ourselves in ways that we find comfortable, we should also do our best to fit in with the existing structures of society, finding a balance between our own sense of identity and the needs of the wider societies in which we live.

Survival of the *fittest* is not merely about being strong and fit, but being a *good fit* to one's environment. I always felt out of place, an *outsider*, if you will, until not only was I able to find a better expression of myself that I was more comfortable with, but also somewhere, some social role or position into which I could comfortably, and usefully, reside. A key works best if it fits the lock. Our serotonin system around recognising hierarchy is hundreds of millions of years old and utterly hard-wired. To find a fitting place in the social order is essential for optimum functioning.

Something like 99.7% of people are gender normative in their personal sense of identity. This is demonised by the Gender Lobby as *cisgender*, from the Latin *Cis,* meaning *this side of*, as opposed to *Trans,* meaning *the other side*. Simply to be in the biologically normative group is now considered an *oppressive* act, which implicitly includes *othering* of minorities.

Othering is a significant part in this as I will explore, and the push for the reversal of all established norms on the basis of political ideology and the forcing of social equality for all sub groups and identities, however anomalous, alien or marginal.

I do not believe that the 0.3% or so of the population to which I happen to belong should have the right or power to dominate the gender values and expression of the vast majority of our society.

And yet laws designed to protect gender identity or expression, such as in Canada, where Bill C-16 was recently passed into law, are claimed by some to potentially allow policing of language around gender, in defiance of other laws enshrining freedom of speech, with the potential criminalisation of *misgendered pronouns*, and there are moves to implement this more widely in other countries with European cultures. Opinions vary[11, 12] about the implementation of

---

11   http://sds.utoronto.ca/blog/bill-c-16-no-its-not-about-criminalizing-pronoun-misuse/ (2020).

12   https://www.lifesitenews.com/news/breaking-canada-passes-radical-law-forcing-gender-theory-acceptance (2020).

these laws, and we shall have to see how the courts apply their verdicts. But this kind of ultra-recognition does not seem to be something that has been taken up by non-European peoples or cultures, interestingly.

Ontario in Canada has even recently passed a law whereby the state can take children from their parents if the child has expressed the wish to be of the opposite gender and parents do not want to submit their child to gender reassignment treatment.[13]

It is already highly controversial for children to receive such treatment with the consent of all concerned, but for the state to intervene so as to impose gender reassignment on minors against parental wishes is troubling in the extreme. Surely a more nuanced approach is needed?

It is not the remit of this work to address in much detail the wider cultural issues we face at this time, but it is strange to me that our governments are implementing laws to deconstruct, to destroy in many ways, fundamental groundings on which our culture is based, while at the same time encouraging and inviting millions from foreign cultures into our lands, many of whom care not a fig for gender identity issues, nor even for what we understand of women's rights.

The claim to be supporting *Transgender Rights* while importing those who have no inclination towards such a thing is a massive self- contradiction to anyone who bothers to truly consider it. It is, however, hollow, for they have jumped on the whole transgender bandwagon, even the media gravy train, which guarantees political capital and profit through virtue signalling that they are liberal and inclusive of oppressed minorities.

Enough. The War on Gender is one of the principal means by which the Cultural Marxists seek to destroy our civilisational values.

The *Transgender Lobby*, the *LGBT* and *Queer Lobby* and *Gender Studies* do not, and probably never did, represent me or my interests. Indeed they are not about those interests, but about taking down the

---

13   http://dailycaller.com/2017/06/05/ontario-makes-disapproval-of-kids-gender-choice-child-abuse/ (2020).

understanding and interpretation of gender which has underpinned the basis of all human culture and psychology.

The total deconstruction of gender does no good for society, and it does no good for me. It is little more than a tantrum in the face of reality, which creates only confusion and chaos.

If I had wanted to be a *gender neutral* or a *non-binary* person, then I would not have sought to travel on the path that I did. I wanted to be as close to female as was medically possible, at least morphologically, and to pass socially, and in so far as that has been achieved, I am content.

It is my task here to expose the false ideology of postmodern Gender Studies, which is rapidly undermining our society and sense of normality, so as to restore the traditional sense of gender, which has been so assaulted in recent time, whilst incorporating into it those very factors which its opponents claim are in contradiction to it. I shall propose a more developed paradigm of gender than existed previously, but which is nonetheless rooted in the biological origins of life out of which gendered life first emerged. Postmodernism wants to destroy this, and with it the stable order of society.

I shall have some recourse to academic works on the subject, but my principal source shall be my own life experience, since the understanding of gender that I have today is not in its foundation different from what I had when I was thirty, or twenty, or even as a child insofar as I had any intellectual comprehension of how my sense of myself might have come about.

And I hope that I shall go some way to re-establishing a natural order to our understanding of gender, while still retaining a niche for those of us who seek to fit with nature, as far as we can, though we may forever be anomalous to its broader designs.

CHAPTER 1

CHILDHOOD: EARLY LIFE AND REALISATION

M Y EARLY LIFE was extremely happy, almost idyllic. My earliest memories are of the searing heat of the African sunshine on the baked laterite landscape of Northern Nigeria, and of my mother, father and elder brother. All was bright Technicolor and an overwhelming assault to the senses. The smell of Africa, unimaginable to one accustomed only to the clean towns and fresh green countryside of England, was omnipresent. The dusty land turned from orange rust to verdant green when the rains came, Flame of the Forest trees would blossom, and mangoes ripen and fall.

A troop of baboons would gather at dusk on a rocky outcrop near our house, where we were the only Europeans for miles.

My father had taken a position as a civil engineer with the Colonial Development Office to build roads through the bush and gone ahead to get established. My mother, brother and I followed on a few months later in the mid-fifties when I was about fifteen months old.

As children we accept the lives and circumstances we find ourselves in. I had no conception that these circumstances were not common to most English children of the 1950s, but accepted the variety and extremes that I experienced without question.

We may have been the only white people for miles, but I never felt the least threat, neither I believe did any of my family. Even the snakes and scorpions, a much greater concern, seemed to be kept at a safe distance, or were eradicated if they came too close. I recall several incidents when my father crushed such creatures with a large, heavy stick that he kept to hand.

He would sit on the veranda in the tropical evening listening to the World Service over the din of crickets, while we stayed indoors reading by the light of the Tilley lamps.

In the daytime, vultures rattled their leathery wings as they scavenged the corpses of dead animals by the roadside, and crowds of Africans would hold out their hands begging, '*Dash! Dash!*'

It was a feral land in which my first memories grew, and one in which twenty-first century Europeans might not feel safe, but the pioneer spirit was strong in my parents. Being exposed to a world of such extremes and challenges made us strong.

The first clear and identifiable memory I have, which emerges from this rich textural backdrop, was the solar eclipse of October 1959. I found recently that this had not actually been a total eclipse where we were, although very nearly, and I recall vividly standing on the driveway of our house in Zaria with our smoked glass looking up at it. My father said, 'You can see the disc.' This occasion, and these first words in my memory, may indeed have some resonance or implication for my later interest in solar religions, and the Ra-Horus Aten of Egyptian symbolism, but I do not think it had anything to do with what I was soon to realise about myself.

My mother, then heavily pregnant with my younger brother, had to return to England for the birth as unfortunately the midwife nun who had been supervising her care tragically died about the time of the eclipse. My elder brother and I naturally went home with her and we all returned a couple of months later. We still have the photos my father took of the four of us disembarking from the Douglas DC-3 Dakota and walking across the tarmac at Jos airport in 1960. He must have felt immense excitement and anticipation at the arrival of his new son, since he took several photos in quick succession, a telling detail for a man not given to impulse, and in an era when colour film was expensive.

We were now to be stationed in Jos, a highly desirable posting in the town famed for its mild climate, being situated on the Bauchi Plateau, a Nigerian parallel to the White Highlands of Kenya. I recall the heavy rains, much heavier than on the plains of the Sahel to the north, as they beat down on the corrugated tin roof, and flowed in a torrent down the slope of our driveway, scouring away at the packed earth.

It was about this time, around my fifth birthday, that the Dreamtime of my early childhood was cracked open and I was thrust unwilling into awareness of myself.

Jos was a large town, and unlike our first few postings at small hamlets such as Kudaru and Dutsin Wai where we had been posted alone in the bush, there was a sizeable expat community. Our neighbours had three daughters. Their eldest was about the same age as myself, and she became my best friend when she came to join the little school which my mother ran for a small number of expat children. We competed in reading Ladybird books, Janet and John and then Enid Blyton.

But it was her younger sister who had the biggest effect on me.

Their parents must have had to go away, or perhaps it was the occasion of the birth of their youngest as with my mother the previous year, and we had the girls stay with us for a little while.

Young children do not tend to have the reticence about their bodies that we acquire as we grow, but perhaps this is because they are unconscious of difference.

The moment of the coming to that awareness is seared indelibly in my memory, when in the bathroom one evening I saw the younger sister naked, and realised that we were different.

In that one moment, which has never left me, I knew that a terrible mistake had somehow been made. I saw her body, and I saw mine, and I knew that mine was wrong.

Perhaps the reader has experienced the loss of a lover or a bereavement which, forgotten in sleep, returns suddenly on waking. The sense of lightness and freedom in which we have been immersed, taken for granted, is ripped away and the crushing truth is brought back to us.

The only difference here was that this had lain dormant, waiting to be discovered, revealed by an external correlate that I could not escape.

I knew of course, instantly, that such a thing could not be spoken of. I had naturally seen that the world was made up of men and women, boys and girls, but had not yet entered into that distinction myself. I, my brothers, and the girls from next door were just children and I had not yet properly extended my awareness of the distinctions, the differences between the sexes.

And so began a lifelong quest to unravel, to solve, resolve and, insofar as might be possible, rectify what a much greater writer than I has described as a 'Conundrum'.

I shall, in due course, explore the medical and developmental aetiology of what I believe to be a birth condition that may be described as a form of neurological intersex. But for now, dear reader, stay with me, as I trace my path through the years, struggling as I did by turns to deny and beat this feeling and sense of myself, and then to run with it, externalise and manifest it through the confusion of my life.

Many years would pass before I would begin to deal with this in any formal way, but there was an incident very soon after the episode I have described above that I have long believed to be related, although I am unable to recall specific thoughts or intentions at the time which would confirm it.

In our kitchen we had the usual utensils for the preparation of food, amongst which was a very sharp knife that our cook kept whetted to a merciless edge, principally for the filleting of meat. I don't recall exactly how I came to do so, but one day I stole it away and hiding at the bottom end of the house cut the index finger of my left hand. I have the scar to this day. It is deep and I recall something of the alarm of my parents when I ran screaming to them.

It is well understood that shock can lead to the suppression or even wiping of memories, and so it is with this. I can recall very little about the healing except that fortunately there was a packet of sterile lint in the toy doctor's bag which I had been given for a Christmas present, and my mother dressed the wound with that. (My mother and father had high hopes for my future career and clearly wanted to set certain role expectations.)

Liberal applications of Dettol by my mother mercifully saved me from a septic infection, but my parents must have been alarmed, not only for my physical safety but there must also have been lingering concerns about why this had happened. I think I had passed the episode off as an attempt by me to dig the hard ground of the flower bed below the house, but doubtless a cursory examination of that piece of ground would have shown no disturbance, but only my blood. The injury itself was no accidental nick, but a much deeper and probably intentional assault. I have long speculated about its motivation, and while I cannot say with absolute certainty, since I have experienced a degree of memory loss around the incident and I cannot quite put myself back into that moment, nonetheless I am inclined to see this as connected to and consequent from the moment in the bathroom, which had probably just preceded it.

If I am correct in my interpretation of the fragmentary memories, which I piece together from this time, then my response was clearly going to a deeper level than mere curiosity at our bodily differences. My alarm had not been that she was *lacking* the male member, but that I *had* it.

This was not the first time I had suffered bodily harm while in Africa. About a year or so earlier I had wandered in front of a swing at the Zaria racecourse and been knocked flying. I can remember almost nothing of this, but the dent in the side of my skull attests to it having really happened. Zaria had a hospital to which I was rushed immediately, and several stitches were applied post-haste, without anaesthetic I am told due to the location of the wound.

I must have been an immense worry to my mother. These accidents could happen equally easily in Sussex, but the added uncertainties and dangers of Africa multiplied the risks manifold. A few years later, when on holiday from boarding school, I got a small cut on my left elbow, and it didn't heal properly until I returned home to England after a month, despite proper cleansing and dressing. But we persisted, and it never once occurred to me that these kinds of incidents and the risks posed in an environment of much greater hazard should prevent us from continuing to go to the Dark Continent.

On the contrary, I am certain that it imbued me and all my family with a robust and healthy attitude to challenge and difficulty, with an ingrained understanding that difficulties are to be faced, challenges to be overcome.

I recall one of my mother's friends saying about this time that one didn't fully appreciate something unless one had worked for it. As a child I mentally rebelled against this — children like to be spoiled and given presents. But the truth of this comment stayed with me and fed itself into my understanding of self over the long years and even now informs my views on how we, as trans people, may best seek not only to fulfil our own self-image, but equally achieve functional integration within society, as I will describe later.

While it is clear to me that Africa had nothing to do with the suddenly awakened sense of my bodily identity, I do believe that it had much to do with my willingness to face things that many would find unimaginable.

Nigeria gained independence in October of 1960, and we had lived there for four years under the setting sun of the colonial administration of the British Empire. Political correctness demands that we look back on that era with shame, but all I knew of it was that my father built roads into the bush and bridges which connected villages that would otherwise be isolated in the rainy season. More than a decade after Independence, I recall a senior member of the Ministry of Works asking him if he thought that there was any chance that he might be able to persuade the British government to come back to run Nigeria again!

I'm sure he would have been quietly amused that such people could have imagined he had the influence to bring about such things, but more importantly, it gives the lie to the commonly promoted illusion that colonial administrations of the British Empire were all ruthless, tyrannical and exploitative. The Nigeria of 1960 was a long way from the Belgian Congo of Conrad's *Heart of Darkness*.

In the twenty years that he worked there, my father and the few dozens of other British engineers spread throughout the country established infrastructure without which Nigeria, and those other African countries that were fortunate enough to have similar invest-ment of skills, would have had no chance in facing the future.

I detail all this to show the pioneer spirit of the milieu in which I grew up as a child. Western society of the twenty-first century has lost touch with its roots, has lost that spirit and become weak. It has become so weak that, unable to face the shame of that weakness, it looks back on the strength of the past, the independence and vigour, with envy and decries it, calling its strength oppression, morally un-dermining the memory of the lost zeitgeist.

In the pages to come I shall return fire on that Politically Correct culture, which has sought to make of people such as myself a politi-cal ideology, which not only exploits our birth condition for political ends, but does this through misrepresentation and sophistry. The broadside attack on our civilisation seeks to bring down all cultural achievement, calling it '*Privilege*'. All differences are to be wiped out, even that between men and women. *Transsexualism*, the sense of be-ing of a mind in the wrong sexual body, has now been turned into *transgender*, whereby people are encouraged to see their identification of gender as little more than a matter of choice of social role, which has nothing to do with the sex of their body. I shall expand on this considerably in later chapters, but the simple view is that many in the LGBT and *Queer* movements seek to eliminate all distinctions of gender, and completely detach gender identity from notions of bodily sex. A position which is entirely at odds with my own experiences from the earliest age and my subsequent view about the evolutionary importance of sexual differentiation and how *Gender Dysphoria* is a neuro-developmental condition, in which the stages of the differentiation of neurological structures in the brain have been incomplete, overdeveloped or interrupted *in utero*.

I had absolutely no idea as a child how to deal with my situation. My likely attempt at self-mutilation, which could have led to serious infection and even death, had, quite fortunately, failed.

No major incidents followed in my memory for some while after this. Perhaps a year later I started at school in Bognor Regis where we had our home in England, and then about my seventh birthday I was sent to boarding school. The one thing I recall about this interim stage of my life was my love for dressing up. I had played a shepherd at a Nativity play while in Jos, and I loved the long robes which my mother made up as a costume for me. I can still recall the smell and texture of the cloth, and was heartbroken when my mother told me that the costume was to be given to the church to keep for future years. And there was a Robin Hood costume which she also made, with a long skirt-like tunic, probably based on that worn by Errol Flynn while playing this role in his films. I knew that this was like girls' clothes and it was my first awareness of my sense of sexual identification through dress. But I am absolutely firm in my memory that this came after the episode in the bathroom, principally from contextual referents in the timeline of my early years, but also because it seems in my recollection to be something I responded to from an already existing awakening.

Perhaps my mother picked up that I was identifying rather too strongly with the feminine elements of these costumes, and back in

England the play suits which she made for me and my brothers were of commandos and cowboys, for which there were now plenty of new toys coming into the shops during the 'Never had it so good' era, such as plastic tin helmets and cap-firing six guns. The television age was upon us, with the masculine role models of the likes of *Rawhide*, but somehow I couldn't be entirely shielded from Robin Hood tunics and tights as our perennial English hero had a popular weekly show alongside the cowboys!

It should be clear I was born into the traditional culture of England, with traditional sex roles, and that I was exposed to no undue or unusual role models of influences in my early years, entirely unlike what is happening today.

Unless one was to include the influence of pantomimes with their cross-gendered actors and actresses.

I recall a performance of *Aladdin* to which I was taken at about this time. It was at the Esplanade Theatre on Bognor seafront and while the deliberately absurd figure of Widow Twanky is part of my memory, I was far more interested in the eponymous hero, who of course was played by a girl in traditional manner as Principal Boy. Her short green tunic was reminiscent of my Robin Hood costume while her shapely legs clad in yellow tights were clearly those of the fairer sex.

This was definitely a slightly later event than my earlier experience, and one which stayed with me. In my imagination I was like Aladdin, a girl playing the part of a boy without anyone knowing.

I must emphasise that this was not some untoward influence that gave me ideas I would not otherwise have had, but only a marker that I recognised, an external referent to which I could relate. I don't think most young boys would find themselves speculating about being a girl from seeing such a pantomime; they would be more likely to laugh at it simply as an absurdity, or as a means of releasing fear of the possibility; it is merely something that is part of the topsy-turvy world of such theatrical performances. One of the means by which our Western society has functionally contained the anomalies of gender is to have such outlets. Mardi Gras, carnival, pantomime, Hallowe'en, the Feast of Fools and suchlike are opportunities for release, a pressure valve for our minds and our reality in which impossible, contradictory and absurd things are allowed to come out of the shadows for an hour, a day or a night. And then they are put away until the next time and we return to our constrained lives of normality and convention.

For most, hopefully this is enough. And had I been born in an earlier epoch, it might have been all that I had, all that I could hope for, but it was not. The world was expanding with new possibilities, some of which might allow the expression of my own inner world.

Most particularly I should say that as a child I was never exposed to any form of inappropriate sexual attention that might have marred my sense of self. In fact, I cannot recall any other sexual experience or awareness other than that moment in the bathroom until quite a lot later. But my sense of how my body should be would not leave me. Despite my sense of guilt about it, nonetheless it was a secret I treasured in my heart. It wasn't just a fantasy, but rooted in my aesthetic sense of my body as being more feminine than was usual for boys.

If my awakening in 1960 was troubling to me, it was nothing to being wrenched out of the protective bosom of my family and being sent to boarding school two years later. It was not quite *Tom Brown's Schooldays*, but it was tough, certainly by today's standards, and perhaps more so for such a young child.

I had been going to small schools locally in West Bognor Regis for a year or so, and my mother had returned to this country for that purpose. My elder brother had already gone to board, and my mother began the juggling of responsibilities, which she maintained until all three of us had left school in the mid-seventies. If we were to have gone to local day schools, my father would have had to have either returned to England permanently and not just for leave, or else my mother would never have been able to go to Nigeria to spend time with him.

These kinds of arrangements were not uncommon in the past. It was difficult for me, and it took me many years to grow beyond that, but modern society has become so soft and self-centred on immediate gratification that it can be too easy to focus on one's own distress and not look at how situations are for others, or how much worse things could be if they were arranged in different ways.

Other considerations aside, Windlesham House was one of the best schools in the south of England and my father was definitely thinking ahead when he had put our names down for places soon after we were born. My father had been in the first wave of the post-Great War baby boom, and so found himself growing up in the Great Depression of the 1930s. Artisan working class, his family had been in canal boat shipping, but this was in decline, and he became a carpenter's apprentice at the age of fourteen. War was declared by Neville Chamberlain in 1939 just a week after his twentieth birthday, and he signed up as a volunteer, rising to the position of sergeant in the Royal Engineers of the Eighth Army, fighting in the North African campaign and invasion of Italy under Montgomery, and invalided out from fighting at Monte Cassino in 1944. This led to a curious coincidence with my own path many years later, which I shall mention when we come to it.

After the war he had returned to the building trade, for which there was much work and became a site foreman for Neill's builders in Chichester, while studying for surveying and construction qualifications. A connection with a friend shortly after I was born led to his applying for a position with the Ministry of Overseas Development, in which he was accepted.

Independence for Nigeria was already on the horizon, and the Colonial Administration was preparing for its exit. I think my father would have probably loved to have gone back to before the Great War and been a pioneer with Lugard in the days of the apogee of Empire, but the bush of Northern Nigeria in the mid-fifties was still quite a challenge. He once said to me, 'The British Empire was the greatest achievement of civilisation in the history of the world.' A statement which in our modern or even postmodern world would probably not go unchallenged. But during the evening of Empire, into which I was thrown, this did not seem such a preposterous proposition as some might contend today.

When I think back now, from my sixties, to what my father endured, and through which he actually prospered and grew strong despite the hardships — the Depression, the War, injury, working alone in the African bush — I am humbled, and just a little ashamed of how little I appreciated all that he did for me.

In the world from which he came, grew up, and faced challenges that I can barely imagine, to be sent to a boarding school of the quality of Windlesham was an opportunity, a start in life beyond the expectation of fortune.

Sometimes others make sacrifices for us which we do not know or understand. Sometimes we have to make sacrifices in our own lives for a betterment further down the line.

It was a masculine society in which I was brought up, and while it was difficult, I bear no grudge for it. It was not *oppressive*, masculinity was not *toxic*. This was the world as it was in the early nineteen sixties, warts and all, plenty of rough edges and perhaps the better for it. People accepted most difficulties as part of life and tried to rub along together with them, only worrying about the serious stuff.

When today I hear about *safe spaces* for people away from others whom they don't like, whom they find too challenging, I recall that I was made stronger by facing opposition, not by running away and hiding.

No one was responsible for *misgendering* me. There were no *gender-neutral* toilets for people who claimed indeterminate or anomalous gender status. To have said such a thing would have gained no more than a strange look or a laugh and then been ignored. Resistance would only have been encountered if you had pressed it on them too much, something that is not incidental today.

The road from there to here has been a long and winding one, but one whose thickets of thorns and bramble patches I do not now regret.

As the youngest child at the school in 1962 I had no hope or idea that I could ever be what my inconvenient dreams told me I should be. Taken away now even from my girl friends in the expat community, I found myself to be stranded in amongst a world of rough boys, the older ones of whom, when in the changing rooms, I saw were entering puberty, and the dim realisation that something like this might be in store for me some years down the line in the distant future began to dawn. I thought of my grandparents and couldn't imagine being old, whether as a man or a woman; it was all too much to contemplate.

But even in this world in which I felt stranded in unreality, as if I had been parachuted into existence in the wrong form, minute details would crop up to give me hope, while at the same time ridding me of some false speculations I had engaged in.

For instance, while I knew intuitively that my secret was forbidden, at the same time I wondered if all boys secretly wanted to be girls; it was so obvious to me that this was the most desirable thing imaginable.

I recall the exact spot by where the cricket bats were kept on which a boy said to me one day not long after I had arrived, 'Ugh! You've got girl's hands.' So it wasn't just my imagination. But also, no, all boys *didn't* want to be girls, that became apparent, and was proved to me again and again.

Many years later, when still struggling with this sense of myself, I read Carlos Castaneda's *Teachings of Don Juan* series and came across the passage where the Yaqui shaman tells his pupil that to wake up within a dream, to become lucid and aware, use your hands as a trigger. When you see your hands, remember to wake up within the dream. This was like a meta-level dream awakening for me, as I recalled that moment by the cricket bats.

On my way down this path, there have been glimpses of some deeper reality which was guiding me, putting down little way markers that I would notice and gain a shamanic sense of this being more than just something that was mixed up on the material plane, or something which I had picked up perversely that moment when I first became aware of myself. That, indeed, not only was it a true part of me, and that I should one day express and realise it, but also that there was a spiritual, other world from which this somehow emanated.

At other times though, these would seem like evil temptations. I had absorbed and taken to the Christianity which was a daily part of life at prep school in the sixties, and while this was never mentioned, I knew without asking that my feelings would be beyond the pale of imagination to anyone there. I even remember speculating, one night after lights out, what it would mean to sell your soul to the Devil, and if my feelings had anything to do with that, but I decided I didn't want to find out. And now, a lifetime later, I don't believe that I did, whatever some may imagine.

Seldom trodden and unfamiliar paths can be dangerous, even though the goal may have purpose, and those who tread them may slip and fall, or lose direction entirely, at least for a while, as perhaps I did at times, if one forgets the destination or ignores the road signs.

If one's path is true, I believe there will be these signs. But such moments were rare, and it was perhaps two or three years later that I came across information which was to give me a little hope. A strange moment it was indeed when one day in the school library, reading a newspaper, probably the *Daily Telegraph*, I found an item which reported that a man had had medical treatment to become a woman. This was my first external verification that such things could happen, that I was not alone in my secret wish, and that at least one had gone before me.

The truly odd thing about this occasion was, however, not the mere fact of what I discovered, but what happened only a few moments later. Some boys were talking nearby, and one of them said about something I had not been listening to: 'That's as impossible as a man becoming a woman!'

Had I been sitting on this knowledge for much longer, and had I given myself time to consider, I might have worried that some might wonder why I would be motivated to make such a rejoinder, but I didn't, and I simply said, pointing to the column in the paper, 'But it is possible, look, I've just read this!' I imagine they were too dumbstruck to suspect my own interest, and I escaped the examination which would almost certainly have followed had we been teenagers. This also confirmed again that not all boys wanted to be girls. The desire was so strong in me that it seemed entirely possible, reasonable, even likely, that it might be common, even ubiquitous.

At least I was able to add the prospect of actual possibility to my inner dream, although it would be quite some years before I dared speak of it.

This was the mid-sixties, and attitudes were evolving rapidly. I don't know where the idea came from, but, what must have been a little after this episode, a rumour went round that Mick Jagger, surely one of the most controversial figures of the time, was to have a 'sex change', the term which had now become popularised in the press. Clearly this was not based on any factual state of affairs, but children can create the wildest stories based on the slightest imagination, and this probably arose from some casual remark made by an adult about Jagger being effeminate or somesuch, conflated with the now general knowledge of what I had already seen in the paper.

What I learned from all this confirmed my intuitive assumption that men becoming women, boys becoming girls, while it might be something that was possible, was not considered normal, desirable or acceptable in the least. On the contrary, it was regarded as some kind of kinky perversion, which perhaps explained its projection onto a pop star known for his outrageous lifestyle.

So my divided life continued. I detested the football and rugby I was meant to participate in and used to 'funk' games, as the practice was known, until I was caught by the school matron and sent for a sound thrashing by the headmaster. Corporal punishment, the strap,

was still practised in those days, and while I certainly wouldn't advocate for its reinstitution, I will not claim that I suffered any permanent
trauma or that it left me emotionally scarred. My teenage years were
to provide ample material for this, unrelated to such treatment.

I knew girls were supposed to be softer and weaker than boys, and
I recognised this within myself. I was certainly much less aggressive
than the average boy of my experience at the time, rough and tumble
was definitely not my thing! And if I had known the word, I would
have applied the term 'androgynous' to myself as appropriate to my
aesthetic sense of self. In fact, I secretly aspired to protect and nurture
this thing I felt.

My early childhood friends from Nigeria were a very long way
in the past, but my social gap was to start to be filled in 1967 when
the school began to take girls, the first prep school in the country to
become co-educational.

The first new thing I was to discover was that boys chased girls,
but that while I wanted to be friends with them, I didn't have that
predator edge which seemed prevalent in boys. As I began to close in
on puberty this became a source of serious conflict which was to last
a very long time. Every night I would lie awake, praying that I would
wake up as a girl in the morning, but always to be disappointed. I have
heard the same story told by many in my position at this age.

It was at this time that I first thought of taking my own life. The
thought of what I might grow up to be and the disappointment that
I could not be what I wanted to be haunted me. I got some herbal
sleeping tablets and took them all in one go, but all that happened was
I slept rather heavily. As the years went by, the torment returned to me
in waves but I knew that it would be wrong to take the easy way out,
and there was the dim awareness that I might one day follow the path
that I knew existed if I held on.

As I entered my teens, I was reading Lobsang Rampa, a supposed
Tibetan monk who had incarnated into an English life and written
books such as *The Third Eye* and *Doctor from Lhasa*. Probably fantasy,

but it was intriguing and gave me some early ideas for personal development. He said that if one repeated that one's desire was coming true every day, then it would become real. Merely a sort of goal setting really, and a technique taught by many in the personal development and success mindset field, but to me it sounded like a magic way of becoming what I wanted to. I remember standing alone outside the science block one rainy evening, repeating out loud that I was going to be a girl. To speak those words, to even frame the thought explicitly had always been hard; it filled me with both fear and anticipation. But I did it. Only a few times, but the statement of that goal, of that intention, stayed in the background of my young mind, despite my endless wavering in the face of the obvious social expectation.

I talked about the differences between boys and girls with my mother when I was in my early teens, trying to rationalise my feelings about myself without actually explaining what they were, and arguing that apart from the physical details our feelings were the same inside. Of course, speaking for myself I may have been right. My mother tried to counter these ideas to some extent, and this was probably one of the few failures in her life, but it was all beyond her ken.

As is often the case, my teens were the most difficult phase of my life. Puberty began to hit around my thirteenth birthday, but besides the developments which disgusted me, I was afflicted with a side effect, not entirely uncommon amongst adolescents, but in my case quite extreme.

As a child I had had beautiful skin and it had been one of my physical characteristics which had assisted me in clinging to the notion that I was, in some secret and mysterious way, 'really' a girl, or that I was at least some kind of creature in between and that I might one day be able to resolve this crisis within myself.

This whole constellation of thoughts, ideas and feelings about myself and how I felt in my body was seriously assailed as I entered puberty. I began to break out in increasingly severe acne that was not just unsightly, but extremely painful. Unlike most forms of acne which affect only the surface layers of the skin, mine was a variety that I now know as *cystic*, although I never came across the term at the time. This involved the development of boils around deep cysts of unexpressed sebaceous material that became severely inflamed. It was recognised as a medical problem and I tried countless different lotions as well as even being given X-ray treatment, and settled eventually with antibiotics and an ultra-violet lamp.

Compared to dealing with my acne as a teenager, going through transsexual medical treatment and reassignment was a piece of cake. In the latter I was becoming the physical being which was, if not perfect, at least closer, much closer, to the image and goal which I had always felt and imagined, despite myself at times, while the former was an irruption into my body of a toxin which assaulted me from inside because it had no way to express itself, waged war on me and left me scarred like a battlefield.

It was exhausting. All that I imagined for myself seemed to be slipping away. Puberty is a difficult time for many children as they begin their transition to adulthood, but for one who has seen this from afar and long feared its onset, it was a nightmare.

I had seen older boys in the school changing rooms and the prospect that I might become like them frightened me.

The principal changes to my body were repulsive to me, and though my face and parts of my back were plagued with the eruption of painful boils, I was granted one aspect of relief. I never developed significant body hair, something which again brought me sneers from the boys around me who were proud of their masculinity and hairy chests, but for that I was grateful despite the consequent diminution of my status.

Though on no occasion did I utter a word about my feelings to a single soul. The boys with whom I was surrounded once I moved up to secondary school clearly picked up that I was not a contender in the dominance stakes, and this, combined with my skin problems, made for several years of extreme social discomfort.

This was all a kind of torture, made worse by the emerging social awareness of transsexualism in the media. One might see references to, or even pictures of, Amanda Lear, notorious for being suspected of being transsexual, or David Bowie, an early example of the gender and sexuality *fluid* culture, which was nascent at the time. I was deeply troubled by Bowie in the early seventies, for a number of reasons, which I did not fully understand at the time.

Principally, he was identified with *gay culture* and *bisexuality*. As my school was a boy's public school, a covert but nonetheless half recognised culture of pederasty had long existed. Older boys, either homosexual by nature, or simply starved by the absence of girls to pursue, would lure pubescent juniors into their studies for tea and toast, as well as perhaps other things, and there were even certain of the bachelor masters, many of whom lived in the gothic pile, who were reputed to engage in this kind of thing.

How far all this went is not for me to say, since I never engaged in it. It probably rarely went all the way, but the homosexual or *queer* culture was a definite thing at the school, and created conflict between the different in-groups.

I always had a strong disidentification from male homosexuality, since my sense of myself had always been about my desired physical, sexual morphology. As a child I had had a crush on Paul McCartney I recall, but there was never really any sexual element to this. I was too young for that, and I'm sure that there were a million pre-pubescent girls who had similar feelings towards this young man, who was considered one of the most eligible bachelors of the time. When the rock band Genesis played at our school in the early seventies, I was troubled by my sense of attraction to their singer, Peter Gabriel.

Exposure to the culture, and implied practices, of the world of homosexuality in my early teens probably had quite a strong influence on my developing attitudes around sex, which were to take a very long time to fully resolve.

Certainly, I was put off by it. I was young enough still to be able to dissociate my feeling about my desired body image from the inevitable eventuality of having sex with someone. Although my skin had a hyper-reaction to the presence of male hormone, I had a late and slow onset of puberty and my body remained fairly androgynous except for the obvious ailment.

So even though I might see myself inwardly in a desired way, the boys in the homosexual culture were clearly attracted to each other as *boys* and to engage in such would be to affirm this identity, something which I felt deeply conflictual about.

Once, at prep school, a boy had followed me out to the toilets at night after lights out and tried to do things to me, but I simply didn't understand what was going on, and the Headmaster, prowling the corridors late at night, heard voices and interrupted us. The boy invented some quick excuse about thinking I had taken his slippers (he was barefooted, while I was not) and the Head sent us back to the dorm with fleas in our ears. It was only years later that it dawned on me what that boy had had in mind, and what the Head had probably guessed.

I guess the boy had sensed something about me which he found attractive, but had I realised what he wanted to do, I would certainly not have engaged willingly.

It seems likely to me that there was an element of social induction in the practice of homosexuality in single-sex public schools. Young teenagers are impressionable and quick to learn. Habits can be acquired through the reinforcement of exploratory or thrill-seeking behaviour. Sexual gratification is a very strong reinforcer; we hear in the modern world of *sex addiction*.

I am extremely glad that I never engaged in any such social learning, since I'm sure it would have caused me more confusion down the line than the actual path I took. But, young and naïve though I was, I was clear in my own mind that wanting to be a girl, feeling that I should have been, however one wishes to describe it, was not the same as being a homosexual man. I use the word *homosexual* since the term *gay* hadn't gained full currency at the time, and *queer* is highly pejorative, even though that was the actual term most commonly used for what formerly used to be known as *pederasty.*

Even more than Bowie's identification with 'bisexuality' was his fondness for cross-dressing, as on the cover of *Hunky Dory.* I recall seeing an item from the *Melody Maker* during 1969 or 1970 in which he had caused an uproar whilst in Texas, having gone out in public in a dress.

The subsequent development of his image over the next few years, through *Ziggy Stardust, Aladdin Sane* and ultimately *Diamond Dogs* caused me so much inner conflict that I completely turned against him.

[It is only in writing this that it came to mind that there might have been an unconscious reaction based on my childhood memory of the Aladdin Principal Boy I had seen at the pantomime, a girl playing a boy, with whom I had felt such a strong identification, while this was a boy, playing, if not a girl, at least an androgynous and somewhat feminine character in a similar silky costume. I was engaged in an inner war with myself!]

Even at the time it was plain to me that he was only playing with crossing the gender boundaries society took for granted. He, as a young man, might play with androgyny, but it was more of an affront to me than a validation. In modern parlance, he was messing with my head. He was taking on a feminine appearance, but only as a role, theatre, while I wanted to *be*, and not merely *appear.*

I also became aware of Lou Reed, formerly of the *Velvet Underground*, through his *Transformer* album, and the infamous *Walk on the Wild Side.* I was always uncomfortable with the whole Andy Warhol scene of the time because there seemed to be a decadence to that culture. The transvestism and transsexuality associated with it seemed to be more an expression of that decadence than of inner truths, whatever the actuality may have been.

And so I retreated from this whole emerging gay and gender-bending scene, seeing not only nothing in it that I could identify with, but rather sensing something that was in many ways the opposite of what I was looking to express in myself.

Looking back with hindsight it occurs to me that my skin affliction may have had an unrecognised benefit. For the early part of my teens at boarding school I was perpetually assailed by my peers with social abuse about it, and taunted with names I will not repeat. Truly awful in my recollection, an inescapable torture, but had I not suffered from this physical condition, which was so unattractive, my androgyny might well have left me vulnerable to the predations of the pederasts.

It is widely thought by many that experiencing molestation at an impressionable age can lead to what one might call 'acquired' homosexuality, or have damaging effects on the psyche, such as poor personal boundaries; and while the social abuse and exclusion I experienced for my skin and perhaps for my unrecognised but un-consciously sensed gender identity damaged me emotionally in ways which it took me many years to heal and overcome, I can now at least be grateful for that protection which it granted me.

I was reading Hermann Hesse, exploring romantic philosophy and metaphysical notions. For a little while I tried to quell my imagination and took to the gym to try and build myself up into a more masculine being. I was torn between trying to become what I was supposed to be, and saving my androgynous body for the medical treatment I knew about and longed to one day achieve.

Even as I exercised in the gym, unlooked for reminders would be thrown at me as both encouragement and taunt. I recall one of the boys who had a natural masculine air, who was not one of the ho-mosexual crowd, glancing at me as I did sit-ups in the gym and com-menting jauntily, 'Sexy navel!' He was not one of those who abused me, nor did he lust after young boys, but I felt rather that this came as a recognition that I really was somewhat feminine in appearance, an-other one of the affirmations which the Universe would occasionally throw at me, and his natural alpha male posture gave him the street cred to be able to say such things with impunity from being called out as *queer*.

My life was thus a torture chamber of unrealised, and perhaps unrealisable, dreams of glimpsed possibilities, parodies of what I sought, and occasional hints that were just enough for me to not entirely give up hope that one day I might become who I felt I wanted to be. And all the while I swung like a pendulum between my secret desire and the guilt which pushed me to try to be a normal boy, however much conflict this might cause within me.

This other part of me was always whispering in my ear that if I could get a girlfriend into bed, then I would be able to establish a male identity, that if I could get a girl to like my body, I would be able to like it myself.

Seeking external validation for something that one's heart is not really in will never be the most successful path to anything, but at least I can say I tried before I gave up on it.

I was truly in conflict, which became worse as my teens progressed.

At the age of seventeen I was exploring both directions. I had begun seeing a girl whom I had met on my summer vacation job, but this only provoked more inner conflict since the more I experienced female companionship the more I wished to be like her.

Meanwhile my father was hoping that I would take up a career in the military. This was so far beyond what I felt about myself that I recoiled from it. The long years of separation due to his tours in Africa and my being at boarding school had sadly disconnected us.

So, I engaged in correspondence with Claire Rayner, a popular 'agony aunt' of the time who worked on the *Daily Mirror*.

She wrote back privately, suggesting that perhaps I felt this way because the boys at my school were more boisterous or aggressive and masculine than I, and that this had caused my sense of gender identity. I responded that my feelings about my body had existed long before, deep in my early childhood, to which in my second reply she suggested that I correspond with a gentleman who was a member of CHE, the Campaign for Homosexual Equality, a campaign group of the time, whose address she sent me.

It seemed clear to me that she didn't really understand my position, but I wrote to the man from CHE and explained that this was nothing to do with feelings of homosexuality, but entirely about my sense of my own body and my inability to feel comfortable with it. I think we only exchanged a couple of letters before I let it drop.

I look back now and can see the competing aspects of my personality that fought to gain control. Had I been successful in gaining a place at Cambridge, my whole life would have been different, but failing that, the tides around me opened new paths of awareness which I could not ignore, and for which I am immensely grateful.

First was the publication of Jan Morris's *Conundrum*. The former *Times* journalist and author (who as James Morris had been the first reporter to make the story of Hillary and Tensing's conquest of Everest, published on the morning of the Coronation) had shocked the establishment by having a 'sex change' in the early seventies.

I remember watching the Robin Day interview with Morris in the summer of 1974 with my mother, who said, 'I know what *I* am!' I grinned, laughing nervously. I went out and bought the book at WH Smith's the very next day. I could hardly wait for lunchtime to get away from my summer holiday job. I hid it, as its startling Op Art cover would have drawn attention from any who might have seen it and caused them to look further. I was more interested in the mechanics of transition, and the culminating surgery than in her philosophical ruminations about the meaning of gender. Had I been so, I might have remembered a reference she made to the subject from the science-fiction novel *Perelandra* by the renowned Christian scholar, author and mystic C. S. Lewis; one to which I shall return.

Not of huge significance in the greater scheme of things, but it certainly meant something to me to find that Morris had gone to the same public school as me, Lancing, although it had been retired to the banks of the River Teme during the wartime evacuation from the highly visible landmark which was the school on the South Downs near the coast that had been requisitioned for the war effort.

Nonetheless, I wrote to her and poured out my feelings. She must have had hundreds of such letters, and so I should not have been disappointed that all I got in return was a grey post card with the words 'Take your time! J'.

I don't recall if it had a return address on it. If it had, my mother might well have seen it. I certainly do remember that over breakfast my mother asked me about it and I brushed it off. My father at the time was still on tour in Nigeria. I can imagine that he would have not taken the Robin Day interview too happily.

Jan Morris's book, however, was only the starter course for what I was shortly to discover when I came up to Leeds as an undergraduate in the autumn of 1974 and a doorway opened before me, unlooked for.

CHAPTER 2

UNIVERSITY: TV/TS AND THE SCIENCE OF GENDER

C OMING UP TO university was one of the biggest disloca-
tions in my life. Fending for myself and having to make all
my own arrangements for the first time was demanding. I
expect that my feelings were perennially common to many freshers,
and as I look back I cringe at how naïve and lacking in social skills I
was.

The opening of the doorway which was to change the course of my
life happened soon. Barely two and a half weeks after my arrival the
moment happened.

Jerry Garcia told the story of how he and Phil Lesh had chosen the
name of their band, the Grateful Dead, from a musicological encyclo-
paedia while tripping on DMT. Something to the effect of 'it flowed
off the page like liquid fire glowing in red and gold'.

This wasn't quite so spectacular, but was an equally arresting and
seminal moment on my own timeline.

There was a row of notice boards in a particular passage of the
University Union that I happened to pass on my way somewhere. I
suppose I must have been idly glancing at the boards as I passed by,
but I was certainly not examining them all methodically.

I recall the exact spot where, on a small piece of paper pinned with brass tacks, I read the words:

Transvestite or Transsexual?

LUU[1] Transvestite and Transsexual Group

Meet Thursday evenings 7.30

Phone 7*****

There may not have been letters flowing in red and gold like fire but those words could not possibly have had a greater impact on me if they had.

I knew I had to follow this lead which had broken out before me so unexpectedly.

As an aside, it may be interesting to note that this was a good example of subliminal recognition. The notice jumped out at me because this was already an elaborated preoccupation in my mind, not least from the book I had read during the summer, and this shows how much of our experience we unconsciously process and screen out or select most of the time.

I nervously made the phone call that evening from a public box in the Student's Union, fearfully imagining that someone might see the number I was dialling. This was entering the Twilight Zone. A friendly lady's voice answered me and handled me very tactfully. Before I knew it I had been invited to their group that Thursday and given an address not far from the university.

Remember that this is the mid-seventies. What I was about to embark upon was entirely beyond the bounds of normal society, and something of which I had no experience and very little knowledge. If social influences were all that shape and drive us, why would I have felt this about myself in the first place? Why should I want to explore what was so far over the edge of all that I had known?

---

1   Leeds University Union.

Even at this early stage, I had formulated to myself the core hypothesis to which I still hold, and which research seems to be confirming, that people like me have some part or parts of their brains which have not developed as they should in terms of sexual differentiation.

But I was not thinking about the aetiology of transsexualism that night when I walked down the footpath over Woodhouse Moor to the garden flat where the group was to meet, although I would be soon.

The moment when I hesitantly knocked on the brown-painted French windows and a face pulled back the curtain from the glass to squint at me is indelibly imprinted on my psyche.

Seconds later I was inside.

I had so built up this moment with anticipation that it was actually something of an anti-climax to find that I was in a large bed-sitting room with several people sitting around drinking cups of tea. I sat on a green chaise longue while the lady to whom I had spoken on the phone and who had answered the door asked me gently about myself, the first time I had ever even acknowledged this subject with anyone face to face.

The group was extremely informal. A couple of gay friends, who just happened to have dropped by, were there, and one or two others whom I guessed were actual transvestites or even transsexuals.

A TV/TS disco had been arranged for that very Saturday and by the end of the evening it had all been arranged that I would join the gang and go there. The lady had promised to *dress* me.

I arrived at the flat mid-afternoon that Saturday and with two or three others prepared ourselves to go out that evening.

I had longish hair so it wasn't too much trouble to style but I had to borrow all the clothes I was to wear, of course, and my make-up was applied by hands other than my own.

This was the seventies, and make-up was applied more strongly. Anyway, it acted sufficiently to bolster my androgyny to passable femininity, and covered my awful skin.

We made it to the prefabricated flat-roofed Medical Students Union, which had been hired for the evening and where the entrance to the General Infirmary's A&E Department is now without any comment and I was amazed at how easy it had been. A perception which was soon to be rebuffed.

I must have seemed a little bit too comfortable or confident with how things had been going, as I was swiftly deposited at the door behind a table and told to take 50p off each member of the public who came into the disco. My unthought assumption that all the guests would be TV/TS or at least gay was soon challenged.

Before long, a burly troop of decidedly un-gay looking and definitely not transanything medical students were lining up to get in, presumably for access to the cheap bar, and with no interest in what actual University society was running the show.

I'm embarrassed to say that almost the first chap that I asked for '50p please' jumped out of his skin when he heard me speak. Apparently my visual appearance was quite good enough to be a cause of shock when he heard my voice! Perhaps it being Hallowe'en gave me a slight pass. But better to learn these things quickly through hard knocks than not at all.

The ensuing few months I lived something of a double life, but the next influence was to bring a link between them, and eventually be a big part of my coming to the wider understanding that I now hope to convey.

My interest in spirituality and my inner world had led me to take Psychology as one of my majors, and I had the great good fortune to have my first-year schedule lectures on Physiological Psychology with Dr John Blundell, now Professor of Psychobiology at Leeds University, and to have him as my personal tutor.

Physiological Psychology included a wide range of material, from foundational research on adrenaline responses to the neurological basis for hunger and thirst and, of course, sex differences.

I had already come across some material on sex differences by Dr John Money the previous year when I had visited a friend at Sussex University which was near my school. Dr Money was a very influential figure in the field of gender identity and sex differences at the time, and he was to be included in Dr Blundell's lectures, but there were also to be covered the actual hormonal and neurological basis of sexual differentiation, and behavioural drives as well, which were already fairly well understood by that time in the mid-seventies.

In countless experiments, researchers had exposed rats and mice to varying levels of sex hormones while they were still *in utero* and found that when they matured into adults, their sexual behaviour had been influenced to be different from the normal course of development.

It was also found that the actual sexual anatomy itself was determined by the levels of hormones it was exposed to at early stages of development.

This provided a readily understandable and scientifically testable model of sexual development. Intersex forms and homosexual behaviour in both sexes could be produced in the experimental subjects and I immediately postulated in my own mind that I had experienced some intermediate neurological effect leading to my own sense of my body.

Absolutely key to the understanding of how the sexing of bodies comes about is the condition of Androgen Insensitivity Syndrome (AIS) in which genetic males (XY) are unable to become virilised *in utero* due to an Androgen Receptor (AR) gene mutation which affects and prevents cells from being able to respond to androgens. There are a number of variations of this condition from Complete (CAIS) to Partial (PAIS). All early-stage embryos begin with female external genital morphology, which is normally accelerated by the androgenising effect of testosterone in XY foetuses so as to develop male external morphology. Being unable to respond to testosterone, CAIS babies develop as morphological girls except that they have undescended testes and no uterus.

The importance of this condition is that it shows that the mere presence of a Y chromosome, while necessary for development into a male, is not sufficient. The developmental pathways in which the expression of the Y gene is manifested have several stages to them, and if they are not all completed, then virilisation will be incomplete. It is possible that in non-CAIS 'male' foetuses with XY chromosomes, interruptions to *in utero* androgens can mimic some of the effects of CAIS, most particularly on the nervous system.

Children born with CAIS are invariably raised as girls, being of a normal phenotypic female appearance and their condition is usually unnoticed until puberty when they fail to menstruate and medical examination eventually reveals the truth. They almost always have an unambiguous female gender identity.[2] This is considered by many to be strong evidence for gender differentiation of neural structures before birth.

Adrenogenital Syndrome is a reverse condition in which, due to other biochemical conditions, genetic females are virilised to some extent, sometimes resulting in ambiguous or enlarged genitals and a tendency to hirsutism.

There are thus clearly strong influences on developmental gender expression by sex and other hormones. Both of these conditions I have highlighted demonstrate that sex is not an *either/or* situation, genetically fixed at the moment of conception, but one that is brought about by precursor influences, and which can become anomalous if these are mixed up or interrupted. The common phenotypes of each sex are

---

2   I had never heard of a person with CAIS experiencing cross-gender identity until I recently came across this study of one who did. The extreme rarity of such an occurrence suggests other factors may be at play which could have negated or overridden the normal effects of this genetic condition. Possibly there are as yet unknown genetic factors on other chromosomes than those so far examined. The researchers also suggest the possibility that functioning Androgen Receptor pathways may not be essential for the development of a male gender identity. See also 5-alpha Reductase intersex p156 footnote 61. https://www.ncbi.nlm.nih.gov/pubmed/20358272 (2020).

only the *optimum* outcomes for sexual development and reproduction, not fixed one size fits all digital categories. This has important philosophical implications, which I will expand on later.

Social learning and postmodern theorists have contested the importance of these influences on behaviour between the sexes, but while not only has much evidence of sex differences in the brain emerged in the intervening decades, there are also the truly ancient biological roots, which we share with rodents and mammals in general, which must be laid alongside the evolutionarily recent overlay of socially acquired gendered attributes.

We also considered how rough and tumble behaviour in young male primates has long been observed by animal behaviourists to significantly outweigh the same behaviour in young females, who have been observed to prefer grooming behaviours. This highly statistically significant observation is seen widely in different primate species, including humans and clearly has some basis in developmental neurology or endocrinology or both, yet to this day social behaviourists still try to cast doubt on the results or the methodologies employed, seeming to insist that such a thing is merely an artefact of experimental bias, rather than admitting the possibility that it might be them who are putting the cart of their conclusions before the horse of the evidence. Evolutionary Psychology was not really yet a fully developed thing at that time as it is now, but the evidence supports its predictions.

Dr Blundell mentioned transsexualism and even Jan Morris's book in the lectures not far into the year. He was a specialist in hypothalamic mechanisms of hunger and thirst. Sex is closely involved with the hypothalamus and he speculated about what, if any, neurological substrates might be involved in transsexualism.

His academic thoroughness in covering all the different aspects of a subject was however to lead down some blind alleys — although it wasn't his fault. The perennial *Nature vs Nurture* debate had to be gone into and this was one good instance of it.

Dr John Money, whom I have mentioned, was already a prominent figure in the world of research on sex differences. He proposed a *Social Learning* model of sex differences in behaviour rather than the previously accepted traditional views.

Perhaps the most influential piece of research that he had to offer had been ongoing since the early sixties; on a certain child who had had the misfortune to have had his penis cut off when being circumcised at an early age. Dr Money had counselled the parents that if the child was surgically altered to appear morphologically female with the sex reassignment techniques which by then had been developed, brought up as a girl and given female hormones at the appropriate time for puberty, then the child would develop as a normally adjusted young woman, albeit unable to have children.

The distraught parents were persuaded, and the long nightmare of the Reimer family had begun.

The world was not to know the truth of this for some decades. At the time, in the mid-seventies, all we had were reports from Dr Money that the child, then about thirteen or fourteen, was adapting well and had socialised satisfactorily as a girl, with no knowledge of 'her' medical history.

I will come to the true story in due course, and the malign influence of Dr Money, but for me in that time frame, this was to become a potent influence. It took a while for the ground to become fertile for this seed, but its bitter fruit misled me for many years.

One other key concept that I was introduced to was more focussed in the lectures on Perception and Cognition, although it had a wider applicability. This was *probabilistic functionalism*, which is really just a fancy way of saying that we perceptually interpret our sense data in ways that will *probably work*. But the concept is relevant to general evolutionary survival adaptation, and ultimately to gender differences. I didn't think about it in relation to that at the time, but later, much later, I realised its importance.

In the meantime, so much was going on that I could barely process and assimilate it all.

It astonishes me in retrospect how much I fitted into that first year at university. Many things seemed to spontaneously fall into place. One in the group had the book *I Want What I Want*,[3] an incredibly well-informed novel about a transsexual transitioning in the sixties. I read it avidly, and then like magic it appeared on television and we all watched it as a group huddled round the black-and-white rented TV.

After that first lecture on developmental sex differences, I approached Dr Blundell and introduced myself. I cannot imagine how I dared but I explained about the TV/TS Group and invited him to meet us! He duly soon came to a meeting one Thursday. I never knew how strong an impact this had had on him until recently when I got in touch to let him know I was writing this book and he told me that he had related the event many times as an example of two-way learning that can occur in the university setting, and one of the unexpected but valuable experiences that can happen to an academic. I was immensely pleased to hear this.

Things developed with the TV/TS Group. The organisers had been involved with a conference about TV/TS at the University Union during the previous spring vacation period, and there was quite a strong Gay Liberation Front (GLF) locally which had supported it.[4]

I was only dimly aware of this recent history at the time, but something I did find out about quite quickly was that my hosts were linked to a network of TV/TS groups around the country. There was a group in Manchester who would meet and come over to visit us, amongst whom was a highly motivated young FtM chap by the name of Stephen Whittle, to whom I briefly became quite close, who was later to become the driving force behind the Press for Change group

---

3   Brown, Geoff; *I Want What I Want,* Putnam, New York 1967.

4   http://www.gender.org.uk/gendys/2007/39ekins.htm (2020).

which many years later lobbied for our legal recognition, but in ways that not all would agree with.

Quite amusingly the local organiser of the Leeds chapter of the Beaumont Society lived just down the road, a short step of less than two hundred yards. The Beaumont Society was a group for heterosexual transvestites, many of whom were married, and which organised events where members could attend *en femme*, using their adopted female names.

A couple of us walked down there one Saturday, and on a Thursday 'she' and a friend would often call in at the group, *dressed* as the argot had it.

This was all a very long way from a boy's boarding school on the South Downs! Also it felt rather bizarre as well. What my roomies at the student flats would have thought I'd rather not contemplate.

It felt like it took a long time, but it was only about February in the following year, my second term that I approached a psychiatrist at the Student Health Centre. One of our group was seeing him herself and so it seemed a logical connection.

He didn't say a lot as I explained, feeling rather foolish, that I had always felt that I should have been a girl and that I hoped to have gender reassignment. However, he didn't ridicule or seriously challenge me but rather sent me to have some medical tests.

Perhaps the fact that I had already started having facial hair removal at an electrolysis clinic in town indicated that my motivation was real. I was only 19 and had just a sparse facial growth, but completing facial hair removal was considered the Holy Grail of *passing* in the seventies; it was painful and took a long time, so one had to get started as soon as possible. Again my friends from the group had pointed me in the right direction to the electrology clinic.

When the tests came back, he wanted to ask me if I had been taking female hormones as my levels were elevated. He might have wondered if I had got them off my friend to whom he was already prescribing, but I hadn't. I expect this all had some influence on how he considered my case.

After about the third appointment, he gave me a prescription for some female hormone tablets and I was over the moon. The first hurdle successfully overcome!

But this was the least of the hurdles I was to encounter.

The hormones had very little effect on my body, and I was later to discover that I had only been prescribed a very low dose, perhaps because I already had a noticeable level, or perhaps because he was just humouring me. I'll never know.

In the April vacation, I accompanied one from the group to the Beaumont Society Conference being held in a hall of residence at Leicester University and here for the first time fully I was to see the divide between the radical and conventional wings of this world.[5]

Not the distinction between transsexual and transvestite, or *transgender* as eventually the term came to be, but between fitting oneself in with the established gender patterns of society or seeking to use one's condition as a justification, a lever to be brought to bear on changing and eventually, as it has become, upending those established patterns.

Most of those attending were discreet people who didn't want to draw attention to their private lives, and there were talks and discussions referring to transvestism as a *condition*. There was, however, a contingent who sought to take a more radical approach, akin to that of GLF, a very small minority though they were.

Already here, in the earliest days of my exploration of the trans world, I was encountering the two parties who still to this day are battling it out. *Nature vs Nurture* wasn't confined to the lecture theatre and the history of Psychology.

Back in Leeds that summer I saw much of this with the political phenomenon of *Radical Drag*, in which gay men would sport ultra-camp attire such as pink tutus with a full beard.

5   Ibid.

The radical sex and gender political scene of the time was completed with the *Radical Feminists* and the *Separatist Lesbians*, with whom I had little to do but heard a lot about, who seemed to be quite influential in our little demi-monde of this alternative scene.

The feminists were by all accounts very hostile to transsexuals, and didn't make any distinction between us and the transvestites. The worlds of the Beaumont Society and the radical feminists were polar opposites in many ways.

The chief antagonism they had with us was that they accused us of *role playing* as females. There was a complicated argument which went that if you weren't born female, you couldn't know what it was like and therefore couldn't want to be like that. This is a troublesome enough idea in itself, since clearly it is an almost universal human experience to aspire to or envy the condition of another, but they then, it seemed to me, contradicted themselves. And this is where they had much in common with the third-wave feminists of today.

They claimed that the only differences between the sexes (other than the actual physical ones, obviously) were due to social conditioning. So, the only reason you knew you were a girl or a boy was because you had been brought up to believe that, and anatomy and hormonal influences and drives had absolutely nothing to do with it.

Thus, they should have been more sympathetic to trans people since, at least in their own reckoning, they could have accepted that we were people who had somehow inadvertently got socially conditioned the wrong way and should belong among them. But instead we were branded as assisting in the enforcement of female oppression in collusion with the patriarchy.

Not that I believe such things. However, in the bizarre world of seventies radical feminism such things *were* bandied about. The disturbing thing is really that people are *still* bandying these things about more than forty years later with far greater effect.

A key to this can be found in a chance comment I recall in a conversation I had with the woman who was one of the principal organisers of the TV/TS group. I remember talking with her about sex differences, what they were based on and the political implications. I said, 'Men and women may be *equal*, but they are *different*', and she replied, 'Yes, but *we can't admit it.*' She went on to argue that only by making the case on the basis that equality of human value meant equality in all other respects could the cause of feminism be advanced.

I reconnected with this lady a few years ago through the wonders of the internet, and she is still a lovely, kind person. But it grieves me that the feminism which has grown and spread from that time has been based on a lie. If women and men *are* different, there should be different conditions allowed when these differences come into play.

And if the sexes *are different,* the radical feminists who claim that the differences exist only through social role conditioning must also be wrong.

I don't want to linger longer than necessary over the disordered imaginings of the radical feminists, amongst whom I do not classify my old friend; these were *much more radical* than even what I have quoted her as saying, but I would later, much later, encounter writings that demonstrated that there were currents within radical feminism which actively promoted hatred against men, *simply for being men* and then went on to blame transsexuals for 'reinforcing' the supposed oppressive patriarchal system. These were the trends of radical sexual politics of the time and, regrettably, such ideas still have much influence.

I was well out of my depth. This was the mid-seventies; the Left was in the ascendancy and Marxism infected everything. I found myself at the meeting point between personal sexual and gender identity and tides of political influence that sought to subdue and exploit it to its own ends.

In my second term I had moved out of the grim student flats in south Leeds and gone to a house with two others from the group. What the working class people of the Beechwoods thought of us I dread to think. Fortunately, I never found out!

This stage only lasted until the summer vac, and I took the opportunity to move into the garden flat newly vacated by my friends who ran the group, since one of them was now transitioning full time and a move to a different part of the city would save too many awkward explanations locally.

I imagined that having a place of my own for the first time would help in my own transition, but I was so young and naïve that I had no experience of surviving on my own in the world.

It wasn't long before the overlap or clash of the different worlds I inhabited started to cause stress and conflict in my life.

On the one hand, I had been making friends with a transsexual who lived only a couple of streets away, who was a total Marxist, and a bit of a mess, frankly. My friends from the group had advised me against her, and probably rightly so, but when they moved away and some of those I was still hanging out with were also friends with her, it was that or no trans friends.

But most of *her* friends were the Gay Liberation Crowd, which meant just about all gay men (except for the odd supportive woman, like my friend from the TV/TS group, who were usually straight). It was primarily through her that I came to know about the radical feminists and the lesbian separatists.

The social changes of the late sixties had brought about an increased tolerance to male homosexuality, especially after the Roy Jenkins legalisation in 1967, but tolerance between male and female homosexuals seemed less prevalent than ever before.

Earlier that year, when my friends were still residing in their flat by the park, I had arrived for the group one Thursday evening to find that a gathering of half a dozen or so angry-looking women were in the flat instead of my friends whom I had expected. I asked for them by name and was brusquely ushered through to the kitchen where my friend who was transitioning had taken the television and was sitting watching it with a cup of tea.

She explained that it was a *Consciousness Raising Group*, a phenomenon of the time with feminists who basically took the opportunity to vent, and the only rule was that others should accept their *material* unconditionally. Many years later I was to find an interesting retrospective view on this phenomenon, when I had achieved greater self-realisation, although that was much, much later, and an early seed of this book. But I digress.

We, as transsexuals, were definitely not accepted, unconditionally or otherwise. In fact we were barely tolerated, even within my friend's own shared flat.

So the culture that I found myself immersed in was essentially that of GLF, and that was a mostly male population. And many of them were of the extreme exhibitionist type, with Radical Drag and hysterical camp behaviour.

Definitely not what I needed.

And then I began overlapping into mainstream local culture when I moved to the garden flat. The girl upstairs would be playing Natty Dread by Bob Marley as she sat in her bay window in the sun and her friends were always in and out; it was summer vacation by the park. Or they would sit on the grass under the trees in the sunshine drinking cider, and Fleetwood Mac or Melanie would find their way onto the turntable as the sash window would be pushed up to let them blare out.

It didn't take me long to slide back into the seventies hippie milieu and resile from that which I had got into so fast.

If I had felt a true connection into the GLF culture of the time, I would have persisted. But after my friends who ran the group moved away, and then moved again, out of Leeds, sooner than I'd expected, parting to the four winds forever, seemingly I was alone in this. There was no one in the gay scene that I could relate to. I wasn't in this for the sexual kicks, which was beyond most of their conceptions, and I didn't want to be some kind of camp queen. Simply, I recoiled from the culture they promoted. I was not some kind of gay transvestite, but someone who wanted to experience being female, or as close as it was possible to do. And I didn't want to *role play* as the feminists would have it. I didn't really have a proper sense of my own identity, but I wanted to be able to find it, to find it by being embodied as a woman.

At the end of the summer term, the two gay men whom I had met at my first visit had helped me present the case to get a second year's funding for the group from the University Union, but I never carried it through. I was already shrinking not just from the responsibility to others in organising meetings, but from what people might think of me. I was too young to take a leading role.

I needed to be much more firmly grounded than I was at the time to be able to cope with all that this entailed.

As the autumn drew on and I returned to university, I remember that moment when I had some new acquaintances around at my place one evening, and some of the gay gang came knocking. I turned them away. Politely, but I was withdrawing from that world. It took me a few months more to stand back fully from my own path, but that was probably a foregone conclusion once my friends from the group had gone and I had to face things on my own.

As the autumn progressed to winter, I went into something of a meltdown. High potency LSD was in plentiful supply in those days, probably from the Welsh factory soon to be raided in the Operation Julie affair, and several times in November and December I engaged with its spirit. Following the last adventure on Solstice Eve, I chickened out. For the best of reasons. I was taken with a dream of romantic love that I felt I should seek to straighten out this aberration in my soul. The eventual irony of this I ignored for years. The couple by whom this acid-fuelled fantasy had been inspired were divorced not so long afterwards.

The very fact that I was dropping lots of acid was probably a strong indicator that I wasn't ready to be making big decisions. I needed to gain a great deal more understanding of myself, of my condition, of who I was, my ambitions and dreams beyond my sexual or gender identity.

I had learnt a lot in my year with the TV/TS Group and even GLF. The technical and medical information about how to seek sex reassignment had prepared me for when I was personally ready, and saved me a lot of trouble at that later time. But I was too young and the culture I was in was not healthy. I panicked. As the Fremen in Frank Herbert's *Dune* say, 'Better to miss an opportunity than risk disaster.'

It was not only my personal path, when I was ready, and when I did choose to engage with it, that it had prepared me for, although that was the most important for me; it had introduced me to many ideas, trends and movements that we shall see come back as we travel along this path.

But from here, I took a step back to collect myself.

CHAPTER 3

SEEKING SELF-KNOWLEDGE

I HAD MANY OTHER interests in life apart from being obsessed with being a member of the opposite sex to that into which I was apparently born, and for several years after the acid binge, which took me back from the brink, I explored my interests in art, and then the Occult, both of which had engaged my attention since my early teens. For readers new to this, the word 'Occult' simply means *hidden*, and since my inner life was itself hidden, it is perhaps no surprise that I explored other hidden things. I hadn't yet grasped the importance of Carl Jung's concept of the *Collective Unconscious,* which linked meaning, symbols, memory and even their biological roots.

And so I had mocked my post-graduate supervisor Mike for his involvement in the University Occult Society. (Leeds University Union has had an Occult Society for many years which has ranged over countless different philosophical systems during its long existence). I was then some years later to find myself drawn to such matters myself. During this time, Dr Blundell continued as my tutor but very diplomatically declined to enquire as to my progress even though it might have been obvious at the time that I had resiled from my path.

Perhaps it was the Unicorn Bookshop edition of Aleister Crowley's *Book of the Law*[1] which sealed my fate. Inside this modest little paper edition was the admonition:

'The study of this Book is forbidden. It is wise to destroy this copy after first reading.'

One of the wilder of my new acquaintances in the local hippie scene had deposited this in my keeping shortly after my acid excess and I had timidly peeked inside. It was to be some time before I actually read the full text, and was not fully yet into the psychology of Jung, which is where a lot of occultists have started, as well as that of Abraham Maslow, Carl Rogers and the like.

I began to consider whether it was possible that I had some kind of psychological illness. Well, to be honest, I had oscillated around this belief for all my life. It was the principal concern on my acid trip when I turned back from transition. Or in a moral sense perhaps I was simply infected with evil. I had to do something about it, and so I explored these ideas and my own sense of fitting in with them. My inner weirdness was driving me to exploration of bizarre worlds. As to Crowley, it was more that I dared to look at his material, however hesitantly, and thereby set myself on a path of daring to face rather than shrink from challenge, regardless of whether there was actually anything in his writing that I took to or not, which there wasn't.

His dictum '*Do What Thou Wilt Shall Be The Whole Of The Law*' does however seem to have become the creed of the postmodern world, whether there are direct routes of transmission of his ideas or not. His other famous saying, taken from Nietzsche who had apparently taken it from Hassan-i Sabbah, the leader of the mediaeval hashishim, '*Nothing is True, Everything is Permitted*', is in much the same vein. Both suggest that Society and Other[2] are things that should be

---

1   Crowley, Aleister *Liber AL Vel Legis (The Book of the Law)*, Unicorn Books edition, c 1970 (first ed. 1925).

2   *Other:* The philosophical counterpoint to *Self* first introduced by G. W. F. Hegel in the early nineteenth Century.

treated with disregard. Strangely, many of his ideas have kept recurring on my path, and each time I have found them less attractive.

Carl Jung had gone through a breakdown of sorts that he had worked through with images from his dreams and alchemy, the first art therapy, and it seemed a good idea to use my interest in art and fuse it with Psychology in order to help heal whatever this disorder was in my soul, creatively, psychoanalytically, and so after graduating I set out to become an art therapist, not only as a professional therapeutic skill, but to fix myself.

I didn't feel safe to share this with anyone and so tried to do it all within myself. Throughout the late seventies and early eighties, I had encounters with the successor generation to the radical feminists of the mid-seventies. Less hardcore, more what I would later define as New Age, but still with a clear antagonism to all things to do with men.

My innate tropism led me to seek out their company, masochist that I must have been, but I would not find my solution there, even though at times those amongst their number would acknowledge my own sense of myself, albeit perhaps unintentionally.

One particular lesbian, who happened to teach a yoga class at the university which I would attend in the years following graduation, once complimented me on being 'graceful'. She had a kind of surprise in the way she said this, as if she was finding it hard to acknowledge in her mind what she felt or sensed about me; there was the same feel as when the masculine boy had commented on me in the gym.

There was also the tension between my own sense of what I felt I wanted to be, and the still existent fact of my body as it was then.

I didn't like it, but felt that I should make myself, that I should accommodate my mind to the conditions in which I found myself.

The hopelessness of most of that era is something I would never wish to relive. I remember trying to adopt a masculine persona and looked for one to model myself on. A friend was a big fan of Clint Eastwood and so I sought to emulate his strong silent manner. This attempt only lasted about a day or two before I realised I could never maintain the front.

Perhaps I had been inspired by my memory of a lecture I had attended in my second or third year at the university, given by the near legendary figure of ethology, Nobel Prize Laureate (with Konrad Lorenz and Karl von Frisch) Niko Tinbergen. Ethology is the study of animal behaviour, and Professor Tinbergen had done foundational work on the study of the mating and territorial behaviour of the stickleback,[3, 4] besides much else. I recall sitting high up in a back row of the packed Rupert Beckett lecture theatre to listen to the great man recount how he had observed the instinctive patterns of mating behaviour between the male and female stickleback.

Certain key stimuli, such as the bright red chest and blue back of the male during the mating season excite competitive aggression in other males, and demonstrate the fitness of the male to mate with females.

This behaviour is driven by internal hormonal conditions. He must also perform a sort of zig-zag dance in order to persuade the female that he has all the qualities needed to be a suitable mate. While there is, of course, a large phylogenetic distance between sticklebacks and humans, there are however what one might call archetypal patterns of similarity across the spectrum of species. The need for the male to prove that it is fit to fertilise the female's eggs above all else. Supernormal stimuli, exaggerated representations of normal appearances, were found to be strong triggers to competitive territorial behaviour, while Fixed Action Patterns were found in the mating behaviours. These are patterns of behaviour which are repeated exactly in response to trigger stimuli, such as the mating dance of the male

3   Tinbergen, N. 'The Curious Behavior of the Stickleback', Scientific American, vol. 187, issue 6, pp. 22–26, http://adsabs.harvard.edu/abs/1952SciAm.187f..22T (2020).

4   https://www.psywww.com/intropsych/ch08-animals/classic-ethology. html#sticklebacks (2020).

if performed correctly. Even in humans we find that both men and women emphasise and exaggerate sexual characteristics for purposes of sexual competition, both in physical appearance and behaviour: women flaunting their physical fitness to reproduce and men not only their physical strength, but also their wealth and its implied competence.

We might say that certain stimuli, whether in physical appearance or behaviour, are essential parts of the patterns which unlock the mating responses, not just in sticklebacks, but throughout the animal kingdom.

I felt that if I could establish myself in a relationship with a woman, a sexual relationship, that I could perhaps learn to love my body that I hated so much. Unfortunately, I was unable to fulfil the necessary displays to trigger the responses in women that I might wish to become involved with. I simply didn't understand what was required, even that something particular was required! I didn't have the inner energy to fully realise the short-lived Clint Eastwood persona. One may read about how women don't like super masculine men but, given the choice, women do tend to prefer more dominant and masculine men because they demonstrate qualities which would be advantageous in survival situations and in providing resources for future offspring. These are deep unconscious patterns, which we do not need to think about, should not think about too much.

If one doesn't like certain characteristics about oneself, one is hardly likely to be able to fully develop them so as to elicit the kind of instinctual responses that they are meant to.

One reads surveys in magazines which say things like '79% of women hate their bodies' or dislike them or some similar negative feeling. When people say this, what they really mean is that they are unhappy with how much their body shape deviates from the societal norm, or the evolutionary optimum, or the most attractive, or simply that they are out of shape, overweight and unattractive. All of which pretty much come to the same thing. They don't really hate their bodies. They are just dissatisfied with them. They would like them to be better but perhaps they can't be bothered to do the work in the gym or cut down on the calories, or they are unwilling to accept those inherited characteristics which are immutable.

But when I hated my body it wasn't like that. I didn't even dislike most of my body. Except those parts which prevented me from being a girl, and which infected the rest of my body with their poison.

I dare say that it is a difficult and fraught pursuit for many men seeking a mate, but not feeling that I really was a man and that I was only engaging in the pursuit in order to try and confirm this thing that I didn't believe in was a path of despair to my soul.

The social group and scene that I fell in with had a couple of bikers who rode Nortons and so I followed that lead and eventually got a small bike of my own. I was constructing a social persona as the Marxist feminists claimed happened.

What I did not know at the time was that the false reporting of John Money that his guinea pig was socially adapted was a narrative which was falling apart at the same time as I was attempting to implement what would effectively be its implications. I should have realised that I had been subject to an entire childhood of male social conditioning and influences and it had never taken in my heart and soul. Research on aversion therapy, which I had read about as a student, indicated that sexual impulses might be suppressed but were still a force that had to be expressed somehow. To be successfully redirected, the sexual impulses must find an at least equally rewarding alternative. And this wasn't even a sexual impulse in the usual sense.

I sought an at least equally rewarding alternative through my mid-twenties. But when I thought I had achieved it, its foundations would collapse like a house built over a pit and I would be pitched into it only to face my own inner cause once more. Through many years in my twenties I would have dreams that I was perched at the top of a high rise block of flats, which was teetering and about to collapse. I would always be trying to find my way back to a beautiful, large, old house that I had briefly lived in, and I knew that this was me perched on my fragile persona trying to find my way to my true home in myself. I would not leave the tower block, which also felt like a prison, for good until this was all resolved.

I suppose I shouldn't really have been that surprised when upon reaching a certain degree of intimacy with a girl that telling her of my secret desire she would freak out and leave me. And it was probably a good thing too, as had they been all accepting and supportive, I might have got trapped in a prison of my own device. Perhaps I could have staved off my inner sense of myself for a bit longer, but it would always have been some kind of stop gap. And what if we had had children? What impact would it have on them? I knew nothing of epigenetics but perhaps this condition had elements that could be passed down. It was something I needed to deal with myself and not rely on someone else to save me from.

And so I set out on trying to fix myself. *Zen and the Art of Motorcycle Maintenance* by Robert Pirsig was big at the time. I read it, and lived it for a while through my motorbike. I learnt a lot about mindfulness and gained more confidence in my ability to face obstacles and fix my own problems.

A couple of years after graduation, I went back to college and took a Foundation course in Art and Design in order to pursue my goal of becoming an art therapist, and after this gained some experience of the mental health field as a nursing assistant on a local psychiatric ward.

Always I oscillated back and forth between seeking to become normal in my feelings about myself and my secret wish that I could not expunge from my mind for one day, for one hour, for one minute or second of all this time. Getting close to women was heaven and hell.

I had practised meditation since my time at university, where I had been introduced to TM, and it had helped me gain some handle on my inner world as I went through all this. I may not have been able to stop or change it, but perhaps I could at least try to understand it as a first step to something.

I experimented with different alternative therapies and techniques gleaned from my study of alternative psychology and esoteric philosophy.

Guided fantasy 'pathworkings' were a safe entry point, which I engaged in and fitted in with the art therapy, but also slow and requiring reflection to explore one's inner landscape and associations. This blended into my more general meditation practice and was the foundation for the self-knowledge that my wilder excursions eventually led me to.

Then there was 'Co-Counselling', a fringe technique that involved 'discharging distress'. Akin to Primal Scream Therapy, it gave a temporary relief from one's feelings, but it was only releasing them for a while and there was no progress with the underlying cause, which never went away.

One of the big ideas which some Feminists of the time had was armouring, derived in part from Reichian therapy. This was based on the concept that trauma and defensiveness get embedded in our bodies and we consequently become rigid in our postures, leading to illness and disease.

This is quite a basic concept, which I think now is widely understood as a psychosomatic basis for some illnesses. However, there are many other learnt things, both good and bad, which get encoded into our bodies and their habitual postures. The actions of riding a bicycle or handwriting are encoded in our bodies as unconscious potential and are of much benefit. A soldier or an athlete will have acquired what a feminist therapist might label as armour that he has spent hard years building up within himself. As we so commonly see, the postmodern culture of critique seeks to destroy rather than refine the objects of its attentions.

This seemed to be the drive of Co-Counselling, to knock down all the walls and release all the hidden material that might be lurking there. I won't argue that people may have buried or conflictual material that they need to bring to light and deal with, but there was, and I believe still is, a dangerous thread in this type of culture which encourages the development of a kind of hyper emotionality that is regressive, atavistic, rather than healing and reconstitutive. I mention this now because this sort of needy emotionality seems to have become a foundational thread in the mindset of Third Wave Feminism and indeed in much of postmodern leftism.

The evocation of deep material without some sense of how to properly channel the energy associated with it is not a path to be encouraged. It certainly did nothing for my own deep feeling of discord other than to make it more pointed, to feel more jagged and raw. And in the context of the type of feminist milieu in which it was happening, in which I was embedded, there was at the same time a culture that would have scorned the expression of these deepest feelings, while having disdain for any sense of masculinity that I was desperately attempting to find within myself at the time.

The roots of feminist anger and projection of guilt are deep, and as I look back over the decades, it seems more and more like a cult. There is always some political firebrand who wants to remake the world in their own image rather than to accept it and try to work to improve it.

I learnt from this experience, but I did not find what I had been looking for, and my learning was eventually only to understand the long-term perspective of how this fits into the protracted War on Gender, which the Left and postmodernism have been pursuing since some time in the mid-twentieth century.

More akin to modern personal growth programmes were the several visualisation techniques which I tried, derived from the various threads of esoteric practice that I was exploring.

I treated this as a depth psychology exercise. I was aiming to release whatever block or hidden imbalance was causing my bizarre life-long preoccupation that I seemed unable to shake, and restore, establish what I felt should be the case, or at least replace it with some inserted goal or programme appropriate, which would correct my aberration.

This reached its culmination during the period of my post-graduate course in Art Therapy, which I undertook in St Albans.

I had by now, at the age of about twenty-six, somehow managed to construct a life wherein I was engaged, my fiancée a psychiatric staff nurse whom I had met while working in the psychiatric unit. Looking back, it was obvious that she was really in love with my motorbike, or the personality which it had led her to project onto me. As I approached a stage where I hoped to be both married and professionally qualified, it seemed that I might have at last settled into a path that I could be content with.

But this was merely the calm before the storm, the hillside waiting for the pebble to precipitate the landslide that would expose the bare truth beneath.

The culmination of my war against myself came as I set about a rigorous practice of daily prayer asking to be cleansed and freed of this curse. I had wavered in and out of religious faith all my life, and my mother at one point suggested that perhaps I should think about entering the Church, although my philosophical inclinations were far too wildly away from orthodoxy.

It is said that men in the trenches who had been staunch atheists would fall on their knees to pray and beg for protection after they had been under fire for a suitable length of time.

I had been 'under fire' all my life and now it seemed that prayer was all that was left to me. Perhaps that brief encounter with the writing of 'the most evil man in the world', as the *Daily Express* had labelled Aleister Crowley, had got the wind up me. Whatever the case, I was down on my knees begging for release, invoking all the powers of angels and entreating the Lord from the depths of my soul three times daily.

To those of my readers who may feel that this is somewhat off the wall, I should mention that Sir Isaac Newton himself was interested in

Hermetic Philosophy;[5] having as a young man developed the calculus and extensively developed the science of optics, he then went off into reclusion and spent a number of years studying alchemy and biblical prophecy. He made prophetic calculations from the dimensions of the Great Pyramid,[6] and if he had died at that point, he would be a significant figure in the history of science, but he would not have achieved the legendary titanic status which he did later, and would perhaps be seen as something of an eccentric who sadly went off the rails.

But not so. His best work was yet to come and upon his return to more concrete and visible matters, apparently having integrated some Hermetic concepts into his work, he was to describe the very laws of the motions of the heavens through the application of his insights.

Whatever objective importance his work on Isaiah or the Great Pyramid may have is not for me to say, but perhaps amongst other things these ruminations allowed his deep unconscious to percolate and process data which might otherwise have remained unresolved. Certainly, the understanding of the Laws of Motion and the putting of this into precise mathematical form for the first time were not the product of a superstitious and irrational mind, but of one which was seeking to find order and pattern in the Universe, to make sense of that which we find before us in our sensory world.

And so I too was seeking to find meaning and make sense, but of my own inner world. As I began my Art Therapy year, I also began the sequence of prayer which I hoped would cleanse me and free the spirit of my Higher Self to be able to be expressed and manifested through me.

---

5   https://www.britannica.com/biography/Isaac-Newton (2020).

6   Newton, Isaac *A Dissertation upon the Sacred Cubit of the Jews and the Cubits of several Nations: in which, from the Dimensions of the Greatest Pyramid, as taken by Mr. John Greaves, the ancient Cubit of Memphis is determined* John Greaves, Miscellaneous Works of Mr. John Greaves, Professor of Astronomy in the University of Oxford, vol. 2 (London: 1737), pp. 405–433. http://www.newtonproject.ox.ac.uk/view/texts/normalized/THEM00276 (2020).

It was in one sense a religious practice, a devotional prayer for aid and healing.

The atheists who promote postmodern Gender Theory will probably dismiss this kind of thing, but I would say that they have lost touch with reality and spun off into a fantasy if they deny the power of the unseen and numinous archetypal forces behind existence. This book may contain scientific facts which I believe support my conviction that there are real medical or neuropsychological factors involved with this phenomenon of transsexualism, but that is not to limit it to such.

If it did not bring me to the very inner ground of my being in an existential crisis whence I cried out to myself 'What am I?', then it would not be such a thing as I had to make this prayer for liberation in the way that I did, to beg for release from whatever powers I was subject to. This was beyond the management of reason or logic. I later would learn the term *thrownness* coined by Heidegger to describe the condition of being thrown into a situation that I had never made of my conscious volition.

Every day, three times each day, I went through the prayer ritual and repeated it silently in my mind if the circumstances did not allow otherwise.

Perhaps I was invoking divine and angelic assistance, or a higher spiritual part of myself, and perhaps all I was doing was trying to brainwash myself into believing that I was and could be something other than I felt.

It is of little matter to speculate at this juncture. I shall come to metaphysical matters later and address them. Here I am concerned to deal with the practical matter of how to cope with seemingly unshakable feelings of revulsion to one's own sexual body and an equally unshakable desire to be like that of the opposite sex, not just physically but in all ways possible. Whatever the metaphysical nature of what I did during those months, it was done with the desperate intent to heal myself, to change this feeling of division between myself and my body.

My fiancée knew nothing of this. I'd restrained myself from saying anything about my inner conflict but whilst recovering from a full wisdom teeth extraction and in a weakened state, I did so. She was trying to be nice to me and had got on to sexual fantasies, so I told her.

Well, truth will out.

I need though to say to the reader who suddenly cries 'Look! I told you it was just a sexual fantasy!' that there is much more behind it than they try to make out.

I don't consider it to be any big surprise that someone, tortured all their life with the awful desire to be a member of the opposite sex but exposed to physical conditions in their own body neither to their liking nor over which they have any significant control, should succumb to sexual fantasies about what they wish they could be.

What might be called a psychodynamic or learning theory of the aetiology of transsexualism was proposed in the late nineties by psychiatrist Ray Blanchard and promoted by a number of his fellow researchers, which I shall explore in a later chapter appropriate to the timeline.

One is strongly inclined to question the ideological basis of this view, which ignores or denies the possibility of organic developmental irregularities and focusses entirely on acquired or conditioned sexual drives. I would note that it is of course a commonplace observation that sexual desire and behaviour is much more strongly associated with concepts of morality than is organic developmental neurology.

At the time, however, back in the seventies, building on the foundation of the lies put out by Dr John Money about his poor victim, I had bought into this guilt-based psychoanalytic model even though it hadn't yet been formalised by later researchers such as Blanchard.

So yes, these strange inner needs might drive one to fantasies that seem strange, but are not simply acquired paraphilias in the sense that ordinary sexual fetishes are, rather they are the expression of colliding forces within the psyche, and the energy must go somewhere.

My fiancée didn't say anything at the time but a week or so later she asked for some distance. I could guess why and although it took a while for me to realise fully, it was over.

I have long wondered whether it would have been easier if she had been less cruel to me in our breakup. Perhaps it was the only way to break through my denial. Nonetheless, I still engaged in another relationship with a girl from the Art Therapy class after we had qualified, in one final attempt, and this was to end in a similar manner.

I had ended my meditation prayer ritual after the stipulated six months of daily practice, and my whole world had fallen apart about the same time. Somehow I made it to the end of the course and won my qualification as an art therapist, but I was on auto pilot.

The next couple of years were chaotic as I tried to figure out where I was, who I was or wanted to be.

In the depths of this wilderness, I ceremonially burned my first edition of Jan Morris' Conundrum in the backyard of my temporary accommodation, seeking to banish all that reminded me of my curse and put it behind me by a supreme act of will, but it did me no good.

I seemed to be at a complete dead end, or chasing false trails.

CHAPTER 4

ACCEPTANCE

I T WAS A COLD February afternoon at Imbolc[1] in Batty's Wood when I stood above Woodhouse Cliff where it plunges steeply to the rushing Beck below and I faced my truth as they say. Like some figure from Greek myth I was beset, hounded by this unwelcome fate. I felt utter aridity; I was in the Wasteland and all was grey. Exhausted, I could flee no longer.

Suicide had often been somewhere in my mind, but I would not do it; I would not run from whatever this was inside me.

I surrendered to myself.

I had no idea what this would actually mean. All that took place at that moment was a recognition that I had to take a different approach to myself from that which I had been pursuing for the last few years. I became more relaxed about my expectations of myself. I started to let myself express my androgyny through my dress and allowed myself to think about the possibility of transition again. I still allowed the possibility that I might not. For brief moments I would explore it in my imagination, perhaps all I needed to do was stop trying — but as the year progressed, it became more and more alien to me.

I began a life-size oil painting of the High Priestess, an image from the Tarot symbolising the path from the Heart across the Abyss to the

---

1   *Imbolc:* Traditional name for Candlemas, celebrated on 1st February.

Crown chakra — from my feelings to my truth — and used this as a projective art therapy method of exploring what this meant to me.

It was a means of Jungian self-analysis. She did not represent me, but rather the clarity with which I must see myself, the severity I must exercise in my self-analysis and the firmness with which I must act. I am reminded on reflection of the interview that the travellers experienced in *The Fellowship of the Ring* when meeting Galadriel, surely a true literary embodiment of the archetype of the High Priestess, who looks into your heart and reveals to you the truth of your own being as you look into her eyes.

What was revealed to me was no surprise, indeed I had known it all along. This path was set before me and to seek to escape it would leave me broken, an empty shell that had thrown away its core, the seed of its purpose for existence.

I had glimpsed it a year or so before when taking a group of children from the mental handicap charity that I worked for to a pantomime performance, and a young woman playing a court jester triggered my psyche with a numinous force. Was she a Trickster reflecting back to me my unconscious being, echoes of *Aladdin*? The memory of her haunted me, pursued me, and it was then that I had begun to understand that this was something I could not escape.

During that summer, I took advantage of my graduate library card at Leeds University to go to the Worsley Medical Library and extensively research transsexualism in the medical literature. Much of the material I found only elaborated on what I already knew from my explorations at the other end of my twenties before I had gone underground.

Probably the most important piece of commentary I found along the way was a recommendation by a psychiatrist that transsexual transition was most viable if begun before the age of thirty. I had often told myself that if things didn't work out on the path I had attempted, to build a male identity, then I would transition when I was thirty-five.

But I now began to realise that the medical advice was sound.

As I entered my late twenties, I could sense that my body was at last beginning to respond to the endogenous male hormone that it had been exposed to since my teens. My hairless chest began to sprout a half a dozen coarse hairs, unnoticeable to any but myself, but still they horrified me. And was my hairline showing some recession at the corners, or was it just paranoia? What sparse facial hair I had was definitely starting to get a bit tougher. I had always felt uncomfortable with this and it was getting worse.

One summer evening that year, I trekked up the Meanwood Beck and sat long in the darkness by the waterfall below the Hollies. The heightened alertness induced by sitting alone in the forest at night brought on a kind of controlled terror while the roar and rush of the cataract lulled me into an hypnotic state, in which I was able to ride above the fear of a situation in which I could expect no help should I be assailed in that endless void.

It was the culmination of my Vision Quest.

I knew it in my soul. In that most shamanic moment of my life, I knew that this path was what I had been born for. All those distant longings echoing from my childhood came back to plead with me. Were we for nothing? Their spectral presence haunted me. The realisation I had been running from and which was the alchemical spirit that had been distilled from my prayers and pleadings was that I could not change this. It was impossible because it was like living rock, no mere irregular boulder of my personality picked up and deposited in the glacial moraines of my childhood, but the foundation on which it was built, and the valley which constrained and channelled my life. I knew then that I could not change this because it was simply impossible.

Strong Gender Dysphoria is like an itch, once noticed you can never ignore it. I had long wondered if it might be a neural body pattern which was somehow imprinted in the cortex. The sense of one's sexual characteristics and their subsequent secondary gendered characteristics simply being wrong seems to be immutable. Many researchers have commented that the sense of bodily dysmorphia is found to be completely resistant to extinction even in those who are determined to continue a 'normal' life in their original state.

It is as if one had an invisible body double superimposed upon one, a Spectral Self that haunted one a nanosecond out of synch with physical consensus reality, but constantly trying to break through.

I had not yet heard of Dr Rupert Sheldrake or his concept of Morphic Fields[2] but when I did, I found that it fit my intuitive sense of myself. I had realised with a deep resignation that it would never leave me, whatever I did.

I was empty of will. To force myself any further would merely be masochism and self-torture. There was another beacon, a Great Attractor that could not now be denied as it became the emergent archetype of my Self and I resisted its orbit no longer.

A moment of both defeat and victory.

It is proposed by Jung that in cases where material is in conflict with the ego structure that one should hold off from making a decision on what to do with it and allow some new alternative to arise from the unconscious as an expression of the Self that can resolve the conflict. I believe I had done that. I had kept this at a distance for nearly a decade, with no resolution. To do so had required that I maintain some kind of conventional male persona for all that time, which I now abandoned. I wore softer, more colourful clothes, let my hair grow again and stopped trying to be that person which I had imagined I was supposed to be.

And so I began again, although slowly. I lingered a little before I was to act, perhaps unconsciously waiting for a cue, a contextual spark, the synchronous moment. I was not yet fully ready to push ahead; I was gestating myself inside. Relaxing, releasing and becoming.

---

2   Sheldrake, Rupert, PhD, 'An Experimental Test of the Hypothesis of Formative Causation', *Rivista di Biologia — Biology Forum* 86 (3/4), 1992, 431–44; 86 (3/4), 431–44, (1992). https://www.sheldrake.org/research/morphic-resonance/an-experimental-test-of-the-hypothesis-of-formative-causation (2020).

I bought a large poster of the painting The Snake Charmer[3] by Rousseau and installed it on the wall beside my bed. This perfectly expressed my sense of exploration into a mystery that drew me on.

I was exploring new ideas in other directions too now, loosening up my horizons. I read the brilliant Space Trilogy by C. S. Lewis, and perhaps the account of gender which he gave in the culminating chapters of Perelandra helped me come to terms with myself, although it was long to slumber in the back of my mind before I was to return and rediscover it.

That cue came in the autumn when a programme on television covered the subject and offered information for help at the end.

In the Jungian model I would see this as the synchronous opportunity. It doesn't always have to come from within; the principle of Synchronicity in Jung's own worldview allows for meaningful acausal connections between the inner and outer worlds. Meaning is found when the image in the unconscious finds an external referent on which to gain a foothold. The analogy in the material world is that of one seeking to climb a mountain. The goal is clear — the summit — but the path is not. I recall reading that C. S. Lewis said if something was necessary, it must be possible. Perhaps this would not hold in a purposeless atheist universe, but such is not the one which I myself inhabit. Man is perhaps above all a problem-solving creature, and that is how I had to approach this. First, to accept the problem, and to understand it. Then to find a way to solve the problem, to find a path; to test footholds and establish that path which was the matching of my inner world through pattern recognition with the opportunities which would allow further progress up the mountainside. Where there is a Will there is a Way is a very old truth.

To me this was the moment when it all began to mesh and I knew that further delay, further tests of this truth, were pointless wastes of time and energy. The charge had found its earthing point. I was ready

---

3   Rousseau, Henri (known as 'Le Douanier') The Snake Charmer (1907) Held in Le Musée d'Orsay, Paris.

to leave the Wasteland; I had found my compass and was prepared to set off.

There was no hesitation now, and I wrote in immediately. Before long I had received the contact information for the Self Help Association For Transsexuals (SHAFT) and a list of possible local contacts.

I followed up on this unhesitatingly and found that the nearest member willing to meet lived in the last house that I had passed on my way up to my midnight tryst with terror in the darkness by the waterfall.

When synchronicities like this join up in sequence, it is as if the Universe is playing Sherlock Holmes with you and waiting to see if you will cry, 'The game's afoot!'

The trail of breadcrumbs seemed an indication that I was going in the right direction, that I was getting back to a path which felt true, and which I would no longer have to fight to maintain.

In my dreams I was climbing down from the teetering tower blocks.

It also proved the adage that we live in a small world, since when I went to visit this contact a short while later, someone I already knew was visiting them too. But this other was from a new group that another friend had invited me to and which I had attended one meeting of.

This was another opening which had turned up for me at that time, and it seemed as though the Universe was offering me a choice between the two paths, even trying to tempt me perhaps. Definitely not a confluence of them, since this was a group dedicated to *Chaos Magick*, and when I got there, I found they were talking about *sex magick* and invoking the *Whore of Babylon* as referenced in Aleister Crowley's works, who had scarily turned up again. I hadn't really grasped what they were about before I went to that first meeting; it had been presented to me like a possible path of development with respect to my interest in spirituality and esoteric psychology. It soon became clear, however, that it was driven by baser desires, simple lust, or at least as it seemed to me, and not the quest for inner knowledge and enlightenment. To say that *Nothing is True* and that *Everything is Permitted* is to declare a world in which there is no law, and no responsibility.

Not a world I wished for or wish to engage in.

It would also obviously have involved promoting the masculine vibration in my being in offering a warped and debased version of what I had sought to establish and confirm in earlier years, but now reduced to just sex; or worse, perhaps become some sort of androgynous object for them to use in their practices, like the image of Baphomet which Crowley is said to have worshipped.

However, the reader might say 'But was it not your Will to follow this path of transition, as Crowley had suggested, that this was the Whole of the Law?' To which I would reply, that just as C. S. Lewis had described himself as 'the most reluctant convert in all England', I might have said I was the most reluctant *transitioner* in all England. This group would have been an easy way of avoiding that.

I turned away from their path and did not go back.

The other path, the one which I was to choose, was the quest for inner self-knowledge and acceptance of it. It was to have far more to do with celibacy and sexual continence than its alternative.

Some might frame it in Jungian terms as the uncovering of the anima. While the sense of my body was at the centre of my self image, there was much more to it. A numinous sense of a reality just beyond the limen of my conscious perception, the Spectral *Self* which sought expression was more me than my apparent self and haunted me with its presence.

I am quite clear this was not my Jungian Shadow. It was certainly not unconscious, and I could uncover no hidden or unconscious motives driving it. It really did seem to be hard-wired or organic. It felt like physical hunger or thirst, organic drives which had no purpose other than to simply drive you to the appeasement of their need.

Professor Jordan Peterson has paraphrased Carl Jung in saying '[t]hat which you most need will be found where you least want to look'.[4] In this online piece,[5] Dr Peterson references Carl Jung:

'Medieval alchemical thought, serving as a bridge between the extreme spiritualism of European Christianity and the later materialism of science, took to itself the dictum *in sterquiliniis invenitur* — in filth it shall be found.'[6]

This exactly describes the sense of fear and fascination with which I found I had to face that thing which most unsettled me. It is the Jungian version of the saying from the Gospel of Thomas that I have quoted elsewhere. Though I feared this thing, it would destroy me should I not bring it forth.

Feminists would argue in those years that people such as myself were simply role playing, that all we were doing was copying, parodying women, and that we could never experience as they do.

I may never know what they experience, but I was not simply imitating. Certainly, social styles were things I emulated, as all do to fit in, but my deeper quest was to find a way of being that mediated successfully between that external world of shared experiences and common values, and my own sense of having a feminine psyche, which needed a congruent physical form through which to express itself.

These kinds of feminists would not listen to our own account but readily imputed motives to us which had more to do with misunderstanding or even projection. We only wanted to be taken seriously so as to be accepted.

One thing which the advocates of Gender Theory will claim is that it is impossible to define exactly what femininity is, or what gender

---

4   Peterson, Jordan *Look Where You Least Want To — Powerful Life Advice* https://www.youtube.com/watch?v=LjIAzKo62MQ (2020).

5   https://semioticon.com/frontline/jordan_b.htm (2020).

6   34. Jung, C.G. *Alchemical Studies R.F.C.* Hull(1967). *(Trans.). The Collected works of C. G. Jung (Vol. 13).* Bollingen Series XX. Princeton: Princeton University Press.

consists in. And yet we have a profound sense of it in our perceptions and interactions with others. A philosophical point which the post-modern reductionist, atheist Left either resolutely fails to get, or simply ignores, because of its inconvenience is that things are not their descriptions, and abstract concepts can rarely be fully pinned down. The way of the true Tao cannot be described.

It is perhaps more helpful to think about Universal principles as they are expressed through Nature, the Yin and Yang as Eastern Philosophy has it. For they are the complementary forces of life and regeneration.

The masculine is expansive, seeking. The feminine is receptive, but also discriminating. We see how the ovum rejects all the rest of millions of sperm to choose just one which has the most suitable signature. And along with this, I always felt, went modesty. The feminine does not flaunt, but is modest.

And the concept of role playing is a negative interpretation. I saw my path as one of finally being able to fit in, to join in harmoniously, intuitively, organically. Of uncovering myself and my potential. Not to copy or invent, but to discover.

I had waited, and now the time had come to me; my destiny seemed clear at last. My pathway was yet to be seen before me, but at least I had accepted where it was that I was going.

This was an exercise for me in survival adaptation. Not only my bodily sense of self, but as I had now realised, my emotional tendencies, my temperament, was more suited to a female identity. I recalled how my mother had said how I rarely cried as a baby, that I always kept close to her and didn't venture away like my brothers, both classical behaviour associated with girls rather than boys. I remembered the rough and tumble of the male primates, while I had always had an intense natural aversion to this, to the point where I had received the strap for avoiding the contact sports the boys so loved.

So I had to set about reconstructing myself — re-construing myself — reinterpreting myself, transforming, relearning ways of interaction and relating.

It felt as if a tremendous weight of expectation was being lifted off my shoulders. I understand that men carry this weight for us all, but it was alien to me. I could not wear the armour needed for those tasks, for that world. I had always found employment around nursing, childcare, therapy and teaching. My brief foray into the world of masculinity with my motorbike had been a psychological body which had required too much energy to maintain, and it melted away like ice in the sun.

CHAPTER 5

TRANSITION: SECOND SERVE

AS MANY TRANSSEXUALS can attest, there is a great deal more to a successful transition than looking the part. I had discovered on my first night out, one word in the wrong voice can destroy the intended impression. Body language, manners, speech, non-verbal cues all contribute to the gestalt one projects.

The Gender Studies theorist Judith Butler has argued that there is a performative element to gender presentation. But this has become gender is performative. Certainly, the performative element is one in which transsexuals must gain skills. But performative statements are certainly more problematic. Claiming that one is of a certain gender is apparently performative these days, without other supporting evidence.

If the performative act comes naturally from one's centre rather than simply from imitation, it will be more effective. I was at a hormone clinic once some years after completing my transformation when the nurse saw my notes and said something to the effect that I had fooled her, to which I replied I saw it more as a case of convincing, rather than fooling. Such a remark from staff would probably be considered incredibly politically incorrect some two decades or so into the twenty-first century, but I saw this more as an expression of surprise at the time than as any purposeful disrespect. And in a roundabout way a compliment that she couldn't distinguish me from all the other women there for their various medical issues.

This phase of my life was one of relaxing, seeking to do what felt natural.

My contact in SHAFT helped me find the Gender Identity Clinic and make an application through my General Practitioner. I was funnelled through the Department of Psychiatry at a local hospital.

I knew from what I had learnt in my short sojourn with the TV/TS group in the mid-seventies that I would be taken far more seriously if I presented as a female on my first appointment.

So I duly went in my best outfit and sat, sweating, in the waiting room, amongst a couple of dozen folk who seemed to pay me no attention.

Until the receptionist came out, looked at her clipboard and said 'C...... Randall', using my then masculine name.

Head down, I shuffled towards the room of the consultant, who happened to be the Professor of Psychiatry.

That trial over, I found him to be very courteous and polite. He asked me a few basic questions and I explained my lifelong experience, what had happened nearly a decade before and how I had not been able to cope with it, but now was determined to go through with it, and that my first goal was to go 'full time' as they say.

His reply flattered me beyond all expectation: 'Well, you look like you're doing that.' I had to explain that this was not every day, and that I was still having electrolysis and going about my daily life in my then other appearance.

This touches on a life matter which goes far beyond the narrow example of my own path to medical treatment.

There is little or no doubt in my mind that the fact that I had sourced my own electrolysis and was going ahead regardless made a significant difference to how I was treated, as it probably had done previously. If one goes ahead regardless of obstacles, then one is far more likely to be treated seriously, in any situation, than if one waits around for someone else to fix an easy path up for you. As the saying goes: Fortune favours the bold. This also figures in the current demands for legal recognition simply on the basis of declaration, which I will deal with in the latter part of the book.

Suffice it to say at this stage that I am of the belief that at some deep level action invites providence.

My progress created a paradox which my mother drew to my attention when later that year I told her my plans. She said that if I did really feel like a girl, then I would accept the situation and not try to change myself. And there is at least a small element of truth in this. I desperately wanted to fit in and be part of things as they were without having to do anything drastic, but this conflict within was so abrasive and painful to me that I simply had to do something to remove or at least diminish the stress that it caused.

I knew from my earlier days that if I wanted to make my way speedily through the triage at a Gender Clinic, I should be proactive. In those days of yore it was not unusual for psychiatrists to offer at times considerable resistance to giving transsexuals treatment. I was firm in my conviction by now and said what I needed to, that I was seeking full reassignment, that I hoped they could offer me a pathway that might lead in that direction, and that I was keen to start on hormone treatment as soon as was possible; and this is what I said to the Professor of Psychiatry.

Blood tests were arranged, and a return appointment a couple of weeks later. I left the hospital in a state of elation. I got home and no one had given me a funny look or stared at me.

One thing that was different this time around was that I had more knowledge, and this included having found out about male hormone blockers from my new contacts. This subject has become highlighted in controversy in recent times because of their use in delaying puberty in some teenagers who have been supported in transitioning early by their parents or medics involved with their care. I shall deal with the medical ethics of that situation later, but for me, at the age of twenty-nine, this was a godsend, and I hadn't realised how much so it would be.

I have mentioned that during my teenage years I had had a severe case of cystic acne. It had begun at the onset of puberty and continued with varying degrees of severity, peaking in my mid-teens, abating a little in my twenties, but remaining a continuous problem that was a great grief to me.

It was one contributing factor that had always made me doubt whether I could make a successful go of transition, since I knew I could never have back the beautiful skin of my childhood which had been ravaged by this affliction for so many years, and which had helped support my sense of myself in those early years.

I knew that female hormone treatment would probably help that a bit but it could take a while to persuade the doctors to allow it. I also understood by now that male hormone blockers would make any female hormones I might take more effective since they wouldn't be in conflict with the hormones my own body was emitting.

But when I asked the registrar who took over seeing me from the consultant on subsequent visits that I would be grateful to start on androgen blockers as a stepping stone, I hadn't realised how dramatically my skin would be benefitted, only that having the blockers would assist the progress of my facial hair removal since any regrowth from the follicles would not be stimulated by male hormone.

The surprise, which I might have anticipated had I thought about it, was that it cured my acne almost literally overnight. Within about thirty-six hours of taking my first tablet, the insistence of the many inflammations on my face simply turned off. For over half my life I had lived with this, whereby, if not on a daily basis, at least several times a week, new eruptions and inflammations would break out. Now, suddenly, it was as if a monsoon had passed over the forest fire and it was quenched.

Had I known about the, to me at least, almost miraculous healing properties of the substance known as Androcur, cyproterone acetate, on this condition, I would have begged the psychiatrist at the student health centre all those years before to prescribe it to me, and I would never have given it up as I did the ineffective low dosage Premarin hormone which he had instead.

But reality plays strange tricks sometimes and perhaps I would have been caught between two stools had I been offered that path before I had properly resolved my feelings about myself.

This elixir of wondrous power also had several other effects which I greatly appreciated.

My skin generally became softer and less greasy. The insistence of male libido abated to my great relief, and post-electrolysis regrowth was less than before I had started the blocker.

I don't know if I have what could be described as any formally recognised syndrome with the effects that male hormone had on me, but I can't help wondering if I did have some kind of irregularities going on in my body chemistry. As may well be the case with certain classes of trans people.

My earlier examinations had shown an unusually high level of female hormone in my bloodstream, and this may have partly been why the doctor only prescribed me a very low dosage of additional female hormone. On the other hand, I had a kind of toxicity reaction to testosterone in my bloodstream as evidenced by the deep tissue eruptions in my sebaceous glands, which began when it did, and stopped just as suddenly.

Whether this has anything to do with the neurodevelopmental hypothesis for transsexualism or is simply a chance may never be certain in a simply material causal way. But for me, at a personal level, my skin condition being such a burden that I had to bear, and then finding that it was caused by the very thing that I had hated all my life, simply seemed to confirm to me that the path I had taken had turned out to be the correct one for me. Here already was an unexpected reward. Something that enabled me to literally feel more comfortable in my own skin was welcome.

About this time I went to an Art Therapy short course run at a local educational establishment, as a kind of way of checking and monitoring my own inner life to ensure that what I was doing was indeed right for me.

One of the exercises was to make a painting of a story we remembered from childhood. I immediately thought of an image of Cornelius the Rabbit,[1] who was lost in an underground cave and found an iron ring on a trapdoor in the floor that, when pulled up, had a gleaming treasure of gold and jewels beneath, lit by cracks through the rock. The secret chamber even had a map of the caves — 'There was no hesitation now about Cornelius's movements, no doubting, no fumbling.'[2] Stumbling around in the chthonic darkness of my inner labyrinths or alone in the night and fear, I had found my treasure and I knew the path to take.

There I met a woman of about my own age who came on to me quite strongly, especially after the group leader had us paint an image related to a sexual secret that we had never told anyone and suggested that participants paired off in order to discuss this privately.

I paired with this woman and described a memory from my early childhood in Africa when I had fantasied wearing a grass skirt and being a girl.

This certainly didn't cool her ardour, and when later I went up to her room in the Hall of Residence, she offered herself to me in the most blatant way possible! An offer I felt obliged to refuse since to have accepted would have betrayed my sense of myself.

Some might say that this was a last opportunity for me to find a path of normalcy, but to reduce it to cheapened sex in this manner

---

1   Flynn, Mary, *Cornelius on Holidays,* The Talbot Press Ltd., Dublin and Cork (1945).

2   Ibid. p. 34.

did not have authenticity to me, it was just a similar temptation to the Chaos group I had only recently turned away from.

We saw each other for a little while after the week was over, but when it finally came to the crunch she said she didn't want to have a relationship since she said it felt like being with a girl.

Which shouldn't have surprised her really, since I told her I wanted that in our private pair session in the first place!

I had just been glad of the opportunity for an intimate relationship rather than a fully sexual one, which is probably a more female type of attitude.

However, the even more curious thing about this brief encounter was that she had confided in me that she had always wanted to be a boy and have what boys have.

I can understand that my failure to fulfil a male role might have triggered that more within herself. About a year later, a mutual friend told me that she had had a breakdown, but didn't give any details, and I never knew if this had anything to do with it or not, but I can't help feeling that it might have.

CHAPTER 6

RADICAL FEMINISTS AND THE OPPRESSION OLYMPICS

AFURTHER CURIOUS link with this is that in later years I have had several women, lesbians, seek relationships with me, who then later told me that they had wanted to be boys. I guess that perhaps my existence gave them some kind of permission, but also I have encountered those who see transsexuals as a kind of fetish object.

Being rather on the conservative side where such matters are concerned, I have never explored the seamier side of this as far as some, but one of the big problems I have found is that we are all lumped together as one class.

There is no denying that nonconforming people from many diverse communities often fall into unwholesome ways through poorly judged association. But that should not be to tar all in the same way. Those who do not flaunt themselves but rather exercise a degree of what I call psychic invisibility are not taken into this account.

Unfortunately, the Law of First Impressions pertains to the general populace when it comes to their awareness of trans people; they see some profligate exhibitionist publicly parading their transition while the media fawns over them and they think that is what it is all about, while the rest of us are hiding our faces in embarrassment hoping we won't in any way be associated with this.

What I sought was to find a way of fitting into society. The schism between my mind, my psyche, and my body seemed to make that impossible.

If gender really had been no more than a construct, it might be expected that I could have fitted in with the feminists back then, but, apart from their rejection of me, the whole thing just made it worse as it reminded me of what I was not.

But their philosophical position was one I could see as being seriously flawed before they even thought about transsexuals.

The 'only physical differences' argument was one which they began with and proceeded from this to contend that men kept women in a state of oppression as home servants and bearers of children, nothing more. This was an application of Critical Theory, even though they probably didn't know the term at the time, and neither did I. Critical Theory is one of the roots of postmodernism and while seeking to find all faults and imperfections in social models and conditions, it seems to offer no remedy or solution to any shortcoming that might be found. This is a Marxist technique which aims at the deconstruction of society in order to 'remould it nearer to the heart's desire' as the Fabians had it, but it was not reformation of an existing system that they sought, correction of the faults and improvement, but rather to bring down the entire system as it stood, in order to replace it with their own idealised model. This is shown in the (in)famous 'Fabian Window', which depicts Bernard Shaw and Sydney Webb hammering an image of the world.

The radical feminists did not want to build on the existing layout of nature, but rather to raze it to the ground as evil and replace it with something made by Man, or in this case, Woman. The neurological basis of gender identity was something they would not look at.

In short, they were unable to understand that they, and all of us, are embedded in an ancient continuity and context of time and being, which has its own laws, forms and momentum and has existed forever in the terrible inevitability of most of Nature.

Besides, the Marxist Feminist account of oppression denies the ancient tradition of love and passion between men and women, of families, raising children, of the great value that most men place on women.

Rather, they create a false social unity between all women, and a false dichotomy between women and men. Just as with the Marxist trope 'Workers of the World Unite' they imagine that the women of England have interests more in common with those in say, Peru, or Macao, or Chad or the Mongolian plains, than they do with the men of their own communities, their fathers, brothers, husbands, sons, families, kin and more.

Surely it is not only better, but more practical, to build strength in a community where one is rather than to create some imagined solidarity with others in communities we may never meet. This is not to disparage cultural links or exchanges; however, Marxism seems designed to undermine established cultures rather than encourage them to be better.

Following only physical differences there was the social conditioning position, which had it that women were kept down by social role conditioning. We hear a lot of this today, but very little about the need for women to bear children while they are still young. Rather, there is social role conditioning to the effect that women should have a career and get on while they are young rather than have babies, which is seen as demeaning and oppressive.

This seems to be where the Radical Feminists from the seventies and eighties wanted to get us, but are women happier? Is society better off, more stable and productive? And are men any happier with it? I would suggest that the answer to all these questions might be no.

By the time they got on to transsexuals, we were dismissed not only as role playing as I have mentioned, but also that we could not know what it was like to be female as we had not been brought up as girls. This extreme behaviourist position is obviously flawed because of the questions it raises about biological boys and girls being raised in the opposite sex roles, or genders as might be said now.

Would they accept a girl who had been raised as a boy amongst their ranks? And shouldn't they accept a boy who had been raised as a girl? What exactly would all this mean, anyway? Social standards might be the same, but wouldn't they notice the physical differences? Wouldn't they realise that made them into different classes somehow?

There have no doubt been innumerable children down the ages raised with little or no distinction between genders. But this is hardly to claim that the girls were actually raised to believe that they were boys, or boys girls. The only way such a thing could happen was in the way of Dr John Money's guinea pig, which I was yet to find out the truth about. Otherwise, the obvious physical differences would surely become apparent. As to the social role behaviour, the well-established evidence of primate rough and tumble has to be suppressed by those seeking to promote gender neutrality in order to produce their equality of outcome between boys and girls. 'Boys will be boys' is a saying that has come into common use over countless generations because it is an expression of the rough and tumble nature of boys in general, not because of some oppressive patriarchy that wants us to believe boys are different.

Recent studies in countries where there is equality in upbringing of sex roles have shown that the greater the social freedom, the more women and men grow up into preferring what are considered traditional sex roles.[1]

---

1   Falk, A. Hermle, J. 'Relationship of gender differences in preferences to economic development and gender equality'. *Science*, 19 Oct 2018: Vol. 362, Issue 6412, eaas9899 https://science.sciencemag.org/content/362/6412/eaas9899 (2020).

So, although this is influenced by a variety of factors, looking at the fact-based evidence, it seems clear that there are indeed genuine differences, if only in preferences, when not pressed by overriding financial drivers, and this agrees with the neurodevelopmental psychology I had learnt about back in the seventies. And in my own experience, despite achieving high marks in science and maths at school, I had veered towards the female preferences, first studying Psychology, and then pursuing my career in related people-oriented professions.

Much work over the decades has demonstrated sex-related preferences for play and work, men having interests more towards things than women, who are more interested in people, statistically speaking.[2,3]

But this was eighties feminism, and the radical end at that. Neurological tendencies were oppressive, like everything else it seemed.

The only physical differences argument also weakened their position because those physical differences were not an exact list and some could be changed. Not all women bear children or menstruate. I have never found out what radical feminists think about morphological females with AIS, mostly, I suspect, because they don't want to consider the idea that the boundaries between the sexes may at times be a little fuzzy and not entirely defined by genetics. The arguments that would later be used by Gender Theorists easily deconstruct Radical Feminism, and would supersede it in its influence, raising new problems of its own. The later school gained wider credence and I shall arrive at that in due course.

2   Su, R., Rounds, J., Armstrong, P.I. 'Men and things, women and people: A meta-analysis of sex differences in interests'. *Psychological Bulletin*. 2009;135(6):859–884.   pmid:19883140.   https://psycnet.apa.org/record/2009-19763-004?doi=1 (2020).

3   Full   paper   http://emilkirkegaard.dk/en/wp-content/uploads/Men-and-things-women-and-people-A-meta-analysis-of-sex-differences-in-interests. pdf (2020).

The term Male Privilege had already entered the vocabulary of the world of Feminism and this was an accusation that was levelled at transsexuals such as myself. We could never experience life properly as women because we had apparently lived a life of privilege and had never been oppressed. The fact that the moment we started passing successfully in our desired gender we were entering the world of Female Oppression was one they studiously avoided looking at. And growing up as a non-dominant individual in an environment where I was brutally treated had already taught me about Social Oppression.

Besides, the concept of Privilege Theory which was beginning to emerge at this time tended to ignore facts such as that privilege in the modern application is what might have been seen as status in earlier epochs. Certainly, if I think about the way the extremely upper middle class headmistress of my old school might have related to the gardener or the janitor or a delivery man in the supposed misogynist nineteen sixties, there is no possible way in any imagination that you could say that they had privileged status or that she was oppressed. Of course this devolves into claims about the patriarchal class structure and so on, which is something outside of my remit, so I shall leave this here, having, I hope, demonstrated that this was something of a minefield that I was entering, and it was almost literally on my doorstep, as I was to later find out.

By the time I began to negotiate my social transition in the mid-eighties, I had reconciled myself to the existence of the radical feminists and their position, was even a tad amused by it. Living in the student ghetto, I could not escape their presence.

Indeed, it is with the greatest amusement that I found out that the editorial office of the Revolutionary and Radical Feminist Newsletter was located next door to me in the back flat approached from the rear.

I have on a number of occasions found myself taking the role of Outsider, even Trickster, and I guess this was one.

It was not until many years later that I was to see the contents of the Rev/Rad Newsletter, as it became known, but it was terrifying stuff. Bound in a volume in the Brotherton Special Collection, I found it to be replete with articles on how the contributors hated men — all men — not just for the things that some had done to them, but simply for being men, and with cartoons advocating violence against them. This was true hate speech.

My own most extreme personal encounter with them derived from an outing I had taken with a friend who knew my situation, on her birthday, with several others who didn't.

We had had a splendid day in the sun at Castle Howard, the peacocks strutted around the fountain and a dog that one had brought with her splashing us all splendidly as he retrieved his stick from the little runnel pond halfway down the rill to the main lake.

Another, the driver of our little band, a rather butch lesbian, had shown interest in me, and I should have been wary, since J, the birthday girl, had already told me not to disclose to this one since she was hostile to transsexuals.

We were not common in those days, and having gone full time about a year before when my facial hair removal had reached the point where it was no longer necessary to shave, and the hormones had changed my appearance, I naively assumed that passing successfully, as I seemed to be doing by that stage, would be sufficient to ensure my safe passage into the citadel.

Not so, as I was soon to find out.

This lesbian invited me to come round for dinner a couple of weeks later, and I duly arrived, bearing a potted plant as gift.

Everything went fine till half past nine, when, after a couple of glasses of wine, she broached the subject of the feminist circles and consciousness-raising groups, which were still somewhat in vogue.

I hesitated, and then gingerly explained that I hadn't been to any of these groups or events in the social milieu to which she was referring.

'Why ever not', she said. 'I'm sure you'd get on well.'

To which I began to explain, 'Well, you see, I'm ...'

I've never seen anyone's expression change so fast.

'I don't allow men in this house, please leave.'

I began to remonstrate and try to make some impression on her, but the entire effort was futile. I chugged down the remainder of my wine in a trice and was ejected, probably within less than a minute of my uttering the Deplorable Word.

Of course the irony is that it was not I who was attempting to seduce her, but entirely the reverse. I had already sensed that, but didn't really take it seriously since such things were new to me, and I wasn't interested anyway; this had just been a social adventure.

She, on the other hand, had perhaps expected to bed this new young prey, who had so recently appeared on the scene, that night. And so this most unexpected revelation had spoilt her plans a little.

Here then was a gender dynamic which was in some way reversed, but in some way simple.

The butch lesbian played the masculine role, and I, passively, the feminine, despite not yet having completely achieved my aspired bodily morphology.

We see this kind of dynamic in the behaviour of the rats who were hormonally influenced during gestation.

Gender Theorists seem to fail to recognise the nature of sexual drives and their rootedness in biology. In single-sex environments, some of those with high sex drives, correlated with higher testosterone levels, will tend to predate on those with lower, regardless of sex, whether male or female. Underlying principles, biological drives, being made manifest into the experiential.

This is the breaking through into the phenomenal world of the noumenal.

The world of thought and epistemology since the middle of the twentieth century has been such that metaphysical realities, the principles behind existence, even the inevitability of material causes, have become marginalised and treated as irrelevant. All that has been seen to matter is social appearance, the surface.

Rather than considering the dyadic situation of the butch lesbian and myself as an anomalous expression of fundamental principles, some postmodern theorists would be happy to see the lesbian as being 'male' and me as 'female'. The latter is what I seek, but not for that reason.

I have often wondered if some of the Radical Feminists who took this approach were what one might call potential transsexuals, but were repressing their own desire to be men, or at least envied men.

It has been anecdotally observed by many that male-to-female transsexuals will often be somewhat androgynous to start with; perhaps this has something to do with self-selection to go forward. Conversely, one might wonder if the opposite might apply to especially butch lesbians. I will deal with how the so-called construction of transsexual identity occurs in my account of my time engaged with Gender Studies.

This particular lesbian likely had high testosterone levels since she clearly had the strong shadow of a small moustache, which she obviously shaved.

I'm certainly not suggesting that this alone is reason to believe she might want to be a man, but she probably had higher male hormone levels than I did by then, and it was plain to me that she was acting out a higher sex drive like the androgenised animals in the experiments I had studied a decade before, or the dominant girls and women in single-sex institutions.

There was a coda to this when I wrote to *Spare Rib*, the feminist magazine, with my story. I was very proud to have had it published, as I felt it gave me a certain degree of respect and recognition.[4]

I didn't find out until over twenty years later that it had led to me becoming probably the only transsexual woman ever to be published in the notorious Leeds-based Revolutionary and Radical Feminist Newsletter, otherwise known as the Rev/Rad Review, when in 2010

---

4   Full text of my letter published in *Spare Rib* included in Appendix A *Spare Rib* date and number not known.

a young woman I knew had been researching radical feminism in the eighties and had found this story. Not realising that it was me, she mentioned that this was an item I would probably be interested in, and so suspecting that it was I, I checked it out and found that indeed it was. I went to the Brotherton Library Special Collections, where these old copies of the Rev/Rad Review were archived, and there was a four-page interview with the woman concerned attacking me,[5] which included my *Spare Rib* letter in full (probably infringing both their copyright and mine) and a cartoon that was entirely unrepresentative of me. By this time it was of course all water under the bridge and I was amused to find that they had made space for a transsexual woman in their rag! (I have included my own letter in the appendices.)

Strongly associated with the wave of Radical Feminism in the eighties was the arrival of the Oppression Olympics, as a friend used to call it.

This has now become a major pillar in the Left's strategy to undo society as we know it in the West.

I was introduced to it by a later-to-detransition friend who was more involved with the alternative scene than I was. We used to joke about the radical feminists, and he would call them Stalinists, not because of their Marxist leanings (they probably wouldn't have admitted that since Marx was a man and therefore innately evil) but because of their authoritarian behaviour.

Their ideology also leaned heavily on the concepts of victimhood and oppression.

This would seem to have had its roots, at least in part, in the Consciousness Raising Groups culture I encountered and that had been around since at least the early seventies, in which members were expected to accept without reservation the tales of their sisters and to offer unconditional support.

---

5   'RRF Collective' and Eileen Carter, 'Trannies', *Revolutionary and Radical Feminist Review*, no.18 March 1988, pp. 11–14 (Brotherton Library Special Collection, Leeds University).

This is all very well as far as it goes, but unfortunately that is not very far.

A culture which is entirely uncritical of itself is one which can easily get bogged down in narcissistic self-obsession.

And women, being on the whole more empathic than men, are more easily engaged with group empathic responses.

Not unsurprisingly, many of the women who participated in these groups will have come seeking an opportunity to express themselves about negative experiences they had had, and this is all to the good if that is what they needed. But it had roots close to the alternative therapies I had experienced earlier, and often had little in the way of managing powerful emotions other than to direct these outwards in a negative manner, simply of blame, rather than finding ways of constructively channelling the emotional energy.

This became dangerous because a culture that was supposed to be supportive and nurturing could easily be manipulated and exploited by more dominant personalities, and even turned to political ends. This was the fertile ground from which Political Lesbians sprang up, claiming that it was the duty of women to reject men and become lesbians. Looking back after all these decades, one can't really help wondering if this was some kind of psychological operation by the CIA or somesuch, as it is so obviously designed to create problems and disrupt society rather than make it run more smoothly for all concerned.

And so playing up your victimhood status in the Oppression Olympics became de rigueur. Of course, simply being a woman was the principal oppression, but there were numerous others. My friend would joke about the status that a ***** ******6 lesbian would have had in these circles. Here we may descry some of the deep roots of

---

6   I have redacted these two 'victim groups' since in the present climate I could well face political attacks and censorship for daring to repeat a joke mentioning them. I will probably get some pushback even for referring to one of the groups in my friend's joke.

modern Political Correctness and Intersectionality, the phenomenon of being able to stack up victimhood points in the radical feminist world by claiming an intersection of various oppressions. In those days it was more about the protection from criticism that it provided, but in the post-millennial world it has become a potent source of status. A recent twenty-first century addition to the Intersectionality and Oppression Olympics armoury is Othering, a concept I wrote about here.[7] It is basically a means of weaponising a simple philosophical concept. The concept of *Other* was originally elaborated by G. F. W. Hegel in the early nineteenth century as a counterpoint to self, and as a part of his concept of dialectics whereby reason and arguments may progress.

But the modern exploitation of this term is to demonise it as a moral crime. In the New Age mindset that many postmodernists inhabit, we are all supposed to be one giant collective; we are not allowed to see ourselves as distinct and consider our own interests (a small matter of survival comes in here) but instead to keep any strange person at a distance through caution or unfamiliarity is to Other them, a mortal sin. In this manner we are morally forbidden to pursue our own interests and adaptation since it involves putting ourselves first, and may involve excluding others, possible competitors or threats. This classic Cultural Marxist technique follows the established pattern of reversing the conventional wisdom of the ages that puts one's own family, tribe, culture and people first in the face of outsiders and claiming that this is oppressive — Othering. I would suggest that this is how they label all actions involving agency that don't follow their own agendas. In other words, they are Othering those with whom they disagree. Such transparent hypocrisy is commonplace in the pseudo-moralist world of the postmodernist who only knows the exercise of power.

---

7   http://pcnewspeak.blogspot.com/2015/11/othering.html (2020).

Some of this may seem a little tangential to my prime subject of how transsexualism has been exploited as a means to negatively impact and deconstruct society, but it is all part of the same weave. For instance, I am accused of Othering those who claim social identities without morphological congruence, but they Other me, because I don't fit their modern transgender ideology. They refuse to engage in debate, while demonising me.

In the Consciousness Raising culture that I have described we have the origins not only of such ideas as that men could, and even should, be replaced, eradicated from the map of existence, but also the poisonous claim that there are certain things which **should not**, **cannot** and **must not** be questioned. Quite something for an ideology which believes there is no such thing as truth but only competing narratives based on power.

This has spread from rape accusations and child molestation to the point where anyone can say anything and it is trial by allegation in the media. Some groups cannot be questioned and others must not be believed.

The conscious and unconscious motivations to be seen as a victim are enormous in our society as the media attention can doubtless be intoxicating.

It is so much easier for some to feign or milk victimhood for sympathy than to do something about whatever their condition or disadvantage is. The next stage is to demonise those against whom one claims grievance.

Now don't get me wrong, people have grievances that need addressing sometimes, I get that. However, there are better ways of doing things than endless complaint and blame, addressed to Society in general. This is the Culture of Critique.

Some years before, immediately following my qualification as an art therapist, I had worked at a residential home for mentally handicapped children in London and one of my co-workers had been a very visible and vocal butch lesbian. I recall one evening, when I was on sleepover duty, after the children had all gone to bed and the remaining staff were relaxing in the sitting room with cups of tea, that my inquisitive conversation led to her revealing the true extremes which some of her ilk espouse.

She explained that she looked for a world in which there would only be women, that men would have become extinct — I don't recall exactly how she proposed this, whether humanely by preventing births and allowing the existing population to die off, or by more, er, active measures.

What I do recall is that what she proposed as a means of reproduction, in the absence of males, was parthenogenesis, which is a type of budding of clones from the mother. I don't think she even bothered with looking to fusion of ova from two women. That would at least allow for genetic mixing, which is the big advantage of sexual reproduction.

This Radical Feminist mindset then is one which is rooted in an ideology akin to genocide on the one hand and transhumanism on the other. It would seek to end, or at least severely limit, genetic evolution through sexual reproduction which has existed for a billion years or so, while eradicating one half of our species.

It is of course, an absurd, totalitarian fantasy that could only possibly be implemented by means of war, and since men are better designed by evolution for war, it is not even likely that the war could be won, except perhaps by deception…

And because it is so absurd I wouldn't waste time discussing it in these pages except for the fact that I still hear similar kinds of dystopian science-fiction fantasies from Radical Feminists.

It is not uncommon in the current year to hear them say that men are obsolete.[8, 9] The word 'toxic' has now been associated through endless Pavlovian association with masculinity so effectively that this is

8   https://www.theatlantic.com/magazine/archive/2010/07/the-end-of-men/308135/ (2020).

9   https://www.thinkinghousewife.com/2010/06/men-are-obsolete/ (2020).

now declared not merely as one type of a wide range of expressions of masculinity, but as the essential nature of masculinity. (I shall deal with essential natures later.)

Masculinity itself then must be eliminated and the Goddess will rule supremely in peace.

But exploiting emotions of hatred against half of your own species to the point of what amounts to genocide isn't functional. It's not survival adaptive but rather a symptom of a deep psychological disturbance.

While in the boring, conventional daylight world my experience is the opposite of what Feminists claim: that most women are, at least in the West, rather than being oppressed, generally treated with respect.

Men always do the rough, dirty, hard things, and women usually expect to be put first. Which would be fine if the position of the sexes had remained as they were in the past and the division of jurisdictions as it were remained, but rather we are faced with Feminists who claim that men are obsolete. Certainly, washing machines and contraceptives have freed women from the drudgery associated with women's roles in the past, but this is not to mandate that women should seek to do and be all those things that men do and are. On the other hand, I am brought to mind of the poster from the Great War, 'Women of Britain Say Go!', surely the most embarrassing excess of the proto-feminists. Humans are highly adaptable and most of the members of each sex can do most of the things that the other does but often not as effectively, and in the past, division of labour has led to specialisation, an obvious evolutionary development that radical feminists refuse to acknowledge.

It should come as no surprise that, almost like a quantum entangled pair of particles reflecting each other, we now see men's advocacy groups saying that women will become obsolete when artificial wombs are perfected.

For myself, I want no part of any of this, although perhaps I am already entangled. It is a curious synchronicity that transsexuals emerged on the world stage in the 1920s with Magnus Hirschfeld's Institute of Sexual Sciences in Berlin, where he was the first scientist to take our problems seriously, culminating in early transsexual surgeries like that of Lili Elbe, soon after First Wave Feminism succeeded in breaking into the mainstream. Coincidence? Or an entangled Taoist balance?

I have come to accept that we are anomalous and that the best we can do is try to find a way to fit into the greater scheme of the two genders of which the two sexes are the expressions, rather than seek to revoke the immutable patterns of nature.

CHAPTER 7

TRANSITION: FINDING MYSELF

W HEN I HAD SEEN the consultant to pursue my course, I had said that I was prepared to take up to five years, and if it wasn't going well by then I would give it up.

Making a successful transition so that no one other than close confidantes knew your status was the end goal in those days. Total Stealth as it became known. After the legal precedent set by Justice Ormerod's decision in 1971 on the Corbett vs Corbett case, when he dissolved April Ashley's marriage, having decided that she was a man, transsexuals no longer had the protection of being recognised in their acquired sex.

We carried on making new identities nonetheless, negotiating the labyrinth of legal requirements as they came up.

Who we see ourselves as is not necessarily how others see us and the complex web of interrelationships, which support and extend that identity, may need to be severed, at least in parts that would offer too much resistance.

One major difference between then, in the mid-eighties, and now, more than thirty years later, is that stealth as a desirable thing seems to have been devalued, even denied as a goal to seek by radical trans activists.

In establishing my new identity, I had to seek new social connections, like dendrites branching out with new learning pathways, while at the same time old ones died off.

And I did lose connections with people I had called friends. But this was a very new thing to most people and I do not judge them too harshly.

The images that circulated around in the collective consciousness about people who share this affliction were often quite lurid. So I suppose it was somewhat inevitable that after the examples of the Andy Warhol scene, Stonewall and the Radical Drag exhibitionists in the years prior to this that people might have had similar expectations of me. But that kind of gay culture was something from which I had recoiled a decade earlier and felt no inclination to revisit.

My only contact with that world was the gay man who had started to transition but later dropped out. At the time when he was still ostensibly transitioning, he had had relationships with other gay men and it had seemed highly probable from this that he really was just a mixed up gay man.

I believe that a lot of current supposed transgender people are quite possibly like this, mixed up gay men who are expressing more of a sexual drive than a larger bodily identity issue. Or lesbians vice versa. I expect some to attack me for this suggestion, but is it not preferable for someone to simply be gay than to have the whole bodily dysphoria and gender identity thing going on?

I didn't have any political agenda as I got into this. It was uncharted territory and I mapped it out as I went forward.

The Feminists would have it that I role played, but I had no conscious template that I adhered to. It was more as if a stone had been lifted off from a plant which had been crushed under it and then begun to grow freely at last.

I sought above all else to be authentic, to be true to myself. It was as much a journey of discovery as anything else. Exploring my own intuitions rather than trying to fulfil a role image. And so I grew into and began to become a happier person, reducing my inner stress and conflict.

It was important that I have some counselling while going through this process and I found a local feminist therapist who was willing to see me. The time when I might have been talked out of my path by an over-directive therapist was now past, but I was still vulnerable to projections and expectations. I don't know what she meant when she said I could become an androgyne but I didn't want to find out. Was this some kind of proto-genderqueer that she was proposing? She probably didn't know what to make of me: I was completely outside of any box she knew.

It took a long time, but my pain eventually melted away. A lot of that was the emotional distress I had experienced with my skin, and the social abuse I had received, which had worsened it.

I felt lighter, that I was no longer carrying around a burden that I didn't want, no longer clad in the armour of a masculine identity. I became open and vulnerable. I led weekly art therapy groups at the local MIND daycentre and I recall a painting I did of myself as naked before the blades of those who would wound me. I was glad to be free of my social burden but I realised that now I had to develop more subtle defences than mere armour. It is at times like this that we are tested and find what we are really made of.

A period of facing challenges and overcoming obstacles is necessary on any path of progress. If things are too easy, anyone can do them and they are meaningless.

Having laid down my burden, I relearned who I was. This was a novel experience as I discovered myself in my responses to the world, how I was treated as an apparent woman, and it was wonderful. There is no question in my mind that it is Female Privilege on which our society is built, not Male. I assume I must have been passing because I can't imagine that an obvious transvestite would have been treated so politely by your average person on the street in the mid-eighties; unlike today when trans people are becoming such protected special snowflakes that to even notice or comment on a trans person's identity might invoke some kind of lawsuit.

I have had my challenges, although only one case where I had to get officious, but we'll come to that. For now, in the mid-eighties, I was finding that blending in and going with the flow was a lot easier than I had ever expected.

There was the delicious moment when I realised that I was passing without making much of a conscious effort. I was wearing unisex-style clothes and haircut as standard when one day, walking on the wide pavement alongside the road which goes through the local park, I witnessed a minor road traffic accident. Little more than a bump in fact, but in a moment the drivers, both young men, had jumped out of their seats and were on the pavement beside me arguing whose fault it was. It was only a second or two before one turned to me and said, 'Ask her, she saw it was your fault!'

I must have made a satisfactory answer as I was not met with the response I had experienced at the disco a decade before and was able to slip away unnoticed.

I was developing my interface with society. My appearance, my communication skills and how to fit in with a system vastly predating my personal issues. This is not, or at least should not be, a political movement. Certainly it is nice to get legal status, but that is an entirely different matter from the movement that has piggybacked on this whole thing and turned it into a wrecking ball with which to destroy the very concept of gender as we conventionally know it.

If a person cannot go through the transition process and come out the other end perceived generally as the gender they would like to be, we must ask ourselves whether it truly can be considered a success.

The Gender Identity Clinic referred me to a service that would be of immense value in my personal development — speech therapy. The Charing Cross GIC had gained some retrospective notoriety for its Deportment Classes and this was a refinement of that. I had an excellent speech therapist, who was an expert in communication modalities and to whom I owe an immense debt of gratitude for the insight which she helped me gain into personal presentation and manner. This was way beyond mere imitation, was rather true education, leading or drawing out, from the Latin root *e-ducere*. I was actually finding myself through this process, an immersion so total that my own long suppressed being was emerging almost through a process of sympathetic resonance, like a dormant string on a musical instrument responding to the note from another string with which it was in resonance. Or perhaps like learning yoga, or dance, in which one's potential is drawn out and developed.

Amongst the trans population one will find a range of vocal deliveries, but after my first night experience, and along the way, meeting several transsexuals who sounded like gay or even just straight men, I knew I had to make it good if I didn't want to stick out like a sore thumb for the rest of my life.

Had I not been able to do so, I would have had to ask myself whether this was such a good idea. Things had got off well at the start, but there was still a long journey ahead.

CHAPTER 8

BORDERLINES

ONE OF THE FOREMOST issues which has been raised under the current trend which seeks to allow people simply to declare their gender with no supporting evidence is what toilets they should use.

Radical trans activists and their supporters argue that all self-identified trans people should be able to use the facilities of their choice, claiming that fears of people exposing themselves or of committing sexual assault are false and that these things would never happen. This is to my mind an unsupportable case, since the law should apply to those things which could happen, in order to prevent them. To say that something or other which people might find unacceptable would never happen and that therefore there should be no laws concerning the possibilities of it ever happening is putting the cart before the horse. This is a mere unsupported claim, and one of a type which is becoming more common in Cultural Marxist-dominated society.

Half the population cannot be exposed to this possibility simply to assuage the demands of an infinitesimal minority. In fact, as I hope will become apparent, I do not even believe that it is a significant proportion of the real transsexual population that are seeking this, but rather the trans trenders and concern vultures who see an opportunity to use this 'rights' issue to slip a wedge into popular culture and set about deconstructing, or rather destroying, traditional notions of gender.

There are also more subtle reasons simply to do with sense of territory. It is not so much about threat as intrusion. Trans people who pass or at least who make a serious effort with their presentation are far less likely to be felt to be intruding. These are female territories and obviously masculine persons should not be intruding and demanding to be allowed there. Those who simply claim a female identity with no change in appearance or manner will be seen as such, regardless of how they feel about themselves. Women tend to have a much more highly developed sense of smell and will detect male pheromones whether consciously or subliminally in those not receiving hormone treatment. Radical trans activists complain about beauty standards, but it is not beauty by which they will be perceived, rather it will be the balance of their masculinity or femininity. Much of this is rooted in the body. And it is women who must decide on where this borderline is to be drawn through their own intuitive perception, not the radical activists. If we are unnoticed, then we are not intruding. But for women to feel that they must remain silent in the face of obvious radical trans intrusion because of political correctness is surely wrong.

Radical conservatives, on the other hand, demand that no trans people whatsoever should be allowed to use the toilets of the gender they are seeking to be a part of. While I am obviously sympathetic to the idea of preventing inappropriate people having access to women's toilets (and let's be clear, this is about male-to-female trans people going into women's toilets, not passing trans men going into men's toilets, at worst you might find some men would be amused), it is simply not practical, and would surely not be politic, to require every person going into a women's public toilet to provide some sort of proof of physical gender.

In my own transition I had to negotiate this minefield, and although it was one which was perhaps more simply laid out back in that time, nonetheless it may still be of some use to consider the path I tracked.

In my early stages I avoided the use of public toilets altogether, this being really the simplest way to obviate the problem. The issue has now got to the point where at schools this is not a viable solution, but I will come to that in a later section. For now I will simply address the adult on the street as it were.

It must have been around the time of the road traffic incident I witnessed that I had another similar experience which prodded me further forward on my path. Being in the mid-eighties, the AIDS scare was at its height, and I was considered by some to be in a high-risk category, despite the fact that I was completely celibate by now and actually more like a no-risk level.

However, the level of paranoia was so high that the principal of the beautician's college where I was having my facial electrolysis insisted that I have blood tests for HTVL iii, as it was known at the time, in order to protect her students. They already wore medical gloves, and at the most a misapplied electrolysis needle would only bring forth the tiniest drop of blood, but concern was high, and I was getting cut-price electrolysis at the college, so I didn't resist. (Today it would probably be considered offensive to require a trans person to have such medical check-ups because of political correctness.)

This involved going to the Genito-Urinary Medicine Clinic, which curiously happened to be in the same prefabricated building as the disco I had attended on my first night out, which had been repurposed. The doctors were accommodating, my blood was taken and tested, and I got a letter for the principal which declared that I was clean.

It became something of an inconvenience when the request became repeated the following term, but to keep in favour I had to go back every couple of terms or so. This did, however, produce some amusing episodes.

I was negotiating my transition quite slowly, not pushing my dress or social acceptance in unfamiliar places, and so the feedback I got was quite informative of how I was being received. There were two incidents at the GUM clinic which were instructive.

The clinic was partitioned into men's and women's sections, with corresponding waiting rooms, and at first I would wait in the men's section because I was not yet full time. On the second or third occasion, there was a man there in the waiting room with me and after taking a long hard look at me came over and said, 'You're in the wrong waiting room, luv', using the local Yorkshire slang. I don't recall how I replied, but I was pleased to be seen in such a way.

Incidents such as this led me to decide that it was time to go 'full time' and I got a letter from the consultant at the GIC explaining that I was undergoing Gender Reassignment which I could carry with me and show in the event of my being challenged by police or other officials. Fortunately, this never happened, but it had been known to, and I wanted to be prepared.

On a later occasion, when I had thus graduated to the female section, I went into the consulting room and the first question the lady doctor asked when she looked up was, 'How are your periods?' I guess she hadn't looked at my notes properly, but luckily I now had my letter, otherwise she might have considered my coming to the women's section presumptuous.

The Department of Genito-Urinary Medicine eventually lost patience with the demands of the beautician's college and the professor wrote a letter saying that they were unwilling to perform repeated tests on a person who was at no risk of STDs due to my at the time complete abstinence from sexual contact. The principal refused to allow me to have treatment there any longer, and our ways parted. I was subject to the spectre of projected sexual promiscuity: she had to be cautious for her students, but would not accept the recommendation of the professor who had infinitely more experience in whether to believe a patient or not. It is often simpler to sidestep a projection and move on than to attempt to rectify it, something that may be impossible.

I had almost completed my facial hair removal and sourced what remainder I needed elsewhere.

But what this taught me was that I had passed into the realm of being perceived in my desired identity. And so, to return to the vexed question of which toilets to use, I now had to consider my own safety as well as the perceptions and feelings of the women I might encounter.

There will never be an exact formula to decide what should be the precise requirements to be able to enter ladies' loos. If I say that trans people should only be allowed to use women's toilets if they pass sufficiently well as to be unnoticeable, then I will be attacked on several grounds.

Firstly, they will say that some biological women don't pass as women, those who might suffer with hirsutism from polycystic ovaries, or some other condition. This is a case where exceptions should not be used to make new rules. Clearly these are anomalous, but while they may have some masculine characteristics, such women are very rarely so masculinised that it would not become apparent pretty quickly that they are indeed women, should they be spoken to or interacted with, not simply on the basis of their facial hair, but on the full spectrum of their being.

Perception cannot be rigidly demarked and prescribed. It is a gestalt experienced intuitively, and too much examination can destroy it, even in the case of the most genuine anomaly.

Secondly, from the other side I will be attacked on the basis that just because a trans woman passes in her desired identity, it doesn't mean she will have completed medical reassignment to the point of surgery, or that this is even their end goal.

This is a problem which is in some ways imponderable. As I have intimated, physical examinations are out of the question. We have to rely on common sense, despite the fact that such a thing is despised by the politically correct.

Indeed, this is one question over which I have had to review and revise my opinions. In an ideal world with no anomalies, where gene expression was always perfect, perhaps trans wouldn't exist, and we would all have had optimal developmental pathways for the matching of our brain sex with that of our reproductive organs. This ideal world doesn't exist, but perhaps a slightly less ideal one (although still a little more ideal than that in which we presently exist) would be one in which only those trans women who have had surgeries to give them the desired female morphology where it matters would be seeking to use women's toilets.

This is a state of affairs which is simply not going to happen, however strongly many different parties may feel about it from different points of view, including myself.

Having learnt over the years to be severely practical, I would rather look to finding a way in which this can best be managed than try to eradicate the situation entirely as some might wish, since that would require an extreme authoritarian imposition of draconian laws to achieve.

We hear a lot from trans advocacy groups about respecting trans people's rights, but we are only about one in every four or five hundred people so far as can be established, and allowing extreme minorities to be able to effectively have the privilege of private laws[1] is invidious.

Let me make it clear that I do not oppose adults being able to explore and express their personalities in whatever ways they may see fit, but this must not infringe on the existing rights of others, especially to their own spaces.

We seem to be faced with an opposition between two basic positions: either we allow anyone to claim to be whatever they like and

---

1   *Privilege* from the Latin *privis* — *private*; *lex*, *legis* — *law*.

allow them to use women's toilets and spaces, or else we have some kind of standard, even if it is only implicit.

This is a fundamental question which applies to questions of other rights and jurisdictions. The kinds of people who argue that we should accept what people claim about themselves without asking for evidence are often the same as those who say that we should have open borders, uncontrolled movement and freedom of settlement anywhere. Or those who say we should always believe women when they say they have been sexually molested when there is no evidence. Some claim that this is about respect for all as individuals, but what it leads to is a carte blanche to abuse any trust. A licence to lie at will.

It is a very small step from open and inclusive trans rights to anyone can be anything, anyone can use a woman's toilet.

In which case the concept of woman itself effectively becomes meaningless, if anyone can claim that identity on the basis of no evidence.

I only used women's toilets most minimally and when absolutely necessary before I was morphologically congruent, but there is also the matter of pheromones which I have already alluded to that adds to the situation. Discretion is surely the better part of valour when screaming demands that you haven't yet earned would only mar your cause.

I have mentioned this on a YouTube video[2] which I made about claims for trans rights. We all have pheromones, hormonally related scent, which is often perceived only subliminally. However, male and female scent can be quite strong in urine passed, and men's urine can be particularly strong.

A viewer made the comment that there was no such difference, and when I inquired, I wasn't surprised to find that this supposedly MtF transsexual was pre-medical treatment and apparently not taking

---

2   My YouTube channel Cosmic Claire *Justine Greening / Tories 'Gender Declaration' Proposals* https://www.youtube.com/watch?v=ymXwDN_WH10 (2020).

hormones at that time. In other words, they were still in a state of having testosterone as their dominant sex hormone, and would not therefore be able to perceive it in the way that a woman does, since one's own state affects what different scents are most readily picked up. This viewer was the somewhat notorious radical trans activist Lily Madigan, whom we shall encounter again later.

So, trans people who are only cross-dressing, rather than taking hormones as part of a medical transition, may be much more easily perceived as incongruent, not from their sexual morphology, which will be hidden, but from their pheromonal cues which could be liminal, but are still there, besides other factors which are influenced by hormones such as skin tone.

My foremost concern here is that the 99.8% or so of the female population who are not anomalous should not be forced to have to deal with an issue which is not of their making. Certainly, they will not wish to be forced to encounter anyone that they would perceive as obviously male, and anyone who enters that women's space should not display any characteristic which would identify them as such in their territory.

It is not my business here to prescribe exactly what the taxonomic distinctions and qualifications for legal conditions on this should be, but it seems apparent to me that someone who passes socially and is advanced in hormone treatment, emitting female pheromones, is far less likely to be found unacceptable, even noticed as incongruent, than a semi-transitioned trans trender who is behaving in an exhibitionist manner and demanding their rights.

The fundamental difference here is one in which people are either to be given everything they demand simply on the basis of unsupported claims, or that they can be guaranteed certain rights on the basis of having qualified for them, having fulfilled certain conditions and successfully adapted to their desired niche in society. The latter is far more in line with the tradition of scientific thought and the need for survival adaptation than the former, which is based on notions of social justice, although this does not start out as a social justice issue and only becomes one once the concern vultures have got their beaks and claws into it.

It's a long way from exclusion by radical feminists to finding that you are in the fashion of the month category, but that it's not for you that the category has been made. Rather it's for another group entirely who have appropriated your identity, revised it into something that you don't recognise, something that doesn't represent you, and from which you are now excluded, because your identity has become problematic.

I didn't find any particular problems in my identity as I completed my transition. I was passing socially and the temporary social exclusion I had experienced became a thing of the past.

An episode which was like a glimpse of the future in which we now live occurred when I was in private practice as an art therapist and I took a client who declared on contact that they were transsexual and were looking for a therapist to help them through it.

I was fine with this, but rashly disclosed my own status. The client had seen my advert that I had special experience with gender issues, but I had not made my situation known publicly.

This client was about a dozen years older than me. Although her early profile was similar to mine, a different path had been taken which had led to marriage. That had now been dissolved, their house sold, and the proceeds divided, with which my client was now looking to fund her own transition.

She seemed to fit a classic profile that I could recognise, not least because I had tried to go down that path, so I agreed to act as her therapist. Having established the ground of her situation and process, we moved on to planning her transition.

It was at this stage that we began to fall apart. My client happened to be a professional, qualified clinician and planned to exploit that to gain early passage through treatment. The protocols around Gender Reassignment Surgery generally entailed the patient undergoing supervision by a psychiatrist as well as some kind of therapist, taking the necessary hormones so that their appearance would become more congruent, all this leading possibly to a referral for surgery when they had completed their Real Life Experience and lived in gender for two years. I had done that, and although at the time it had seemed frustratingly slow, it was helpful in the long run. There is a tremendous amount of social readjustment to go through, and the hormones can lead to an increase in emotionality to which one must adapt.

But there was apparently an exclusion to this qualification process which was allowed to doctors and clinicians. The basis of this wasn't entirely clear to me but seemed to be a mix of two reasons. Firstly, to facilitate in the transition of professional identity. The second being that these highly qualified professionals could be trusted to be firm in their conviction that they had irresolvable cross-gender feelings, and that they would adapt swiftly.

As the overseeing therapist myself, I was unable to endorse my client's plan, which entailed arranging *Sex Reassignment Surgery*, together with a *rhinoplasty* to help feminise her appearance, and that this would all take place on the day of transition.

It may be that some can get through the necessary changes in under two years, but this client had a strong beard shadow and an obviously masculine voice, both of which could be dealt with, but it would take time. I urged her strongly to do as Jan Morris had recommended me a decade and a half before — *Take your time.*

But she would not. It was not my place as a therapist to deny her wishes or try to prevent her in any way, but I had to offer some advice, although this was rejected brusquely.

She went ahead and did it all at once. I had to stop seeing her professionally, due to my reservations about what she was doing, but saw her informally several times afterwards. Clearly she was pleased with the procedures, which I hadn't doubted would be the case, but she seemed high and a little irrational. It soon became apparent that she resented the fact that I had encouraged her to take longer over the business and eventually accused me of trying to prevent her from going through with it, an allegation that was entirely false.

It is not uncommon for transsexuals to have intense emotional experiences following reassignment surgery. I myself recall having what might be described as spiritual or religious experiences whilst recuperating in the garden outside the ward when I had my own reassignment. But I had retained a sufficient grasp on the mundane world to realise that these were experiences for me alone, and not something I could really expect to carry outside or share.

My assessment of this former client was that she had simply gone through it all too fast and had precipitated what was at least a minor psychosis. Our ways parted finally when she sent me a letter detailing her accusation and demanding that I never contact her again.

This was not, however, the last I heard of her.

I myself had dallied on the edges of the radical feminist world, but one rebuff was sufficient for me to understand that I was on a hiding to nothing with that.[3] My former client, on the other hand, got bitten by this bug a great deal more seriously than I had ever been.

Over the next few years, tales would occasionally find their way back to me through mutual acquaintances that she had got involved with one of these separatist enclaves. The word was that she had got past their resistance by telling the tale that when she had had her reassignment surgery, female organs had been found inside her and that she had been pronounced to be a hermaphrodite, or possibly intersex.

I can say with a reasonable degree of certainty, or at least high probability, that this was a lie, since it seems most unlikely that if this had been the case that she would not have proudly told me in the aftermath. I only ever saw her once again after this, on the street in town; I don't think she saw me, and she still had that strong, dark beard shadow.

---

3   Note: 'on a hiding to nothing' — British expression meaning to be unlikely to succeed.

So many issues are touched on by this that I thought it would be instructive to share them, starting with the matter of psychological adaptation. It does not seem likely to me that someone, who had, despite feelings of wanting to be a woman, maintained a male identity until the age of 45, would be able to psychologically adapt as if by the throwing of a switch.

I have, over the years, heard numerous transsexuals, usually in the upper age groups, maintaining that they felt entirely comfortable socially as a woman only months, weeks, or even days after transitioning or having reassignment surgery. This seems to me to be almost entirely delusional.

Even some of the younger transsexuals I have known have told me how, at least at first, they experienced — and needed — a transitional period of what I might call cognitive realignment as they readjusted the parameters of self-apperception and expectations in social interaction.

It is not my purpose here to seek to prevent people from presenting themselves as they will. I desire that no more than I desired to prevent my former client from transitioning.

But there are limitations and practicalities to this that need to be taken account of.

As I approached the end of my twenties, I had realised that if I left it much longer, I would no longer be able to exploit my androgyny for transition. My body didn't seem to like the influence of androgens given the reaction of my skin, but their influence was beginning to have some other effects, and I knew that the longer I waited, the harder it would be to reverse. Also, one's social persona is beginning to become more fixed by the time one is thirty. Until that age we are like a sapling which can be trained into shape, but afterwards we become more set.

If we are to avoid the complaint by some that transsexuals often stick out like sore thumbs, then those who seek to pursue this path should bear all this in mind.

I shall develop this later, but for now let me return to the link with the radical feminists. Early on in my own process, one of my new contacts had told me about *The Transsexual Empire* by Janice Raymond. This was a book based on a PhD thesis which portrayed transsexualism as the invention of doctors who wanted to replace women, a kind of proto-transhumanism.

Transsexuals themselves were portrayed as evil men who sought only to penetrate [sic] the sisterhood but were also victims themselves of the patriarchal medical system which had entrapped them. The notion that there might be something behind our experience was forcefully denied, and the usual feminist rhetoric employed to both deconstruct gender and at the same time maintain essentialist differences between women and men.

There was no accommodation for the feelings of transsexuals, and no debate was to be engaged in. The fundamental misunderstanding that transsexuals are merely trying to socially mimic female roles was put forward and the recurrent theme of 'feeling like a woman in a man's body' was dismissed with the claim that we should find some space where we can accept ourselves rather than pander to the medical agenda which tells us we need to mutilate our bodies in order to become women. We should, like good behaviourists, look at our bodies and accept that we are not women but men, forget your inner experience.

She wrote '...the issue of transsexualism has profound political and moral ramifications; transsexualism itself is a deeply moral question rather than a medical-technical answer. I contend that the problem of transsexualism would best be served by **morally mandating it out of existence**.'4 [My emphasis.]

'...What this means is that I want to eliminate the medical and social systems that support transsexualism and the reasons why in

---

4   Raymond, Janice. *The Transsexual Empire.* The Women's Press Ltd 1980 ©1979
     Beacon Press, Boston.

a gender-defined society, persons find it necessary to change their bodies.'[5]

She wants to **'eliminate… the reasons why in a gender-defined society, persons find it necessary to change their bodies'**. [My emphasis.]

She simply doesn't understand why this is and imputes motives for which she has no evidence. She wants us to stop wanting to change our bodies, but thinks it is some kind of moral or social problem, when even by the early eighties there was already much evidence indicative of neurodevelopmental causes, as I had seen as an undergraduate, and which she, and the politically diametrically opposed Gender Theorists today refuse to entertain. And she would like to remove the medical means to fulfil our wishes.

Various versions of this have been put to me over the years, all founded on the notion that we should just accept it, like the person who says 'why can't we all just get along'. To offer such solutions is to give no solution at all. If you have a stone in your shoe, you need to get it out. If someone says that you should just accept it you would think they were crazy. The parable of the Lost Coin[6] says it all. One cannot rest when one is so troubled, and an answer must be found.

This is in no way to suggest that radical changes to one's life, even to one's body, should not be seriously challenged and tested before they are made permanent, but to put one's feelings into a state of perpetual limbo in order to please someone else's idea of what is and is not acceptable to do is not a solution.

What this was saying is that transsexuals should be ignored and discarded.

The countermeasures that some transsexuals have employed in response to this are both inevitable, and somewhat amusing.

---

5   https://janiceraymond.com/fictions-and-facts-about-the-transsexual-empire/ (2020).

6   Luke 15:8–10.

Trans exclusion spaces have existed since at least the mid-eighties when I first encountered this book. In the late eighties, I went to a Bisexual Conference in which one of the workshops was a discussion of transsexuality which excluded transsexuals. To do this at a conference was somewhat provocative when there were likely to be transsexuals there. The Michigan Womyn's Festival dates from around this time and is infamous for denying access to trans women. The founder and organiser for forty years, Lisa Vogel, has said that it was never stated policy to exclude trans women, but after one was asked to leave in 1991 the reputation was assured. In later years, this became a millstone around its neck despite continued claims that there was no policing of status, only an 'intention' that the festival was for 'womyn-born-womyn', and put 'the onus on each individual to choose whether or how to respect it.[7]

The fact that trans men were accepted didn't help the impression (these individuals not even claiming to 'identify' as women), and after high-profile bands, such as the Indigo Girls, started dropping out due to this policy, it seems its days were numbered.[8]

Predictably then, every year it was considered a badge of honour to be earned by as many transsexual women as possible to be able to gain entry and last the duration.

This is all a bit of fun and games, and after my run-ins with the radical feminists over the years, it seems something like masochism to associate with a bunch of women who would hate you if they knew the truth. Why would one want to hang out with women with whom it would be impossible to have a reasonable debate should one want to?

I had flirted on the edge because I happened to know one who was accepting of me, and only engaged through another's invitation, and then disclosed. But I was falling into hubris. The desire for the

---

7   https://www.advocate.com/michfest/2015/04/21/years-michigan-womyns-music-festival-will-be-last (2020).

8   Ibid.

acceptance of others can become self-destructive if it is allowed to drive one too far.

Doing it at a festival event is one thing, but embedding oneself into such a social network in one's home circuit really does seem like some kind of crazy to me, especially if it involves lying about one's medical history to gain ingress like a military operation.

Unfortunately, this is one of the points which Janice Raymond somewhat belabours, and has a small amount of substance, although she extends the projection to all without evidence.

The substance is that there are those, like my former client, who do really seem to want to gain entry to separatist feminist spaces in this way, by deceit. Perhaps she did this from a need to compensate for her lost years. Fortunately, Ms Raymond has an exaggerated belief as to the number and importance of such feminist social groups and their spaces and this is little more than a sideshow since most women aren't radical separatist feminists.

However, there are sensitivities about women's and men's spaces which do need to be addressed, but not in the extreme way that they manage. Trans women should be modest and reticent about involvement in women's spaces so that they are not seen as invading, which is a classic accusation that is made against us.

We must have a balance of rights and responsibilities. We cannot have people transitioning one day and demanding all the traditional rights of women the next. We cannot have people demanding these rights who do not pass as women, or at least who are not making some effort towards such an end, as this will sour relations.

The Transsexual Empire is a greatly flawed work, not least because Janice Raymond was later widely believed to have been having a relationship with Mary Daly, her academic supervisor over the PhD thesis on which this was based.[9, 10]

---

9   https://radicalbitch.wordpress.com/2010/01/05/rip-mary-daly/ (2020).

10   https://zagria.blogspot.com/2008/04/mary-daly-1928-2010-feminist-theologian.html#.XJ5Za6Snyoo (2020).

So, Ms Raymond should perhaps not have been granted her doctorate. And the book contains very little evidence on which its claims are based; it is largely a feminist polemic against transsexuals with little inclination to understand the phenomenon of transsexualism itself.

The various issues raised around this area have bubbled along through the ensuing decades but have now resurfaced in various mutated forms and confront us still today.

I am glad that the idea of morally mandating transsexualism out of existence seems to have been taken off the menu in the current year, but now we are faced with almost the exact opposite.

The pendulum of social opinion swings back and forth, but we shall continue to exist, and so some legal accommodation must be made which balances our own needs with those of the remainder of society, so as to stabilise the situation. Societal relations work best when boundaries are clearly understood. Exemption and immunity from the customs and responsibilities to which the rest of society are subject is a step towards social chaos, as protected groups proliferate, and the tyranny of minorities holds sway over the silent majority.

Without firm boundaries we have a recipe for significant pushback from the extreme end of conservative interests. Pushback which could easily go too far if that which they are pushing against is not seen to be reasonable.

CHAPTER 9

FREEDOM!

COMPLETING MY TRANSITION was a big relief. To be free not only of the requirements of the medical programme but also of those aspects of my body I had hated for so long and no longer to feel myself as incongruous.

Another one of those curious coincidences turned up around this time, which I found out shortly afterwards. I completed my treatment at Seacroft Hospital and it turned out that it was the same hospital that my father had been sent to when he had been invalided out of the Italian campaign in 1944, having been seriously injured in the assault on Monte Cassino.

He had written me a letter shortly before I went through with surgery, telling me that I would regret it. I remember reading a story in a magazine I took in with me which covered a 'trans' person who had regretted having surgery, and I wondered how someone could get into something like this with so little self-understanding.

And lo and behold, I went through with the procedure and felt no regret, no sense that this had been any kind of mistake, only a deep relief that I had finally actualised what had been in my mind all my life.

I had never properly talked about this with my father, and that I regret, but he was a man of few words, and this was something so alien to him that I can understand how difficult it was for him to even contemplate, let alone engage with.

He may have been reticent of his feelings about this to me, but I felt I had had some level of success, when a year or two down the line I was visiting my parents and we stopped near some shops that I used to know so that I could go and see them. Later on, my mother told me something I shall always treasure. She said that when I had left the car and walked down the street, he had said, 'He does look like a girl'. She then went on to add that he would be too embarrassed should I ever speak to him about this and strongly cautioned against it, saying, 'This is the most you'll get!', advice to which I adhered.

Relations with my father improved after that, and there seemed to be a measure of acceptance that I had not turned into a disaster. I felt more comfortable knowing what he had said and while what followed was mostly implicit, when he passed away some years later I was mercifully spared unresolved feelings or a sense of permanent estrangement.

My mother had been more accepting at a personal level, but fearful of social reactions. For many years, while we still maintained our relationship, she kept me as a secret from my brothers and their own families after my father's passing. I was unpersonned despite my frequent entreaties to be restored. On one of the rare occasions when I visited her, which had to be done under cover of darkness, she said, 'If your brother comes round unexpectedly, please go upstairs and wait until he goes', I had literally become an 'attic child'. Upon her death my extended family had to face that she had fed them a fiction about me for decades beyond any understandable period of hesitation and planning of explanations. By comparison, my passage through the bureaucratic officialdom required was a breeze, even in the eighties, long before any legal reforms came over the horizon.

I was free but had paid a price for my liberation and felt marked in my soul by a sense of being an outcast, something I had experienced in many phases of my life, and this played into the experiences of psychodrama I relate in *Waking The Monkey!*[1] Perhaps this also influenced my attitudes in later developments.

But this was deep background which took many years to work through. In the foreground of the moment I had got to the waystation I had long envisioned, and it was a relief. I had reached an oasis in the desert.

As the dust settled I was nonetheless soon engaged in turbulence as I was obliged to move when a new owner took possession of the house in which I lived and he harassed most of the tenants out in order to refurbish the property and take new tenants at higher rents. The former owner had told him about me and there was an element of what might now be called transphobic bullying, but this was opportunistic in that they wanted to get all the tenants out by hook or by crook.

It was certainly an unpleasant few weeks before I found a Housing Association which sourced me new accommodation, and which I would not like to have to repeat, but the new owner and his brother were really just knuckle-dragging primates who made no distinction about whom they harassed. I felt much sorrier for the elderly lady downstairs who was too old to be moving.

My new abode was in a much better area and was a dedicated block for single women. I had explained my situation at the Housing Association office and there had been no problem. This was yet another instance of an unwelcome challenge which led to a series of opportunities which I would otherwise have never encountered.

Although not seriously distant from my old place, my new location nonetheless allowed me to continue to leave my old identity behind and develop without some of the former social expectations. I made new friends and was as close to deep stealth as I was ever realistically

---

1   See my book *Waking The Monkey!* Lulu.com, 2015 http://www.lulu.com/shop/claire-rae-randall/waking-the-monkey-becoming-the-hundredth-monkey/paperback/product-22175832.html (2020).

likely to achieve. I became involved in local community affairs and began to develop my career.

I detached from the world of gender clinics, transsexual support groups, feminists and the like and was able to think about other things, leaving the torment behind.

At last the thoughts of suicide, which had long lurked at the back of my mind, began to fade. I was no longer at war with myself; I was free.

CHAPTER 10

A NEW CENTURY: INTERPRETATIONS AND PROJECTIONS

I PAID VERY LITTLE ATTENTION to developments such as the emergence of Gender Studies in the nineties, or the major change in usage implied by the adoption of the term transgender as opposed to transsexual, the term I had always applied to myself, not only since my time with the TV/TS group in the mid-seventies, but from my earliest discoveries about such things as a child in the sixties. It seems that I had got through just before this became politicised and exploited.

My first intimation of what was in store was on a late-night open-ended talk show about the turn of the millennium on the UK's Channel 4, a TV station dedicated to alternative views, supposedly, and minority arts. The programme, *After Dark*, had unusual guests, and one of these was a person who self-described as transgender. This person appeared to be a woman, but as the discussion ensued it transpired that they were anatomically male, and what was most extraordinary to me, had no desire for sex reassignment surgery.

For me it had always been axiomatic that to want to be female was to want to be morphologically embodied as nearly to the female as was medically possible. Transvestites might act out, but I had always known them to return to their masculine selves. Various religious beliefs have it that we are embodied as male and female through our physical bodies, and that these are parts of our identities which we must recognise.

Even though I acknowledge that I could never be fully female in this body, it was plain to me that if I and my fellow travellers were to be able to achieve the degree of acceptance that we sought, then we should be as bodily congruent as possible, not only for our subjective sense of self but also for the greatest authenticity.

Here was a person who didn't share this opinion, clearly.

Way back in the eighties I had corresponded with a transsexual who had transitioned but had had no medical treatments. We never actually met, so I can't say what her presentation was like, but she sounded like she managed all right. She had tried to get onto a medical programme, but she lived in a remote part of England where this kind of thing wasn't yet recognised by the local health authority. This was someone who would have liked to be physically congruent but hadn't found a suitable pathway to achieving that goal.

The guest on the late-night talk show, on the other hand, clearly wasn't in the least bothered. This was the first time that I encountered a serious full-time transgender person who wasn't transsexual and it boggled my mind. Was this what we were to expect in the new century?

It would be a little while before I was to see the proliferation of this reality, but as the new era progressed, it did, hugely.

An experience which has recurred in many different guises over the decades is being interpreted by others. Not just in the ideological manner in which the radical feminists of the seventies and eighties did, but in many other ways.

This has ranged from old friends asking simply 'Couldn't you just be gay?' to Gender Studies doctoral students telling me why I had this experience and online critics stating that all trans people have an acquired sexual paraphilia around fetishes for women's clothing. Really!

I am happy that not all of these assumptions can be true at the same time! In fact, very little of what has been projected onto me by others during my passage through life has been correct.

I mentioned elsewhere the young gay chap who identified as a woman for a while and attended the Gender Clinic. I had always suspected that being gay was all that was up with him and was most relieved when he dropped out of the programme before he went too far. It had always been apparent to me that he was more interested in the social identity and boyfriends than he had been about any sense of being ill at ease with his body.

My own sexual attractions were of less importance to me, and my own body, more. I had never found engaging in physical relationships easy and the childhood shock of the older boys in the changing rooms remained with me. I had found women attractive, but that was mostly filled by longing to be like them rather than to actually relate to them sexually as a man. I did have girlfriends in my mid-twenties, and I did have sex with them, but I would spend the whole time wishing I was the girl. I felt that I was having to learn some obscure pass code like Tinbergen's sticklebacks, and then when I got told that it felt to them like I was a girl anyway, it was clear that sex wasn't the main part of this.

'Why can't you be…?' was the easier to deal with, partly because the answer was simple and partly because despite the embedded assumption about sexuality, it was posed as a question, allowing the opportunity to explain.

More difficult to deal with were those who believe that they have a comprehensive explanation for this phenomenon and are determined that I should be fitted into their box. This is largely why I went stealth and retreated from the world of trans and gay activism in the nineties after completing my transition. But as time has gone by the world has changed and I have found myself in a different position with a different perspective.

One critical hinge on which my path turned was my experience at the 2002 Art Therapy Summer School at the nearby college.

I had attended this short course several times in the past, both before training and qualifying as an art therapist in 1982, and afterwards; it had been an important part of the self-assessment of my problem, even leading to that experience with the woman who had said being with me was more like being with a girl.

The 2002 experience was to be no less of a milestone. I had chosen to go back and have a look at how far I had come, in view of the fact that I had reached a quiet spot in my life and was seeking direction for the future.

Perhaps the Imp of Perversity got to me but I chose to attend the workshop group of the psychiatrist whose group I had attended on the previous occasion when I had revealed my sexual secret to that woman with whom I had briefly been intimate.

One of the most important things I had learnt as an art therapist is to be sensitive to what may be brought to the surface. Closed circle workshop groups can elicit deep and controversial material. Partly this is facilitated by the confidential nature of such groups, partly by the little tricks and games which the facilitator may use to get participants to drop their boundaries in order to share this information, and partly by the presumed assumption that this material will be respected. I guess if someone started relating material of serious criminal behaviour from the recent past, there may be questions raised about confidentiality and this information going beyond the group to the relevant authorities, but I have never been involved in such a situation.

He was rather adept at getting his group members to loosen up and drop their boundaries in order to relate their deep tales, but was less good at withholding excessive judgement.

Remember that this was a practical workshop aimed at those who were already professionally trained art therapists, mental health workers in general, such as occupational therapists and nurses, or those with a serious interest in the subject who were either doing it for reasons of personal growth and career advancement or as preparation before entering upon art therapy training themselves. This was not taking place with psychiatric patients or in a Therapeutic Community, where people with serious personality disorders were obliged to take responsibility for their sociopathic behaviour.

I began the week like the others warming up into the process gently. By the middle section, we were discussing life maps in the open group — visual representations of our lives' timelines and events, before getting into them individually in more depth.

It was at this point that I disclosed my story. He queried why I had not alluded to it earlier, to which my reply was that I was cautious about the response I might get. It was not lost on me that it was only shortly after I said this that he, in speaking towards the others in the group who were observing the process, referred to me as 'he'.

I froze rigid and was afraid to challenge him, or even point out what he had said.

Fortunately I had, earlier that summer, bought a Sony minidisc, a little gadget which was obsolete well before the end of the decade, but with which I had much fun in the noughties. And which I had used to record my individual session, discussing my images and material.

I had done this for the purpose of self-reflection, as was the purpose of my whole attendance at the week's event, while the idea of needing it for self-defence had been wholly absent from my mind.

One of my fellow group members was kind enough to review the audio with me later that day, and she confirmed that I had heard aright.

Upon putting this to him in one of the later sessions, he not only failed to recuse his personal opinion on the matter as being inappropriate to the group situation, but he doubled down and asserted that I was not, and never could be a woman, and that he was correct in addressing me as 'he'. He was determined to make my gender identity the subject of his analysis despite the fact that from my position it wasn't a problem and I hadn't come there to examine it as such. Unfortunately, he seemed unaware of the kind of formal constraints on expressing his personal opinions in group therapy, which really should have been taken for granted.

It also later became apparent that he assumed I was still not physically reassigned, which surely must have played into his judgement of me. It may have been partly my fault for applying the term transgender to myself at one stage, a word which I had used because of its then increasing currency, but had never intended that it should be interpreted to mean that I was like that person on the late night TV show, or the character Dil in the film *The Crying Game*, which he mentioned came to his mind. I almost never applied it to myself again.

I made a formal complaint against him to the college, based principally on the inappropriateness of a psychiatrist exploiting my disclosure to impose interpretations on me (in front of the whole workshop group), and it was on this that I won it, being awarded compensation and refund of fees.

In retrospect, I find myself wondering if I was just being a snowflake like the trenders who complain about misgendering. Had I been more confident and assertive from the moment he referred to me inappropriately, he might have backed down, but I doubt it. This was before the Gender Recognition Act, long before the Equalities Act, which I mistrust deeply, and long before I ever heard the term misgender. I was alone, psychologically naked like in the art therapy painting I had made some years before, and I had to defend myself in whatever ways were possible. Nonetheless I should have been more assertive and argued back more strongly that I didn't care about his judgements.

Fortunately, there were Standards of Care in place for the course which I was able to demonstrate had been breached that would have applied generally to all complaints of inappropriate treatment of confidential material. It had been bad practice, regardless of the particulars.

I recalled the group many years before in which he had encouraged us to share sexual secrets. He liked to play with fire, to walk on the edge, to take risks which were not always calculated fully, and sometimes he would slip and get burned. Or his clients would.

I reflected that facing my demons alone, as I had done previously, had been the best thing for me to do when coming to my decision. The kind of resistance I had experienced here would only have delayed me.

In amongst his power trip and resistance to the existence of the phenomenon of transsexualism there was an interesting point which he made that I am bound to agree with to some extent as an hypothesis arising from evolutionary psychology, but which was nonetheless no justification for his authoritarian position as a therapist.

He observed that categorisation of gender was probably an innate perceptual recognition factor (in the same way that perspective depth and paired eye tropisms are in neonates). But I would add that if one is told that someone is of a particular gender, it is hard to unsee what you have been told; you project this onto your previous interpretation and cognitive dissonance is created. He meant that my disclosure had reset his perception of me and he now saw me as male. This can of course even work with a natal woman when the expectations and interpretations of the perceptual systems are misled or tricked. It is akin to figure/ground illusions in which one sees either one or the other image but not both at the same time. I would add that his own forthright views on the matter are likely to have also played a part, whether unconscious or not. In fact, I would strongly suspect that his opinion on this was the deciding factor. We often see what we want to see.

I stated in the Introduction that it was with a good deal of reluctance that I set about writing this book because of this very problem. The two factors become entangled: the perception of real or imagined gender markers and the rigid prejudice of the observer. But the latter can come to override and determine the perception, even in instances when there has been an error.

This was one of my largest challenges of this type, but by no means the only one. I see purpose in them now since they have obliged me to both strengthen myself in the face of opposition, but also clarify in my own mind even more than I already had what it was that I actually believed about myself, and how I, and people like me, fitted into the world. In an unexpected way I had made my assessment of where I had got to, albeit in a much more challenging way than I had ever anticipated.

It would be a while before all the divergent aspects came together, but in the end they did.

One of the major tasks on this path is learning to skilfully avoid people's projections of what they think I or we might be.

We must negotiate our way between numerous obstacles and challenges but, as we shall see later, the law has now become such a tyrant to the ordinary population, and those who exploit it so arrogantly in their assertion, that those who now claim transgender rights don't have to have done any more than that. I am glad to have legal status in my desired gender, but do not wish to be in a protected category which seems to be above criticism, as has now been established by the 2010 Equalities legislation.

The tables seem recently to have been turned to the point where merely claiming to be transgender establishes a hegemonic status which may not be challenged. The balance has swung too far to the other side.

There are certainly those who see us as a threat to society. Those we must face and challenge, but since the emergence of transgenderism as a form of pseudo-transsexualism in the nineties they have failed to understand that there are different groups here, with fundamentally different self concepts, behaviours and ways of being. Perhaps the old school shrink had already uncritically bought into the new trend, judging by his cultural references, and that was why he projected it onto me when I used the fatal term — transgender.

I was not yet ready to understand how far this new ideology of gender had colonised, and indeed was poised to replace, the original phenomenon, which I had believed myself to be a part of. It was not until I was almost colonised myself that it truly dawned on me how far this concept of transgender had moved the frame.

CHAPTER 11

LGBT AND NEW PERSPECTIVES

S OMEWHAT EMBOLDENED by winning my unexpected challenge with the psychiatrist, and following the progress of the new Gender Recognition Bill (GRB), which would recognise the de facto legal status of the likes of myself, I ventured out into contact with the LGBT world. There had been mounting pressure, since the recognition a couple of years earlier of intersex people who had been inappropriately assigned, to encompass transsexual people as well and a directive from the EU Court of Justice made it necessary to put this in place.

The passage of the GRB through Parliament in early 2004 was something that I watched with interest. This was triggered by the decision of the European Court of Human Rights in 2002[1] in the case of Goodwin vs The United Kingdom, when a post-operative MtF transsexual claimed that her right to privacy was being infringed since she was being treated as a man for the purposes of National Insurance. This seemed like a good thing at the time. The decision that '[a] test of congruent biological factors could no longer be decisive in denying

---

1   https://swarb.co.uk/goodwin-v-the-united-kingdom-echr-11-jul-2002/ (2020).

legal recognition'[2] was helpful, but was taken a lot further than was required by the ECHR.

Problems soon became apparent.

I was by this time in several Yahoo email groups, a kind of early social networking format, and a couple of these were for transsexuals. Opinions varied widely, but amongst those of us who had been transitioned long-term and were fully medically reassigned there was concern about the terms of the Bill, which only required that someone had been diagnosed with Gender Dysphoria and that they had lived in their desired gender for two years for them to be legally recognised as being of that gender.

Unlike all previous Gender Recognition acts in other countries, no requirement was made necessary for any surgical reassignments, and the then Labour government made much of this as being a truly ground-breaking piece of legislation which would set a model for future laws both at home and abroad in that it removed the absolute link between the body and legal gender.

Deeply involved with the government's consultation had been the trans lobby group Press for Change (PFC), who had taken a radical new approach to the standards which might be deemed fit for the recognition of transsexuals, or rather transgenders in their desired gender.

One level on which they had argued and sold their position was from a premise of absolute equality between the sexes. In other words, that the law should require the same standards of recognition for both male to female trans people as for female to male, rather than the highest reasonable standard in each case.

But it was not until much later that I understood the deeper legal reasoning why that was employed. The paper *'Sex Changes'? Paradigm Shifts in 'Sex' and 'Gender' Following the Gender Recognition Act?*,[3]

---

2   Ibid.

3   http://socresonline.org.uk/12/1/whittle.html (2020).

written in 2005 in the immediate aftermath of the passage of the GRB into law as the Gender Recognition Act (GRA) and published in early 2006 by Stephen Whittle and Lewis Turner, is for the most part a scholarly exposition of the history of the various standards of recognition of gender which have pertained in historical societies over the centuries. These almost always involved some reference to the body, as well as requiring that those individuals who had revised gender status historically should remain in that gender and not revert. Only as the paper progresses into the later parts does it, I would argue, deviate from common sense.

My old friend Stephen Whittle had in the time since I had known him qualified in law, become the dominant force in the Press for Change group and lobbied for the recognition of transsexuals. Which was all fine and dandy, except that by now we had moved into *newspeak* territory with the *transgender* terminology, which was associated with the wider umbrella that did not consider medical reassignment necessary for recognition.

Making much of Lord Winston's reply to Lord Tebbit[4] in the Lords' debate on the GRB, Whittle and Turner over-egged the pudding of their argument. Whilst Lord Tebbit is regrettably limited in his understanding of developmental gender expression, and Lord Winston was correct in pointing out that it is more complicated than chromosomes or gonads, the latter's case should not be exploited to separate gender entirely from the body, and this is what Whittle and Turner do.

I would argue that their statement that '...although the distinction between sex and gender was re-mobilised through biological discourse by Lord Tebbit, that same discourse drawn upon by Lord Winston *removed* the distinction ...'[5] [my emphasis] is false. He only made it clear that the determination of gender is a complex process in which both biology and psychology participate. Lord Tebbit's

4   https://api.parliament.uk/historic-hansard/lords/2004/feb/03/gender-recognition-bill-hl (2020).

5   http://socresonline.org.uk/12/1/whittle.html (2020).

comment that Lord Winston 'is over-elaborate in his cautions'[6] is one
with which I agree wholeheartedly.

It is worth remembering that the ruling from the European Court
quoted in this debate was that '[t]he court had found under Article
8 of the Convention that a test of congruent biological factors could
no longer be **decisive** in denying legal recognition to the change of
gender of a **post-operative transsexual**'.[7] [Official Report, 13/1/04:
col. GC 5.] [My emphasis.]

We should bear in mind that all previous gender recognition acts
elsewhere had required genital surgery requirements, at least for MtF
transsexuals to gain recognition; this was the first in the whole world
not to, so it was not working on the basis of existing precedent, but
sought to create a new precedent of its own, overturning previous
decisions.

Lord Tebbit is thought to be probably antipathetic to most aspects
of gender reassignment, but, recognising that he can't buck the ruling
of the European Court, he focusses on marriage. There was a certain
amount of confusion injected into the debate since the government
was also putting through its Civil Partnership Bill (2004) at the time,
but in the wake of the GRA, rather than before, which would have
saved a small number of transsexuals a great deal of trouble in allowing them to convert existing marriages into Civil Partnerships. Lord
Tebbit attempted to throw a few spanners in the works but was unsuccessful.[8] Ironically it enabled *transgender* people who hadn't had reassignment surgery to get married after recognition while gay people
who were anatomically in the same position had to be content with a
Civil Partnership. (I am not convinced that *Gay Marriage* is a legitimate epistemological concept, but in view of what follows it perhaps
becomes redundant.)

---

6   https://api.parliament.uk/historic-hansard/lords/2004/feb/03/gender-recog-
    nition-bill-hl (2020).

7   Ibid.

8   Ibid.

The Whittle and Turner research document states:

8.3 What Lord Winston is suggesting is that biological sex cannot be changed, but neither can it be relied upon to definitively categorise. …for the purposes of the gender recognition act, 'changing sex' was never about changing biology but about changing legal definitions of what gender recognition/legal sex was.[9]

The key word here is *definitively*. Biology is not *definitive*, but it is *indicative*. Any two factors, such as gender identity and biological sexual characteristics, which are so closely associated, at a level of correlation in excess of 99.5%, should be treated as though they have some functional relationship beyond mere happenstance and coincidence.

One comment which Lord Winston made in the debate demonstrates that despite his long medical experience and erudition, he does not, or did not at the time, have a definitive knowledge of the subject, if I may be so bold as to say. In the Lords' debate he also quoted retired endocrinologist Robert Jaffe: '…the gender identity (that is how the patient views himself or herself) and the sex of rearing are paramount in determining the patient's sexual identity…'[10] The second part of that assertion, that the sex of rearing is *determinative,* is demonstrably false given the clear evidence of the dreadful David Reimer case, at which we shall shortly arrive. Some have argued that Jaffe was saying that the autonomy of the patient needed to be taken into account, which may be the first half, but that's not how I read it in full: '…gender identity… and the **sex of rearing are paramount**'. [My emphasis.]

Suffice it here to say that despite the extreme efforts of Dr Money, young David never acquired a female identity. One wonders if Jaffe and Winston were still labouring under the false impression that he had? This dangerous belief seems to have poisoned the wells all around the subject.

---

9   http://socresonline.org.uk/12/1/whittle.html (2020).

10   https://api.parliament.uk/historic-hansard/lords/2004/feb/03/gender-recognition-bill-hl (2020).

So, while dismissing the importance of physiological aspects of bodily identity in gender, he replaces it with social determination. This is an immensely clever intellectual sleight of hand, but a logical fallacy, one which I am not even sure he will have been conscious of making, since he had probably already been primed by contact with gender ideology through PFC campaigners and others.

Whittle and Turner want to remove all the indicative factors, which Lord Winston allowed contributed to physical sex, chromosomes, genetic markers, gonads, hormones, genital morphology and so on, and replace them entirely with behavioural ones.

While recognition of surgically reassigned trans people was the minimum requirement of the instruction from the European Court, Paragraph 5.9 of Whittle and Turner draws attention to the fact that recent decisions in that court had not concerned itself with morphological or surgical status but with daily living, in other words social performance alone, above all else.[11]

The early Gender Recognition panels were apparently concerned with surgical status, but the paper suggests that (as early as late 2005 or early 2006) this was not acceptable (to some) and that the attitude changed.

'8.7 For the Gender Recognition Act, the body is irrelevant, as neither bodily modification, nor the presence or lack of a penis is determinative. Moreover, the Gender Recognition Act is performative (see Butler 1990), in that as a form of speech-act, what it **does** is makes gender into sex in law'.[12]

Again, I would point out that the presence or lack of a penis may not be *determinative* or *definitive*, but surely it must be *indicative*. There may be anomalies but to refuse general pragmatic rules and principles on the basis of these is wrong. Gender is a gestalt of several factors, some more heavily weighted than others.

---

11   http://socresonline.org.uk/12/1/whittle.html (2020).

12   Ibid.

Butler's ideology removes all that for so-called *performative acts.* I have referred to how some behaviour is performative; feminists would call it *role-stereotyping* or somesuch, but it goes much further than that. Apparently, merely *saying something* is performative. That is what they mean by '...the Gender Recognition Act is performative'... a... 'speech-act'. They have *redefined* what we understand by gender — *in law!*

Make it so, Mr La Forge!

This is an incredible act of hubris seeking to legislate for how people perceive reality, like O'Brien in Orwell's *Nineteen Eighty-Four* holding up four fingers and demanding that we see five.

The problems with this quickly began to become apparent.

An example of this reasoning is shown by the blogger Stephen Young in his *Critical Legal Thinking* blog,[13] who claims that merely saying that someone is a boy or a girl is a *performative act*, even when the boy or girl has done nothing. Going further, he claims that to say of a child when it has been born '*It's a girl*' is imposing a gender on the child, which is initially described as being without sex or gender. I would say in reply to this that Mr Young has a shortcoming in his understanding of the English language. '*It's a girl*' is a colloquialism, which to parse is not saying 'This thing shall be made into a girl' but rather '*Behold! A girl!*' If the unknown author of *Beowulf* had been saying it, he would have declared '*Hwaet! Maegden!*' The sex or gender is not being *imposed*, it is *declared* or *described* on the basis of the available evidence of morphology. At birth the child can do or say nothing on his or her own account, and so must rely on the best judgements of their carers — the *probabilistic* likelihood of their gender being in excess of 99.5%. As they grow up, should they feel that they do not fit this assumption, then their performance needs to be *demonstrative.* That will be true *performativity*, not a mere verbal claim which bears

---

13   http://criticallegalthinking.com/2016/11/14/judith-butlers-performativity/ (2020).

more resemblance to magical thinking — *Thus is it said, thus mote it be!*

When I was in my deepest state of conflict in my early twenties, I played a game with myself. I imagined that I was an alien from another planet who had come here to find out about Earth life perhaps and this was why I felt so alienated. This was merely what I would call an art therapy fantasy, but it helped relieve a bit of my stress if only by being a little amusing.

But had I then gone on to claim to people that I actually was an alien from another planet, then short of being laughed at, people at least would have asked how I knew this and if I had any supporting evidence.

Whittle and Turner make much of how the law conflates gender and sex into one and the same thing. This is an incredibly dangerous step, since the law has now redefined the meanings of the common language terms which it is using. I believe that this is exactly the same thing that Eric Blair — pen name George Orwell — describes being done by the *Ministry of Truth* with its *Newspeak*, revised terminology with politically correct meanings, designed to control what can be thought, in his monstrously important work *Nineteen Eighty-Four*.[14]

As we see in paragraph 8.8 of the paper, Whittle and Turner state that:

8.8 We share Sandland's (2005)[15] view that as we can now have men with vaginas and women with penises, the act does undermine the binary of two morphologically distinct sexes.[16]

---

14   Orwell, George. *Nineteen Eighty-Four* (Penguin Modern Classics). Secker and Warburg, 1949.

15   Sandland, R. *Feminism and the Gender Recognition Act.* Feminist Legal Studies 13: 43–66. 2005.

16   http://socresonline.org.uk/12/1/whittle.html.

This explication of the 2004 Act must form a large basis for the claims I started seeing shortly after by transgender people claiming to be happy with their *female penises.*

In paragraph 6.6 of the paper we see that those who have not undergone surgeries because they are *unwilling* are conflated with those who for medical reasons are *unable.*

> 6.6 However, as a minimum line, it was perfectly possible for a government to go one step further [than that required by the ECHR for post-operative transsexuals] and to make legal recognition available to those who are pre- or non-treatment and thus include those trans people who for health, disability or other reason are unable or **unwilling** to undergo surgical intervention.[17] [My emphasis.]

This statement exposes the disingenuous nature of the step taken to allow those who have recused themselves from surgeries to be granted recognition. It is not simply a compassionate measure to allow those who want and have already been referred for surgery but were turned down on medical grounds to receive recognition, but rather a sleight of hand using this group to allow an entirely different set to be excused from being required, and thereby to let the entire surgical requirement be set aside. A classic Cultural Marxist ploy — create a loophole exploiting the compassion of others, then leverage it to take down the entire system with nothing to replace it but chaos. Chaos and power. The postmodernists love power.

Originally, I had assumed that this policy was based on the fact that genital reassignment surgery for female to male transsexuals is a much less frequently performed procedure, because it is much easier to surgically reconstruct from tissue that you have, than from tissue that you don't, and so I had considered this a reasonable, practical approach. But I thought it a mistake to extend this to both genders on the basis of equality, a concept that I find inapplicable in this instance.

---

17   Ibid.

I have been berated online by trans men who objected when I have said that the procedure is less successful than for MtF, but I stand by this assessment. I'm sure that many are pleased with it, but without stem cell grafts it could never be as convincing as for the MtF procedure.

It seems entirely reasonable to me to recuse FtM transitioners from this requirement for this reason. But the presence of a penis in an apparent woman is surely more challenging than the absence of one in an apparent man, and to say that it doesn't matter at all is to separate the gender of a body from its physical sexual characteristics entirely. Which is exactly what the paper by Whittle and Turner argues.

I had been acquainted with Professor Stephen Whittle, who was the chief PFC policy advisor, as far back as the seventies when we had met through the TV/TS Group network, and had loosely kept in touch from time to time, but I wasn't aware of his political line on this. In the online networks which I frequented at the time there was a suggestion that Professor Whittle had lobbied for this because of his situation as an FtM transman who, it was rumoured, didn't want to risk the surgeries involved, and I don't suppose many of my then network would have objected too much if this had only applied to FtM trans men, due to the practical difficulties, but we couldn't agree with applying it to both trans conditions. To me this looks like leftist equalities dogma sneaking its way in by stealth, even deception, when to rigidly apply an equality ideology is inappropriate.

Certainly, it was based on the idea of equality, but one cannot make apples and oranges equal.

To be blunt, and may I apologise to my readers in advance for such bluntness, but women do not have penises, despite what the legal sophists might argue. I will hear kicking and screaming at this, but it has always been taken as the case until recently when Gender Theory has tried to make it not so. Indeed, a teaching assistant was recently suspended for saying as much on social media in response to a rash of declarations and claims that 'some women have penises!'

Not in my reality!

I could not have felt that I was a woman in any meaningful way if I was still so embodied. Potential and inner worlds are one thing, but if they are not actualised, manifested, brought into reality then they remain within that spectral realm and have no more substance.

We cannot and should not say when in the condition of a chimaera that we are all and only that hidden part of ourselves while the contradictory outer shell remains.

In the minds of most people therefore, if it should be possible for an apparent 'man' to become a woman in any sense of actual embodiment, then that must involve no longer having a penis. A state of affairs which is not absolutely required by the Gender Recognition Act of 2004.

Whereas, on the other side, while clearly having a penis is an attribute which is generally considered to be an important part of being a man, it is possible for a man to lose this part of his anatomy through injury or disease and still be seen as a man. This is acknowledged by Whittle and Turner in their paper. It might hardly be something he would wish known, but it wouldn't change his identity to be that of a woman. This could probably be expressed in some form of logic gate which permits an 'if > then' in one direction but not the reverse.

So, it is a strange situation when two very different conditions have the same laws applied to them. One condition which is super difficult to reconstruct and never entirely satisfactory because of medical considerations is exempted for what I consider perfectly reasonable grounds, although this is not the reason given, while the other condition, which has had established procedures for many decades, and which is widely considered by many to confer at least some element of feminine status upon the recipient, is also made not necessary because there must be equality between the genders.

The outcome was predictable, although the MPs who sponsored the Bill, David Lammy and Lynne Jones, both denied that it would come about. In the debate on amendments to the GRB on the 25th May

2004, which I watched live on the Parliament TV channel, Andrew Selous, MP, put it to them that the provisions of the Bill would not prevent non-surgically reassigned transsexuals from gaining access to women's changing rooms, potentially communal.[18]

The replies from the two MPs sponsoring the Bill were such as to cast scorn on the suggestion that a transsexual person would do such a thing. Shock! Horror!

And yet Mr Selous drew attention to the case of a Diane Parry, a trans person who was described as being of 'a somewhat masculine appearance',[19] and how this Diane Parry had forced 'herself' onto the ladies of 'her' local community. The Hon Mr Selous was concerned about male-bodied trans 'women' not being as discreet as they might.

This is hardly an example of how 'mild-mannered' most transsexuals are, as Lynne Jones argued. Clearly there are mavericks within the population and surely one must expect a greater likelihood of mavericks of this nature if highly unorthodox conditions are allowed for the recognition of gender and the net is too widely cast.

Mr Selous' concerns were dismissed as being of no importance, since it was argued that these things simply wouldn't happen, a classic deflection which the Left often employs in situations such as this.

We mustn't be mistrustful! People will do the right thing! It is offensive to suggest that anyone might take advantage of this and exploit it for nefarious purposes! Have more faith in people's better natures!

And so on.

I include the relevant portion of this debate in an appendix as it is highly instructive to compare how this was slipped through, and how the weaknesses in it have been exploited.

Unfortunately, it is virtually a law of nature that unless something is hermetically sealed, airtight, watertight, there will be leaks. If

18   See Appendix A. https://hansard.parliament.uk/commons/2004-05-25/debates/36c03d5e-4aa1-42ea-860f-877bc85d9ca7/OrdersOfTheDay (2020).

19   Ibid.

there is a loophole, someone will manage to aim their arrow straight through it in due course. It is only a matter of time.

While David Lammy admitted that it would be legally possible for a supposed MtF transperson who had not had reassignment surgery to gain a Recognition Certificate, he claimed that it would be unlikely, and ridiculous to assert that anyone would deliberately subvert this process. Why would anyone want to get recognition if they were not genuine? Surely only people who were refused surgery on medical grounds would follow this route?

In the intervening decade and more since then, the traditional, conventional association of anatomy with gender has been sufficiently eroded by those who have been indoctrinated in postmodernist thinking and who want to deconstruct gender out of existence altogether that we now hear the absurd statements about women having penises and men having vaginas. This is the ideological background of new proposals by radical trans activists and their supporters in Gender Studies departments for supposed 'reforms' to the 2005 Act, to 'simplify' the legal process, which might allow gender to be recognised simply by means of a Statutory Declaration, or less, with no corroborating medical or psychiatric evidence, detaching it entirely from bodily status and historic established identity.

A Council of Europe Parliamentary Assembly Resolution 2048 (2015) Discrimination against transgender people in Europe,[20] which in many ways should have been a straightforward document, became problematic when it stated that it welcomed 'the emergence of a right to gender identity... which gives every individual the right to recognition of their gender identity' (paragraph 5) but failed to properly explain what this was.

In paragraph 6.2.2, as concerns legal gender recognition, it calls on member states to 'abolish sterilisation and other compulsory medical treatment, as well as a mental health diagnosis, as a necessary legal

20 http://assembly.coe.int/nw/xml/XRef/Xref-XML2HTML-en.asp?fileid=21736 (2020).

requirement to recognise a person's gender identity in laws regulating the procedure for changing a name and registered gender'.

Nowhere does this report seem to say what is actually required. Calling gender reassignment sterilisation is newspeak for not requiring genital or morphological congruence with the claimed gender. The absence of any form of medical treatment or diagnosis being required ensures the slippery slope will be slid down to the very bottom.

This is exactly what MPs Lammy and Jones had said would not happen, and yet a mere decade later the ground was being prepared by the EU for it to be cemented into place. Indeed, Whittle and Turner had already established this legal ideology with their paper in 2006.

In February of 2018 a Report of the European Parliament on the situation of fundamental rights in the EU in 2016 (2017/2125(INI)), Committee on Civil Liberties, Justice and Home Affairs,[21] stated that it '...deplores the fact that several Member States today still impose requirements on transgender people such as medical intervention in order to have the changed gender recognised... and ...calls on Member States to recognise change of gender and to provide access to quick, accessible and transparent legal gender recognition procedures without medical requirements.'

This is the culmination of years of attrition following the UK GRA, compounded with academics propounding the legal fictions invented by Whittle and Turner. The Yogyakarta Principles, an international set of principles of human rights for LGBT people, have been used in this process. Professor Whittle was involved in the production of this set of principles back in 2007 (a busy year for him), as he has been in so many of the revisions of what we used to know as transsexualism.

The legal and conceptual conflation of sex with gender, which has then been exploited to exclude actual physical characteristics, has been severely criticised by feminists of all stripes. I am no fan of Sheila

---

21   http://www.europarl.europa.eu/doceo/document/A-8-2018-0025_EN.pdf,   p.
     12, paragraph 64 (2020).

Jeffreys,[22] who could probably be described as the Queen of TERFS, but it is possible to have overlap with people sometimes, even when you disagree on many other things.

The Yogyakarta Principles, when applied to trans identity, would seem to support the concepts of gender promoted by Whittle and Turner, not least because the senior member of that partnership was engaged in developing these principles, shortly after he had the paper I referenced above published, that you can have a man with a vagina or a woman with a penis and Dr Jeffreys is concerned about how this will impact on women's spaces. I have no problem with that. Surely there must be a distinction between those MtF trans women who have had reassignment surgery and those who have not? Dr Jeffreys would prefer to exclude us all, but many feminists recognise that this is a distinction worth recognising. While sadly some trans women determinedly insist that it is not, like Christine Burns, long-term campaigner with PFC, who argues that it makes no difference, at least for 23 hours and 57 minutes of each day.[23] She is also proud to have been involved in contributing to drafting legislation (the GRA) which didn't require surgical intervention.[24]

One could be forgiven for coming to the conclusion that the Honourable Members of the House, Lammy and Jones, misled the House when they said that such things were most unlikely to happen. Those most unlikely things seem to have now become universal rights, fairly de rigueur.

But all this was only just beginning to unfold. Having been out of the academic loop as well as the world of trans for over a decade

22 https://www.objectnow.org/news/2018/7/27/yogyakarta-principles-international-threat-to-womens-rights (2020).

23 http://ai.eecs.umich.edu/people/conway/TS/News/23%20Hours%20and%20 57%20Minutes%208-12-06.pdf (2020).

24 https://theheroines.blogspot.com/2014/01/interview-with-christine-burns. html (2020).

before my return to it, it was all a lot of change to digest, even at that early stage.

Following the passage of the Bill through Parliament and into law, I began to engage with the world of LGBT and got in touch with the University Union Gaysoc. In retrospect, hanging out with post-grads half my age was a pretty crazy thing to do, but I'd become a little reclusive due to my encounter at the art therapy course, so it was an interesting new experience, and one that would introduce me to a world which would later grow and get out of control.

I remember a particular conversation I had with a final-year student in which I was introduced to the world of Foucault and Derrida and all my concepts of how I believed gender worked were taken apart and deconstructed to me. I was entirely new to this way of thinking, having grown up on experimental, evidence-based psychology, with a dash of Jung and Maslow thrown in for leavening, which had then led me on to Rogers, Transactional Analysis and so on, and completely unprepared to deal with what I should have seen was little more than a souped up Cartesian philosophy of doubt.

I would say now to the postmodernists, my text for this whole book, what Gandalf said to Saruman when the master of Orthanc declared that he was now Saruman of Many Colours!

'And he that breaks a thing to find out what it is has left the path of wisdom.'[25]

This is said in response to Saruman declaring that he is now no longer of the White, but of the Many Colours. White light may be broken into the rainbow he says. To which Gandalf replies that then it is no longer White.

What the postmodernists fail to understand is that by deconstructing everything into its influences and sources, which retreat into an eternal regress of blame and excuses, they break that thing which they were apparently trying to understand.

25 Tolkien, J.R.R. *The Fellowship of the Ring*, p. 272. George Allen & Unwin (Publishers) Ltd, 1954.

Reality is a fragile thing. We build our understanding of the world from the bottom up, making sense as we can of what began as a blooming buzzing confusion, to use William James's description.

Nature abhors a vacuum, and if one is created, then something new will rush in. But what is to become of us if our understanding of the world is taken apart and nothing is put in its place? If it is taken apart and left in pieces lying around discarded, rather than putting it back together, maybe even with a few functional improvements, then there will be nothing, just a vacuum ready for the first opportunistic idea that happens to be taken up to be exploited by someone with enough power to do so.

I have seen online criticism of this line of Tolkien's, claiming that it is anti-science, that knowledge does not advance without breaking things. I would disagree. Some of our greatest scientific advances have come from non-invasive observation. Perhaps smashing atomic particles to bits in a collider is not so wise if it risks creating a Black Hole which sucks in and destroys everything. I use this as a metaphor for Gender Studies.

What is at question here is that something that is supposed to work in a particular way cannot do so if it is broken. Not taken apart, understood and reassembled. Broken. Postmodernists don't care about taking people's realities apart with their critique, offering no improvement. This is not examining the world and how we see it in order to better understand things, this is telling people that everything they believe about the world is wrong, and they are stupid for believing it.

Meaning is only an artificial construct you invented to avoid looking at the emptiness of your soul, apparently. They don't care about the death of the culture which they cause; they don't care about anything except proving how clever they are, and that their nihilistic deconstruction of everything is the only reality in town, which is no reality at all. It is cynical nihilism.

The point that I think my young student acquaintance didn't realise she was making to me was that this way of thinking effectively meant that I was deconstructed in the same way as the concepts of gender that she was doing this to.

One of the strangest phenomena I have noticed with this over the years is that young feminists like this will deconstruct gender to their hearts' content and yet never reflect on the fact that they have an extremely normative gender identity of their own. I notice this especially with feminists who are very feminine and attractive in conventional ways in their appearance, as if they are trying in some way to compensate and prove that they aren't what their appearance might have led people to believe.

They would probably say that they admit to succumbing to their social influences and how great it is that I overthrew mine and established an independent identity, but I would have given anything to have been able to have felt congruent and to have fitted into normative gender modelling. Sometimes they shave their heads, have bizarre tattoos, facial piercings or whatever, and look as ugly as possible in order to protest that they are not well-adapted young people, who would probably be attractive to young men and potential good mothers.

It was not until later that I fully put all this together and understood the influence of Critical Theory and Cultural Marxism on postmodern Gender Theory. At the time I just felt that they had missed the point about physiological psychology and how gender was a product of neurodevelopment.

Along with deconstruction, there were also constructions.

According to postmodernists, gender and the social conventions around it are only constructions. The trouble with this position is that the whole of human culture, civilisation and the societies from which they have arisen are constructions in this sense. To say that something has no value or meaning because it is a construction is to miss the point of human existence in my view.

This is bound up in postmodern thought, so far as I can tell, with Oppression theory and its sister, Privilege theory. Under the bonnet of all this is the assumption that the only thing that matters is power, that there is no meaning other than power and that the constructions of gender and the patriarchy are oppressive systems based on nothing but power. Functional survival adaptation is apparently irrelevant.

Like the Logical Positivists of the last century, who failed to understand that their assertion that all statements are either logical or empirical is neither logical nor empirical, the postmodernists fail to understand that their critique is based on nothing but their own assertion of power, whereby they seek to overturn all that went before them.

In the greater scheme of things, this critique has forced us to develop our positions on these things, but it cannot be allowed that gender is **only** a construction based on power as this obliterates any larger or wider meanings, or even the biological survival adaptation for reproduction which it enables.

My own critique of constructions is that they sound like things that have been assembled from a box of Lego, rather than living concepts which are part of the mind that uses them. Concepts rather than constructs are ideas which grow in our minds organically, holistically. We are biological creatures and even the simplest learning reinforcement is a biological occurrence within the nervous system. Concepts are contextually embedded maps of reality that grow within us as we extend our understanding through knowledge, while constructs sound more like inventions that are put together piecemeal. To construe is not merely an invention, as the term construct suggests, but to interpret, to understand, an internal sense-making of something we experience; to apprehend archetypes of pre-existing eternal dynamics embedded in our race memory. The difference between a synthetic a priori judgement and an a posteriori assemblage, I would suggest.

This mindset of deconstructing reality finds nothing at the foundation. It is all just an accumulation of brute facts, which have no greater meaning. Cultures and civilisations arise merely from the application of power relations and are inherently oppressive.

Every first-year Philosophy student should be familiar with the example in Russell's Problems of Philosophy of the table which upon examination is found to be comprised of trillions of vibrating electric particles which bear no resemblance to the brown thing with a polished surface that we see before us. We must be careful not to say nothing **but** atoms and electric particles because besides the fact that there may be more that we do not know about, our experience of it through touch or sight is an expression of how we relate to it and what it means to us, how it fits into our reality.

What the postmodernists have done is to take us down to the level of the pixels from which our lives have been built up, the atomic particles of reality, as if it were all entirely arbitrary, without allowing for any greater patterns of meaning, and left us there.

Any sense of cohesion, identity or purpose is dismantled and lost. Or rather, all traditional concepts of these things were to be proved wrong, constructed, oppressive and so on, and their opposites implemented in their place. I wasn't ready to see the broad political perspective on this yet, and hadn't developed the tools with which to dismantle their constructs. And constructs I believe they were, rather than real concepts.

The eradication of any notion of essence or essences or essential qualities was a big part of the argument. This is kind of old hat. It is like early Greek philosophers who believed that the world was made of four elements — earth, air, fire and water. In the early stage of their scientific endeavour, they had not yet understood the difference between the materials of which matter is made, and their qualities. Of course the term element preceded the modern discovery of the ninety-two natural elements by a very long time, and so originally meant one of these four qualities. We see the meaning surviving in usage referring to the weather, lightning, or a storm-tossed sea. Primal forces of which the world is made.

When a postmodernist says there is no such thing as an essence of the feminine, they are almost falling into the error of imagining that people such as myself believe that there is some magical quality which can somehow be described, labelled and absolutely defined in physical or even psychological terms. This is one of the huge problems with postmodern thought altogether, in somehow imagining that the information and nuanced understanding of perception which we all experience on a daily basis can be defined in strict and simple linguistic terms.

Linguistic thought, while of immense use in the practical advancement of our societies and their technical achievements, still struggles to map our inner worlds, emotions and intuitions and is often capable of little more than a thumbnail sketch of what goes on there.

It is in shared external experience that language comes into its greatest success, because that is what it was evolved for, not the kind of self-referential analysis for which it has become a tool for postmodern thought.

The postmodernist sees gender as nothing more than an accumulation of accidental, or even incidental, qualities, which, since none of them are absolutely essential to the perception of that gender on their own, therefore doesn't actually exist except as this construction they talk about, a kind of arbitrary invention.

This is the opposite of the holistic, gestalt view of both personality and perception in which I had my grounding. It would be some while before I understood how to defeat and dismiss this Marxist-based approach. I would need to take this to a higher level of existential philosophy and Jungian archetypes, which would put this in a larger, and clearer, perspective.

CHAPTER 12

DESCENT INTO HELL

OVER THE NEXT FEW YEARS I developed my network of connections in the gay and academic world. Postmodern deconstruction of gender was not so avidly pushed by so many others as by my young acquaintance following the passage of the GRA into law, and I did not realise how it was becoming so deeply imbued into the thinking of this world as to be almost unconscious, although I would occasionally come across remarks on webpages such as that I have referenced previously from the transgender person who said that they were quite happy with their female penis, but I didn't really take them seriously.

I was eventually drawn into the orbit of the Centre for Interdisciplinary Gender Studies (CIGS) at Leeds University; I had got to know several post-graduate students of the local department and the picture began to develop. I briefly got the notion that I might be of assistance to a gender identity clinic if I had a qualification from this department, and probed deeper.

In 2009 I took the preliminary steps towards applying to the department. I had already been told by one of their graduate students that my interest in biological and neuro-developmental aspects of gender differentiation was not what the course was about, but I had naively thought I could bring this into the field.

Dr Sally Hines, then Director of CIGS, kindly agreed to meet me in a café opposite the University front and we had an hour or so in which I expressed my belief that the then emerging trend for transgenders, like the one I had seen on Channel 4 around the millennium, should not be conflated with full-blown transsexualism and mooted the term Intergender for people like this who apparently had no physical dysphoria, but only social identification. She said that if she ever used the term that she would reference me. In retrospect, it seems that in my enthusiasm I let her probe my ideas whilst giving away little herself.

Some while later I had another conversation with her, in her study in the Social Sciences building at the University when I picked up an application form and discussed my possible entry to her department in more detail. I was at the time at another crossroads in my life, and was looking for the right direction. This presented itself as a seductive option and I went some way down that path before I realised that it did not go to a place I wanted to be.

In retrospect, it reminds me of the time twenty-five years or so before when I had been tempted to get involved with that group of Chaos magicians and Crowleyites. Curiously, the ideologies were not *that* different as I was later to realise. Postmodernism and Chaos Magick both hold that there is no *Logos*, or that it is an *artificial construct* held in place by power alone, that the Universe is infinitely malleable and all values are entirely relative. Quite a remarkable congruence of ideas between something that dominates our conceptual world today, and an esoteric belief system that most people have never heard of and would think bizarre if they had.

What I had not known, but which I found out fairly rapidly, was that this *gender is only a construct* was the Kool-Aid that they were selling, and that my own understanding of sex differences that I had learnt under Dr Blundell was despised. Critical Theory demanded that they critique to destruction the conventional model of sex and gender that has existed since the beginning of time, and throw it out. All that would be left would be a hollow shell of performative acts, with no anchoring in biology, sexual reproduction or bodily morphology, least of all psychological archetypes. There was no *objective grounding*. This is remarkably similar to the saying adopted by Aleister Crowley that *Nothing is True, Everything is Permitted.*

I soon found I could go no further with this since it denied the importance of the sense of my own body, which had been so vital to my identity, that it insisted that this was a simple matter of a choice to model on my mother rather than my father, and that anyone could do it. The point where it became entirely unsupportable was where some hold that boys are only supposed to learn to identify with their anatomy through social experience, that biological instinct has nothing to do with it, and that it is apparently only a statistical fluke that most children end up with congruent gender identities, that they acquire cis gender. I parody this as a logical reductio ad absurdum, of course, but this is what it amounts to. And we shall see that there are those who wish to take it to this.

The tragic but highly evidential David Reimer case is ignored. He was the poor unfortunate boy on whom an involuntary gender reassignment had been carried out as a baby, after he had been the victim of a botched circumcision. Dr John Money, sexologist at the Johns Hopkins University nearby, had recommended this procedure and in subsequent years had reported that the child had adapted well to being brought up as a girl, as I had heard when an undergraduate with John Blundell, who referenced the case.

This was, however, not so. The horrific story was finally told publicly in the early 2000s in a documentary television programme[1] after he committed suicide, and the world found out that the reports had all been a lie.

David had been uncomfortable in his imposed gender identity, and Money had engaged in practices which blended brainwashing

---

1   *The Boy Who Was Turned into a Girl* BBC documentary https://www.youtube.com/watch?v=9LQBcAVghu4 (2020).

and virtual sexual abuse in order to force a proof for his theory that
psychosexual identity was malleable in early childhood.[2]

Long-term researchers into transsexualism and gender identity
Milton Diamond and H. Keith Sigismund reviewed this case in 1997
whilst the victim was still alive and concluded that 'there is no support for the postulates that individuals are psychosexually neutral at
birth'.[3]

The Gender Theory belief system has very little explanatory value
and no predictive value as we have seen with the sad Reimer case, and
so we must seek elsewhere for ways of understanding sex and gender.

Firstly, we must place our foundation in the fact that all life produces its characteristics in accord with survival adaptation. Not all
life survives, but there are patterns which lead to survival and which
optimise survival.

Sexual reproduction leads to greater opportunities for survival adaptation. A billion years down the line, we are confronted with certain
anomalies which seem not to fit with a simple view of two sexes.

This is where I would have recourse to the notion of *techne* as first
noted by Aristotle, cited by Heidegger and revisited by Dr Jason Jorjani
in his epic *Prometheus and Atlas*.[4] They present the vital insight that
human culture has advanced through *techne* — skill or art — rather
than *scientia* — abstract knowledge. Palaeolithic man did not need to
investigate and describe linguistically the structure or origin of flints
in order to be able to make tools from them. What he needed was
the skill to fashion them into what worked. All engineering proceeded
from practical experiment rather than theoretical understanding of

---

2   https://samanthakatepsychology.wordpress.com/2012/04/28/david-reimer-
     possibly-the-most-unethical-study-in-psychological-history/ (2020).

3   Milton Diamond, Ph.D. and H. Keith Sigmundson, M.D. *Sex Reassignment at
     Birth: A Long Term Review and Clinical Implications:* https://www.hawaii.edu/
     PCSS/biblio/articles/1961to1999/1997-sex-reassignment.html (2020).

4   Jorjani, Jason Reza Ph.D. *Prometheus and Atlas* (2016). Arktos, Arktos Media
     Ltd, London.

mechanics, which came later, derived from experience. It may have refined practice, but was not the starting point. Farmers had been shaking apples off trees long before Newton set to wondering how or why it happened, or before Einstein took the science to a new level.

Nature — *physis* — works unconsciously, but produces secondary effects, which are solutions to problems of existence and adaptation, such as sex.

Sex, in a sense, is nature's techne. It is a tool of nature, that is all; nature becoming more aware of itself, its possibilities and how to realise them. Reproduction is the task, and sex is the method, the acquired skill.

The Gender Theorists seek to define gender by looking at what are in a vernacular understanding supposedly essential characteristics, and then when they show through deconstruction that this is problematic, we are told there are no essential characteristics, so there is no essential gender.

What they are doing is making a category error, a little like the one that conflates the four elemental qualities of fire, air, earth and water found in nature with the substances that have these qualities.

Gender Theorists are like eighteenth-century alchemists who have forgotten that their true quest is for the spirit, but have not yet reached an understanding of physical elemental chemistry.

Since gender is a concept we associate with sex, and sex is a dynamic produced by nature for reproduction and survival adaptation, then gender, they claim, has simply arisen out of this as the qualities embedded around it. Mere association, what the mediaeval world would have called accidents. Incidental details of no especial importance that could just as easily be otherwise. This, I believe, is the reverse of the actuality.

But what about the anomalies, you cry?

Nature is abundant, nature mutates, nature experiments, not to mention unnatural influences, such as hormone-disrupting chemicals, which are omnipresent today.

Nature often takes a scatter-gun approach. In its very willingness to experiment and mutate it allows for errors, for pseudomorphs and quasi-normal appearances.

Gender is a synthetic a priori concept deriving from the constellation of qualities around the core functions of sexual reproduction and its dynamic. It is what drives, and what works. It is metaphysical, it is part of the structure and organisation of the world. Besides, life in our own species, and many others, can only be conceived by the union of gametes from a male and a female, a spermatozoa and an ovum. I don't believe I have ever heard anyone involved in Gender Studies mention this glaringly obvious and foundational fact. The adjectival gender is surely to be associated with biological organisms which combine to procreate, is it not?

My naturalistic approach had no place in the new reality of Gender Studies and the material I was to encounter was so radically different to almost everything that I had ever known academically that it took me a while to find a relation to it.

Early in that year I was introduced to some of the strangest material that I have ever encountered on the long, strange trip that I have been on around this.

The CIGS Annual Lecture was by Professor Judith Halberstam, Professor of English and Director of the Center for Feminist Research at University of Southern California, on **Queer Feminism and the Art of Masochism.**[5] Queer Theory is hard to pin down in short terms but developed around questioning of normative gender concepts and the behavioural transgression of these. I would contend that in recent times the theory itself has become normative in its never-ending quest to deconstruct and destroy everything in its path; an example of Marxist perpetual revolution rather than evolutionary survival adaptation, which is benefitted by stable forms.

---

5   https://gender-studies.leeds.ac.uk/queer_feminism/ (2020).

Coming from a mental health, therapy and personal growth background as I did, I found it hard to believe that this was actually serious. It was not a clinical analysis of the Art of Masochism as a Jungian or an art therapist might do, but rather a promotion of it as a legitimate art form. A key term was refusal, that is the refusal to engage with something that is going on around you. As deliberate emotional disengagement it was argued that this was a final resort as a means to self-empowerment and taking control.

It seemed to me that the extension of this attitude beyond local situations could be entirely the opposite, and would be better described as denial, even the promotion of catatonia. Or just simple sulking. She was certainly promoting masochism as a legitimate state of mind and behaviour. Perhaps I can't say healthy, because it seems that that would be a concept that would be problematic. The concept of Happiness was critiqued by Professor Sarah Ahmed at the lecture[6] the following year. Not simply 'What is happiness?', but the paper 'proceeds by suspending belief that happiness is a good thing, or that happiness is what we want'. Certainly this does not contradict the advocacy of masochism. This is what we are up against.

The central text of Halberstam's presentation was the showing of video of Yoko Ono in her 1965 performance 'Cut Piece', in which she sat on stage and the audience was invited to cut her dress with a pair of scissors provided.

This is usually interpreted as a feminist piece about how women are treated as objects, and in addition to this Halberstam argued about the value of the masochism involved.

I would critique both of these interpretations: firstly, in that Ono invited the audience to cut her dress; they did not think it up for themselves, and the argument that she was promoting passivity didn't jibe with me since I found that it evoked powerful feelings of wanting to intervene and stop it. Secondly, Ono's own barely repressed

6   https://gender-studies.leeds.ac.uk/sara_ahmed_cigs_annual_lecture/ (2020).

non-verbal nuances as she shrank from the cutting indicated to me that there was a lot more going on here. I am not a huge fan of Yoko Ono, but I do appreciate that some of her work at least seeks to get her audience to think and question situations; and that is what I saw this as being about, a much larger concept than the narrowing into passivity that Halberstam's interpretation of masochism suggested.

In the Q&A at the end I said that as a therapist the only value I could see in the kind of refusal that she was advocating was as a precursor to the emergence of some new energy from the unconscious, otherwise it was psychological defeat and would surely lead to depression, if maintained as a fixed attitude.

But no — Professor Halberstam replied that it was a valid response in and of itself, and rejected the value of my desire to see a revival through this. In effect, she seemed to me to be saying that there was no difference in value between radiant psychological positivity and strength and abject withdrawal and disengagement. The abandonment of any form of agency.

I wouldn't bother describing this if it wasn't so emblematic of the culture in which Gender Studies propagates itself, promoting a sense of victimhood.

What it comes down to is the abnegation of all value by a method which seeks to tear down everything formerly established as of social worth — a monumental sulk against reality.

Dr Halberstam teaches courses in queer studies, gender theory, art, literature and film. She is the author of *Female Masculinity*, *The Drag King Book*, and *In a Queer Time and Place: Transgender Bodies, Subcultural Lives*, amongst other books. I also discovered that she has a 'masculine' persona known as Jack.

I was starting to encounter Queer Theory as a subset of postmodern Gender Theory but was still far behind on understanding its social implications.

Although in one way I look back on my time associating with the LGBT and Gender Studies crowd as something of a mistake, a wrong turning, at the same time it gave me immensely valuable experience and insight into the mindset of those who inhabited this world.

I would find that these youngsters would make strange faces at me, evidently trying to indicate that I had made some dreadful social faux pas when I had merely asked them a question or expressed a particular opinion.

I recall one young lesbian who, I heard, had decided to transition and had started using the male pronoun. I mentioned that if he wanted to talk about it or if there was anything I could do to help I would be happy to do so. I was quite taken aback that the response amounted to shunning me, as if I had made some dreadful insult.

At the same time I noticed that this person, who had formerly been quite a friendly and jolly individual with whom I had occasionally enjoyed brushing shoulders at music events and so on, had now become morose and grumpy, performing songs at open mic nights complaining about the Gender Police.

But the strangest thing to me was his social circle, which was clearly still a bunch of lesbians. So what? someone might say, to which my reply would be that surely if one is assuming a new gender identity, then it is likely that one's social group will be affected to some degree. Lesbians aren't too renowned for including, even inviting, men into their circles. Far from it, they often do their best to avoid men and keep them out.

In addition to this, it seems that by now, 2010, FtM guys were being allowed in women's and lesbians' spaces for reasons I found extremely hard to grasp. Had I been offered honorary space in a gay men's or men's rights group, I should have fled!

I shall address the issue of trans women in women's spaces further in due course, but what I will say here is that if one wishes to be known as being of a particular identity — male, female, artist, musician, whatever — one should surely at the very least adopt some of the behaviour patterns usually associated with that identity? Seemingly, performativity does not even demand this.

I know the postmodernists will reply that the patterns of behaviour associated with men are merely constructs, but I refute this assertion with reference to the evolution of our and every other species in the phylogenetic tree of life, in which survival adaptive gender patterns will be seen.

As anomalous creatures we do not fit exactly into those patterns, and some of us may not wish to, but those patterns exist for very good reasons in our ancestral pasts, those reasons being ones of survival and reproduction of our species as a whole. In the greater natural scheme of biology, the individual is expendable.

And fulfilling those patterns, even though they may not lead to reproduction of the individual, will contribute both to our own survival as well as that of our group, since it will more seamlessly integrate with and support its lifestyle.

Traditionally, young men would seek to make their mark on the world and this would often involve them setting out on their own in order to prove themselves. Remaining embedded in the lesbian subculture seems contrary to that dynamic. I had rather myself left the gay scene entirely in the mid-seventies because of the felt pressure to conform to gay stereotypes.

This young FtM transitioner was the lead singer of a band of otherwise lesbian, or at least cis, in their own terminology, women musicians and was a regular at the women's open mic night I used to go to at the time. When I enquired of one of the organisers about this I was told something about how they were being inclusive of trans people. After my experiences of the past I was grateful that this inclusiveness was applied to me, but to a supposed trans man I found it inappropriate, or at least rather odd.

So far as I was aware at the time, my young transgender friend was not engaging in any medical or hormone treatment. He certainly didn't show any physical characteristics indicative of it.

I find myself asking then, in what functional way was he participating in masculine archetypal behaviour?

I also met a performer at an alternative social centre who had taken a male name and pronouns and disclosed at some point that he was not taking male hormones because it would cause him to have body and facial hair as well as possibly start balding.

Although I found this performer both amusing and engaging on a personal level, again I have to ask, in what way was this person engaging in a masculine archetypal identity other than assuming a name and pronouns?

It seems to me that this really is an example of performance, as Judith Butler puts it, but that is all it is. I mean no ill to people who only want to perform gender, but it is clear to me that there is more to it than only performance. This is mere Behaviourism, and I believe in the soul, the depth of Being.

Someone who avoids taking the hormones that would transform them into a being who would be perceived unambiguously as a male, because of the fact that this would give them those unambiguous characteristics, does not seem to me to be fully engaged with the concept of a masculine identity.

Along the way I have known other FtM transsexuals who have for instance taken pride in their male pattern baldness, facial and body hair, muscle and skin tone after taking testosterone, since these give them such obviously masculine appearances. So I ask, which of these will fit into society the best and thus be more likely to find personal fulfilment: the one who will be perceived as an androgynous lesbian that likes to be called 'he' or the one who has physically masculine characteristics and presents an unambiguous image?

It was also around this time that I attended a workshop during the University's LGBT History Month events and was introduced properly to 'multiple genders' and their pronouns for the first time, although I had no real understanding then of how this would spread like a virus in the coming years.

The workshop event was led by a young FtM person, or so I believe he presented, although their identity might have been just of a smart, slightly butch tomboy lesbian. It can get very confusing about how people present. Especially when the subject matter of the workshop was to explore the participants' concepts of gender variations.

The principal exercise we participated in involved thinking up as many types of gender expression as we could, and these were written on a board at the front. It started out with masculine and feminine, then varieties of trans, but after this it got into things like 'femme tomboy', 'pangendered', 'non-gendered', and more too strange for me to remember.

What seemed to be going on here is that perfectly ordinary types of personal expression were becoming reified as actual genders rather than simply as subsets of variation within existing larger patterns of human behaviour.

Or else it was being proposed that there are no actual natural patterns, in other words that it is all just a matter of 'social constructs' and that everything is entirely fluid and malleable…

It was not until 2014 that I came to hear about the Frankfurt School, its offspring Critical Theory, and what had become known as Cultural Marxism, but in the last few years leading up to that I had a series of these type of experiences that demonstrated to me examples of this mindset.

A seminal moment on this path was in the spring of 2010 when I went to an LGBT night at a bar down by the river and got ensconced in a comfortable seat with a table and a view and became involved in a series of conversations with the young people there, one of whom was nearing completion on her PhD thesis.

I had discussed it with her briefly once prior to this and knew that it was about the Consciousness Raising groups of the seventies and eighties. I had on that occasion offered to share some of my recollections of that culture, having actually had experience of it, albeit from the edge looking in, but nonetheless I felt it was an angle that added some extra depth and perspective, especially in retrospect of three decades and more.

She had declined my offer, saying that she had completed all her research material. From a technical point of view, I would say this is a poor attitude to research, lacking curiosity, complacent. She wouldn't take time to informally listen to material that had some potential to be of value or interest to her.

I later found other research which was less than exhaustive in its methodologies.

Her — what I deemed to be — snooty attitude, the kind of thing you get from immature people who think that they know it all, was apparently still installed in her personality without any upgrades that spring evening by the river, and when the conversation got round to the subject of trans I expressed my position that there were at least two types, what I would call social and physical, or acquired and innate.

She said that she thought I was transsexual since she believed I had modelled myself on my mother because I wanted to be like her.

As a therapist I would never put such a thing to a client in such a way, even if I really believed it to be true, because it would be intrusive, judgemental and probably counterproductive. But for a student to put it to someone twice their age who had begun their transition when she had been an infant was, I felt, frankly insulting. This was raw Gender Theory uncloaked.

I took the opportunity to ask her what her PhD subject was, and she said about the *Consciousness Raising* groups, so I asked her again what the rules were in those groups.

She hesitated for a moment and so I reminded her, although she clearly knew: 'To respect the material that the participants bring and not judge it.'

'Uh, so it's condescending....', she replied.

'Exactly. You know nothing of what you are talking about, while I come from a lifetime of experience.'

'Oh, I just want to go to the bar...'

'Come back and we'll continue this conversation.'

'Okay.'

I am still waiting for the opportunity to complete our little conversation; this young lady chickened out and never came back from the bar to continue it. I saw her briefly on a number of other occasions but only in busy social situations, where it was hard to engage, and easy for her to evade. Of course, because she had run away from a debate knowing that that was the only way she could avoid being trounced.

I was coming back from my discombobulation at the hands of the postmodernists half a decade before. It was not only that I had stronger arguments — since I believe the developmental neuro-psychology model is one which is supported by the empirical data, and that therefore my position is properly founded in comparison to the social gender theory — but also that I came from a position of my own lifetime of experience in this.

Postmodernists will sometimes say that there is no truth but only competing narratives. Combined with the assertion that truth is a function of power, then perhaps she had realised that my own personal narrative gave me a greater power with this subject than her mere second-hand academic discourse.

The more advanced or progressive version of Gender Theory, which had gained traction amongst the students of Gender Studies, was Queer Theory, an evolution from Lesbian and Gay Studies, which basically rejects all normative values as social constructs that are oppressive and enforced. This is postmodern Critical Theory taken to its logical conclusion, in which it sees its task as the deconstruction of normative behaviours and identities — even their destruction — in order to free them from the complex array of influences which have led them to be this way. The term Queer, which has its origin in both the meaning *odd* as well as the former slang term for homosexual, focusses on what it terms deviant behaviour and critiques normative sexuality as hegemonic and oppressive, encouraging instead transgressive behaviour.

Essentialist and biological theories of sex and gender are also rejected.

This is not academic study as we know it, researching and exploring a field so as to better understand its subject matter, seeking pattern, structure, meaning. This is political activism and polemic, which offers nothing but rage against what already exists.

There are probably hundreds of university departments bringing this ideology now into the Western world, thousands of lecturers and professors teaching it, tens of thousands of students cloning these belief systems so that they can continue to propagate them to future generations, and hundreds of thousands influenced unconsciously spreading this mindset to the wider world.

I know I stand against the entire edifice of the postmodern belief system, but I must challenge it.

Like most things that postmodernism does, we have here a case where the minority groups, who themselves are not homogeneous, and the anomalous who fit only like square pegs in round holes, are set as the example for all to follow in their transgression of everything that has ever been established.

The talk of enforcement makes it sound as if the gender police really are going around checking up on everyone to ensure that they are entirely gender normative in their presentation and behaviour, but this is simply not the case. In the past there may have been social shaming or ostracism for what were considered deviant behaviours, but there is very little of that in Western society today. What might have been considered deviant a couple of generations ago is now positively encouraged. I stopped going to Gay Pride street events around this time since I found them so embarrassing, with half-naked men in gold lamé underpants gyrating on the upper decks of open-top busses to the sound of music blaring from pubs. Pictures I now see online demonstrate that it has gone far beyond that.

There does need to be a social space for this behaviour, because if there isn't, it will find one, and it will be even less savoury than what is flaunted here, but there is a difference between social acceptance of non-normative behaviour, and its active promotion. Mardi Gras,

Hallowe'en, the Day of the Dead, the Feast of Fools, Lords of Misrule and other forms of carnival allow a release, but it is understood that it is a temporary release, accepted even within some of the most formal societies. Perhaps it is in those that it is most needed. But no society could survive if this was its everyday reality. We need the structure and form of normative, shared behavioural values for society to function. Like gravity, it constrains us but also gives us direction. In zero gravity there is nothing to push against. The 'freedom' which postmodern thought claims to give us is a purposeless void.

The evident contradiction here is that what was once considered deviant is now becoming normative and vice versa. So, are the straight majority now deviant or even non-normative?

This all seeks to upend the values on which our civilisation was built. But neither the postmodernists nor some on the Right will allow space for those transsexuals who are attempting to be normative as best they can; the former accusing us of seeking to bolster the oppressive heteronormative cisgendered patriarchal power structure, and the latter imagining that we are trying to overturn it.

I reject the assumptions of the first on the basis that heteronormativity is survival adaptive. A homonormative society which rewarded homosexual behaviour and discouraged heterosexual behaviour would not last very long. I expressed some view about this on social media a while ago when a gay English PhD graduate I know referred to how Oscar Wilde hadn't been able to fit into the heteronormative society of his day; I said jokingly that the term 'heteronormative' had probably not even been thought of in his day, to which I was treated with the response that heteronormativity has always existed! Perhaps, but the term has not, nor critiquing it as oppressive … Besides, Wilde had managed to father two boys in his marriage, to whom he was said to have been devoted, so heteronormativity cannot have been that oppressive and hard to fit into. We all must make choices between different options.

Wilde was something of an outlier, and while he had tremendous success with some of his work, he was nonetheless louche and over-estimated his skill in dealing with adverse situations. It was his own raffish nature and its imp of perversity which led him to his downfall, not the simple fact of his homosexual liaisons, a practice which had probably existed amongst such classes as he inhabited since the beginning of time. As a parvenu to English society he was careless of its values, and fell foul of them, but his homosexual behaviour was only the occasion, and not the cause, of his downfall. That was in his nature from the start. Had he not been a promiscuous homosexual, he would have been a promiscuous heterosexual and taken risks in that way or another instead.

Society has always had standards that are socially enforced, to use the postmodern jargon, but it is these standards which maintain the society as it is, and why indeed it came to be that way. If they are to change, they must evolve to a higher level, not merely be abolished and replaced with their opposites.

I detached myself from the social networks around this in about 2012, but not before I had had sufficient education in their ideologies and the social impact they had.

I recall a warm summer night sitting in the backyard of the alternative social centre talking to some young women who were deeply embedded in this world. One had earlier that year been promoting a Trans Remembrance event and I had met her to talk about it, but it had come to nothing. Now she was talking about how she wanted to queer up FemSoc (the University Union Feminist Society). Apparently, the current brand of feminism wasn't going far enough for her, and she wanted them not only to engage in some deconstruction of gender and related ideas, but also to seduce them into being queer even if they had had no previous inclination to homosexuality or non-conformist sexualities.

In fact, her devotion to social anarchy went much further and she declared that she despised all those who had social capital and wanted to destroy it. Such attitudes are rooted in Privilege and Oppression Theories, and Intersectional Feminism, which in turn came from application of Critical Theory. Perhaps she knew about the intellectual background, or perhaps not. I was completing my ground level research, but when in 2014 I discovered the Frankfurt School and their Cultural Marxist ideology, it all started to make some kind of aberrational sense.

The zeitgeist of this world was amplified by one of the other participants, who at the beginning of the conversation hadn't understood that I was transsexual. I had for a while been exploring the psychology of success mindset and increasing my degree of agency by recognising self-limiting misconceptions and replacing them with more functional paradigms. I suggested to this young woman that becoming aware that we can change our lives by changing our attitudes and thus ourselves was a big key to how I had managed to go forward.

She was very stuck in her belief about social determinism and victimhood, but when some comment I made had her realise I was trans, she was left poised at a 'But, but, but…' moment.

'But you're both victim and privileged….' she gasped! My having had a good education being apparent, doubtless from my accent. But I was not just a privileged oppressor from the well-heeled middle classes — I was a victim of society at the same time!

What could be done? How should I be treated?

My Intersectionality was surely problematic!

This concept is about how factors of gender, class, race, sexuality and so forth can intersect to create different life conditions. But that's just what makes us individuals, you say. Intersectionality could also suggest the meeting of conditions, experiences and interests which might be shared between those from different backgrounds. On the contrary. This is the basis of the Oppression Olympics and its hierarchy of victimhood we encountered earlier, wherein victimhood grants power; the reverse of a true hierarchy of competence or success.

And like most concepts in the ideology of Cultural Marxism, it was actually the reverse of what it claimed to be. It didn't promote what can be gained from examining where our experiences intersect, but rather encouraged division between those of different backgrounds on the basis of attributed privilege, thus envy, resentment and so forth. This has more to do with dissection than intersection.

It has been propagated and bred in colleges throughout the Western world for long enough now for it to have escaped from the test tube and become a plague on the general population, who are terrorised with political correctness by a new generation of Stasi and Witchfinders.

This was to be my last social engagement with the world of what I would today see as SJWs — Social Justice Warriors — although I did remain on the CIGS mailing list and attended one or two more lectures to stay aware of what was going on. But now, when I did, I would be shunned by those students who remembered me.

One other episode which had already passed earlier that had jaded me towards this little world somewhat and thus primed me, was my participation in an experimental study carried out by Dr Sally Hines through CIGS.

I had been invited to be a subject in a research study in 2009 which she was carrying out on the impacts and outcomes of the 2004 GRA. This involved answering questions on both my history of transition as well as my views on the effects of the new law. One of the main points on which the research focussed was people's views on whether there should be requirements for reassignment surgeries in the GRA, and how they felt about their own status with regard to that.

I was also told that should I have any afterthoughts, I could email them to the research assistant, who was carrying out the interviews and transcribing them.

I did have some afterthoughts, and I sent them in.

On consideration I realised that I had pulled my punches on my views about reassignment since I knew what the prevailing view in the

department was, and while I was still considering my application felt
that it might adversely influence it.

Far more important was the honesty in the research and so I sent
in an addendum which was acknowledged, and ended with the following sentence.

> The bottom line being that someone who not only has not **acquired**, but
> does not even **aspire** to have the morphology of the desired sex cannot
> possibly in my view really be considered to be of that sex. [Full addendum
> included as Appendix B]

That should have been the end of it, but when, in early 2011, the draft
of the paper was sent round to the subject participants, I found that
my additional comments and views had not been included and were
not even factored into the statistics.

The paper stated that of the subjects interviewed, none had
expressed the view that reassignment surgery should be required
by the law. Since my addendum had a statement that in my view
physically congruent morphology should ideally be part of a male to
female transsexual's end status for legal recognition, it had thus been
excluded.

I wrote to Dr Hines, telling her that the results had thus been falsi-
fied since my position had not been included in the data set.

When my addendum was mentioned, a fairly quick response came
back that she had not had it, so I dug it out, sent it on, and it was
included as part of the data for a revised and corrected version, albeit
amounting to one short remark saying that only one subject disagreed
with the statement that '[a]ll of the participants felt that it was positive
that the criteria for a GRC did not involve surgery'.

Obviously, my remark about falsification of the results no longer
stands after the correction.

However, the reason for my data not being included at first was
never fully resolved to my satisfaction. It seems that certain comments I had made in the initial interview about the unequal nature of

reassignment surgeries between the two genders had been taken the wrong way for the first draft before she saw my addendum; presumably Dr Hines had understood me in referring to the unequal nature of the surgeries to mean that they should thus be disregarded, when in fact I had meant the opposite, that the same standards should not be applied to both directions of travel. An interesting example of how expectations or desires can influence interpretations — confirmation bias.

I asked Dr Hines how it had been that my addendum had been overlooked, but it was never explained. The research assistant had by now moved on to a position at another university, her contact was no longer active, and I felt it should have been dealt with internally by the department.

She did, however, include in an email on 22 February 2011 a comment that 'subsequent academic publications which are better suited to dealing with these complexities will be forthcoming', suggesting that I would have the opportunity to make contributions to later research. I was never invited to participate in any further studies into the subject, although Dr Hines has, as she indicated, continued to do research in this area. Interestingly, in 2018, she expressed the view to me that she did not want me to engage in the consultation she was carrying out with regard to the review of the GRA, but we will come to that.

At best this is sloppy work, and at worst might suggest the possibility of purposeful exclusion and bias. The research assistant had implied, although not fully explicitly, that she held to the prevailing view in CIGS that gender recognition should not be dependent on surgical or morphological status, and it was this implied position which had influenced me to pull my punches on this at first in making vague remarks about unequal treatment, since I was at the time possibly applying to the department.

Fortunately, I am something of an outlier in an Asch[7] conformity experiment setting, perhaps due to some of my life experience, and I am not afraid to step out of line in such matters, giving more independent responses under conditions of group pressure to conform rather than yielding as the terms of the experiment put it. Also coming from a background in experimental psychology and the rigour of the methodology on which it relies, it seems to me that that being applied here was not so rigorous. There seemed to be very little control for confirmation bias in the experimenters, and the results were indeed confirmatory of those views already known to be held by the faculty members of CIGS.

Looking back now at the report, I am disappointed to see that the sampling methodology had little to commend it either, relying heavily on focus groups, which are a highly flawed means of data gathering that tend to the subtle reinforcement of conformity, Groupthink, and of the individual participants clearly none of them had been sampled from the kinds of networks I myself frequent, because it gives the impression that almost no one holds the views I do myself, even though I know that not to be the case.

Neither was there any control group from the general population. Some might say this should be irrelevant, but we are talking about the standards which are being set for society, what Joe and Jane Public are expected to accept, and so they must surely be acceptable to the largest possible demographic. Feedback on experience is fine, but should be balanced with wider views, otherwise it is in danger of becoming a self-confirming echo chamber.

I would say that my main critique of the paper is that it sets its own agenda. My understanding of the aim of the GRA 2004 was to

---

7   Asch, S.E. (1951). 'Effects of group pressure on the modification and distortion of judgments'. In H. Guetzkow (Ed.), *Groups, leadership and men* (pp. 177–190). Pittsburgh, PA:Carnegie Press. https://en.wikipedia.org/wiki/Asch_conformity_experiments (2020).

provide a pathway for transsexuals to legally assimilate their identity into society in terms of the existing gender structures.

Starting out with the claimed intention of examining how the GRA 2004 had impacted lives, it ends up seemingly moving the goalposts so that those who had non-binary identities were able to express dissatisfaction with the new law by advocating 'gender diversity', a concept I do not recall being discussed in the Commons, as well as being an early staging post for the ideas and arguments which led eventually to the demands for Gender Declaration. This goes way beyond the things that MPs David Lammy and Lynn Jones argued for in 2004, and indeed way beyond those things they argued would not happen as a result of their Bill. It has become an endless mission creep where last year's accepted norms have to ever be replaced by more radical, progressive and transgressive behaviours because they are out of date and oppressive in the current year.

As with so much of the material I present here, if this had no further impact, it would be a minor thing which could be ignored by society in general as being of marginal importance.

But there is a clear line of progressive evidence here.

Lammy and Jones argued in 2004 that it would be absurd to imagine that a non-surgically reassigned male to female transsexual would allow themselves to be exposed in a women's changing room, on the basis that firstly, most transsexuals will be reassigned by this stage, but also that the rare few who get through the system without reassignment surgery are only there because they would have had the surgery but didn't because of some medical impediment that made it too high risk or somesuch.

The next stage is getting transsexuals themselves to say that it doesn't matter if someone has had reassignment surgery or not, which is now enshrined in the paper by Dr Hines and her research assistant. The paper did not address in any way the attitudes or concerns of the general public on this subject, as there was no control group. Some of the participants had not had full medical reassignment, and only 50%

of the subjects had GRCs under the 2004 law; thus it was almost like asking students what level they have to achieve to pass an exam, even to ask those who had failed how far the bar could be lowered to allow them to pass. So it is quite to be expected that this self-assessment produced results of the type that it did. We are reminded of those individuals who were not only unable to have reassignment surgery, but were unwilling.

Consequently, it should be no surprise that we are now faced with a final stage in which, since anatomical reassignment isn't considered necessary, and social presentation can be entirely arbitrary these days, anyone can simply declare themselves to be of the opposite gender to that in which they were apparently born, with absolutely no triage, physical or even social changes, and that is considered to be quite satisfactory. To some.

This progresses by a means of confusing the observer, and shifting the goalposts when they aren't looking. The old Bait and Switch as some call it, or the Totalitarian Tiptoe as others have it.

A lot of work had already been done behind the scenes in the world of academia, waiting to roll it out on an unsuspecting public.

When in 2014 I discovered the Frankfurt School, it suddenly dawned on me that this thing was a lot larger than some nutty academics promoting silly ideas about gender and having kids experiment with their gender presentation.

Whether someone in the Frankfurt School, as it became known — Marcuse, Horkheimer, Adorno or another — actually coined the term Cultural Marxism, or whether this is a term which was only retrospectively applied by its opponents is of little importance.

Its method is acknowledged to be the same as that which Marxist economists apply to capitalism, critiquing all its shortcomings and proposing solutions based on moral ideology rather than practical experience, the only difference being that they attacked Western culture, rather than its economics.

One of its core and most influential texts is *The Authoritarian Personality* by Theodor Adorno et al,[8] who gave himself away on the second page when he stated his intended conclusion, that white American men were authoritarian and anti-Semitic, as his main premise.

This work of ideology, propaganda and indoctrination has been at the root of postmodernism and its attitude permeates academic thought.

The principal thrust is to destroy the idea of objective values by calling them authoritarian and thus oppressive, then associating it with the bugbear of anti-Semitism since this is generally expressed by authoritarian people. Reverse reasoning thereby associates a belief in objective social values with anti-Semitism. Objective values are thus to be shunned as akin to anti-Semitism. This ideology when applied to sex and gender seeks to deconstruct them and demonstrate that they don't exist except as social constructs, much like social class. That applying objective values to sex and gender is oppressive as are all objective values.

This is a Marxist-based political ideology which has been passing itself off as an academic school of thought for most of the time since the Second World War, and very successfully infiltrating it into every nook and cranny of our thinking. And is it not now the case that transphobia is demonised as being on a par with anti-Semitism?

A good example of this came into my inbox in June of 2015 through the CIGS mailing list that I was still on, informing me of the conference stream on Radical Transfeminism in the London Conference on Critical Thought, held at University College, London, Anthropology Department, one of fourteen parallel streams on a wide variety of topics.[9]

---

8   Adorno, Theodor W.; Frenkel-Brunswik, Else; Levinson, Daniel; Sanford, Nevitt. *The Authoritarian Personality,* 1950 p. 2. Harper & Bros. https://archive.org/details/THEAUTHORITARIANPERSONALITY.Adorno (2020).

9   https://research.gold.ac.uk/25567/1/LCCT-Full-Program.pdf (2020)

From the language used it was apparent that the panels on the stream were comprised of trans activists, and some of whom I have been able to establish were trans themselves, perhaps most or even all.

Many years ago I might rashly have called myself a trans feminist, in the sense that I was trans, and at the time I thought I agreed with feminism, but the addition of the Radical prefix makes it a little, as they say, problematic.

The full texts of the available abstracts, which I gleaned online from the link in an email I received through the Gender List sent by Dr Hines, are now regrettably unavailable but I include quotes from them in Appendix F.

One feature which the publicity material for this stream shared with Judith Butler and many other postmodernists was the opaque language, which seems to be used either to dress up banal truths as profound insights, or else to disguise political tropes as critical analysis.

I could spend whole chapters getting lost in taking apart the political leanings and understrata of the ideology behind this conference, but this book is not intended as an academic work, so I shall just lift the kind of quote which is pregnant with the implications of where they seem to be trying to take this.

For instance:

'By emphasising trans*[10] as an open-ended category without a core, a potential radicalisation of perspective and action, as opposed to erasure, is actualised.'

And thus, in one assertion, the entire narrative which transsexual women at the vanguard of this phenomenon for the last sixty or seventy years have been telling is swept away and replaced by a political movement built on the ground we cleared. Trans*, now magnified

---

10   The use of *trans* with an asterisk * is just another example of the endless obsession that some have with politically correct labels, but has now apparently been abandoned as being *problematic*. http://www.transstudent.org/asterisk/ (2020).

with the inclusion of an asterisk to denote inclusiveness of all varieties of transgender, has been eviscerated of any actual content that it had acquired from the actions of those of us whose life experiences and agency built it in the twentieth century.

As if to say: There are no gender boundaries. We are all trans* now. 'Transsexuals' as a 'privileged' group are no longer recognised. Their identities are problematic to the wider Trans* population.

So many variant types of people now claim this identity under the newspeak term transgender that as the founder population we have been dispossessed of our ontological, even our epistemological territory. The name we used for ourselves since the earliest times has been abandoned by both Gender Studies and Psychiatry. The first claiming it is problematic, their favourite word for things that don't fit into their worldview and the second because recognising it as a condition rather than a mental illness gave them less opportunity for moral intervention.

Elsewhere I have seen the idea of real transsexualism, or true transsexualism derided as not only exclusionary and oppressive, but also impossible to define. How can you say who is a real transsexual, they will say?

And so the postmodern deconstruction continues its takedown of scientific method.

The taxonomy of transsexualism and related conditions is quite easily managed, since it is simply descriptive. If someone has had strong gender dysphoria since childhood and starts doing something about it in terms of seeking not only social role changes but also medical treatments, including hormone treatments, and so forth, we can say with some likelihood of certitude that that person is high on a postulated scale of transsexualism.

If, on the other hand, someone says that they feel out of place, that they aren't quite sure how to express themselves in gendered terms, or that they do so in radically unconventional ways and then say that they don't mind their body but want to be socially of the other gender, then we can say that they are low on the scale on which the former postulated individual is high.

Of course there will be people who have varying degrees of such feelings to the extent that it is sufficient to cause them some distress at times, but not so much as to feel motivated to make permanent changes to their life or their bodies.

The different groups do not comprise an 'open-ended category without a core' but rather are distinct categories with core characteristics. There are boundary conditions which define the differentiation between them. This is not essentialism, merely the statement that there is a hard core of people who have irremediable gender dysphoria, who may be helped by transsexual medical treatments, if they can ride the stress of transition.

The knife edge between feeling this degree of physical dysphoria that is a nightmare of torture and that degree in which it is transient or mild is a boundary condition which may be amenable to the agency of the individual or not. There may or may not be things to be done, actions which could be taken to ameliorate the feeling in this twilight zone, but most are to one side or the other. Nature likes stable patterns and groups and they tend to constellate. Promoting transgender as the latest fad, and gender fluidity as some kind of reified gender identity in its own right beyond simple individuality is likely to influence those of a malleable nature, the suggestible and the immature; those whose gender dysfunction or dysphoria is mild should not be encouraged by fashion to experiment too far. The presence of a population of transgender regretters is testimony to that. Even one regretter is one too many. There are many more than that.

And if someone doesn't have this unshakeable dysphoria about the sex of their body, then they aren't transsexual; they aren't in that constellation, that part of the pattern.

What the postmodernists are doing is deconstructing the existing gender patterns only to put them in the blender, then repackage the resultant chaos with *57 varieties*[11] of invented gender names, while dismantling the existence of the very population on whose back this whole circus has been built.

The Scientific Method is supposed to invite debate on theories and to be willing to test those hypotheses which have been raised by people who have researched matters and are able to provide evidence. The most important breakthroughs have often been made by independent thinkers who have not been constrained by the dictates of conventional institutions. Modern academia has much in common with the Church when it opposed the likes of Galileo who provided evidence that conflicted with their models.

I had a similar experience when Dr Hines approached the organisers of a local event at which I had been booked to give a preview of some of the material in this book in order to shut it down and censor me.

The blurb for the lecture was as follows:

> Transgender rights have recently come to the fore as a social issue, and yet there are many who feel that this is being pushed too far and too fast. Claire Rae Randall is a transsexual woman who transitioned over thirty years ago and is deeply concerned about this precipitous rate of change. Can this have a happy ending?

> Claire Rae Randall's forthcoming book *The War on Gender* examines the progress of trans from a personal perspective that has seen it come from being a marginal issue to one that is now having a disproportionate influence on social values.

Shortly before the event was due to take place, the organisers received emails making preposterous accusations against me, such as that I was involved with transphobic hate groups who went around organising public meetings where trans people were abused and transgender rights were attacked.

---

11   This joke based on the old 'Heinz 57 Varieties' label is now out of date. At the latest count Facebook offered 71 gender choices.

It seems that whoever started this was in touch with Dr Hines since the final email was from her making allegations against me, such as that my views were 'entirely subjective and without evidence' and that I had failed in my application to the CIGS.

I find it curious that the Director of Gender Studies should complain about subjective views since clearly the position that she was willing to advocate in her 2011 paper was one in which radical subjectivism was accepted as a basis for the recognition of one's gender. Furthermore, she knows little of my own evidence because I had not presented it to her, although she should be aware of the field in which I have my background, Physiological Psychology, which I had discussed with her. I understand of course that she may have done little research in that field and so is perhaps ignorant of much of that evidence. But she should have remembered correctly that I had told her I was not pursuing my application to her department because I disagreed with the ideology.

It was clear that she was unwilling to enter into discussion but retracted some of her allegations and got rather sketchy about others where she had perhaps just gone on the hearsay of her students.

The organisers of the event had asked me to postpone it until I had the book published, but also were clearly concerned that there might be a flashmob of trans rights activists and Gender Studies students that could turn up and disrupt proceedings.

My correspondence with Dr Hines petered out because she would not engage with the pushback I gave her on the criticisms she had made, but this was not the end of it.

When, some time later, information was circulated on the Gender mailing list about a consultation event which was to be held at the University on the then proposed changes to the Gender Recognition Act, I wrote in asking for the location so as to attend. The venue had not been published due to concerns about possible disruption from TERFS.

I had a terse reply from Dr Hines herself stating simply:

'For reasons which should be obvious, I have to say that you are not welcome at the event.'

Naturally I had to reply and say that it was not obvious to me at all. I have intermittently been involved in the trans world in Leeds since the mid-seventies, including having been a member of the first University Union TV/TS group in Britain as well as other groups and support networks which I haven't mentioned here. While I was not currently involved with the University, the event also invited members of local community groups and if, as was professed, the event wished to canvass opinion as widely as possible, my own life experience would have been of some relevance.

However, there was clearly never going to be any mileage with Dr Hines and the correspondence again petered out with her making vague allegations against me, which she declined to substantiate when I challenged her to be explicit.

The event went ahead and despite being unable to attend, I managed to gain an idea of the frame in which it was put forward.

In the blurb from the initial email to the Gender List from Professor Hines we have:

> This workshop seeks to cut through confusions around, and deceptions about, the proposed changes to the GRA by:
>
> 1.   Addressing why trans rights are important for everyone
>
> 2.   Providing an overview of what the Consultation is about — and what it's not about
>
> 3.   *Setting out the importance of getting a large positive response to the Consultation from *all* sections of society*
>
> 4.   *Giving practical guidance and hands-on assistance in sharing thoughts as part of the Consultation* [emphasis theirs]

Dr Ruth Pearce, the other academic running the workshop, is an out trans woman academic, something I did not know before doing further research, and the following two pieces are her suggestions to people as to how they should respond to the online government Consultation.

The following model responses are put forward on one of her webpages.[12] (Further critique which seems to indicate that she has particular outcomes in mind is to be found on other pages of hers.[13])

> Question 3: Do you think there should be a requirement in the future for a diagnosis of gender dysphoria?
>
> A: There should be no requirement for diagnosis. Gender should be predicated on self-determination, not medical decisions.
>
> Question 4: Do you also think there should be a requirement for a report detailing treatment received?
>
> A: There should not be a requirement for a report detailing treatment received. This is intrusive…

Much of what she has to say in her own personal blog is in this vein.[14] It is not only that I disagree with her opinions and her reasons for them, but more importantly it seems unlikely that she would run a workshop for people who want to find out what the Consultation means which would not be coloured by the views she so firmly expresses in her blogs. Doubtless she *would* 'outline what it's all about',

---

12   Dr Ruth Pearce 'The Gender Recognition Consultation'. https://transactivist. files.wordpress.com/2018/10/gra-consultation-suggested-starting-point.pdf (2020). Also, https://web.archive.org/web/20200908133215/https://transactivist.files.wordpress.com/2018/10/gra-consultation-suggested-starting-point. pdf (2020).

13   https://transactivist.files.wordpress.com/2018/10/gender-recognition-wherenext.pdf (2020). Also, https://web.archive.org/web/20200923121302/https:// transactivist.files.wordpress.com/2018/10/gender-recognition-where-next.pdf (2020).

14   Dr Ruth Pearce website promoting her views on GRA consultation. https://ruthpearce.net/2018/10/13/gra-consultation-a-guide-for-feministand-lgbtq-academics-and-allies/ (2020) also https://web.archive.org/ web/20200908133335/https://ruthpearce.net/2018/10/13/gra-consultation-aguide-for-feminist-and-lgbtq-academics-and-allies/ (2020).

and help her audience to enter the *right* responses, the *positive* ones she had suggested to them.

Although I have never met Dr Pearce and know little of her, perhaps the fact that certain views were going to be promoted was an influencing factor in Dr Hines' wanting to ensure that a voice such as mine would not be there to critique, not just the ideas, but more the *bias* that would be *implicit* in the delivery by the academics who should be impartial.

I certainly believe that trans people need to have legal status and legal protections, and that the 2004 Act could be improved. It's just that my version of this isn't the same as the activists'.

I am no fan of the anti-trans feminists or palaeo-conservatives, but they are members of society too and need to be taken into some sort of account. It is highly ironic to me that both I and the TERFs were excluded from the workshop. Postmodernists like to control the narrative as tightly as possible and not allow dissent.

It was no surprise to notice shortly after our correspondence about the consultation event took place that I was no longer receiving emails from the Gender List; I had clearly been removed.

CHAPTER 13

THE LYNN CONWAY
EVIDENCE (AND MORE)

N THIS CHAPTER I SHALL endeavour to give an overview of scientific research into and medical views on transsexualism and transgender, without getting too deeply into the detail of the background. For those interested, there is ample material here to use as starting points for searches.

When I was undergoing my passage of transformation in the seventies and eighties, the incidence of transsexualism was thought to be in the region of 1 in 30,000 of the population. However, this figure was based on statistics gathered in the nineteen-sixties and with the wave of those who, like myself, had followed the icebreakers, by the end of the century it had become obvious that the incidence was much higher.

The proportion of the population commonly believed to experience severe gender dysphoria to the extent where they will take action in their own lives to appear socially and live in the desired gender role was calculated to be about 0.2% of the population in the West when researcher Lynn Conway published her paper on the prevalence of transsexualism at the turn of the new millennium (Conway 2001). This updated figure was derived by taking account of the number of reassignment surgeries recorded in the USA and statistically extrapolated from that.[1]

A further steep rise in applications to clinics in the last few years, especially amongst children, could well be due to media promotion, since this rise has been so rapid and is associated in the exact same time frame as the media and LGBT focus on the subject.

Socially progressive channels, such as the British Channel 4, have gone out of their way to promote the phenomenon with programmes such as *My Transsexual Summer*,[2] *Genderquake*[3] and so forth in the UK and elsewhere in the West.

The former naively promoting transsexualism in a reality show format, and the latter, a debate following a series on trans experiences, degenerated into a mêlée.

The figure of 0.3% is now often quoted, a realistic adjustment to Lynn Conway's figures, rather than the massive burgeoning in numbers we see, especially with a 2,500% rise in just seven years for referrals for prepubescent girls in the UK, which surely must be queried.[4] Total referrals rose from 97 cases in 2009–10 to 2,519 in 2017.

Estimates vary, but clearly there has been a massive increase in referrals in all categories.

The Guardian, as far back as 2016, reported that

> [a]t a GIC in Leeds, referrals tripled from 131 in 2009–10 to 414 in 2015–16. The increase put such a strain on the service that last October it estimated that new patients would have to wait four years for their first appointment.[5]

---

1   https://www.researchgate.net/publication/237519830_On_the_Calculation_of_the_Prevalence_of_Transsexualism (2020).

2   https://en.wikipedia.org/wiki/My_Transsexual_Summer (2020).

3   https://www.dailymail.co.uk/femail/article-5708261/Viewers-slam-appalling-Channel-4-Genderquake-debate.html (2020).

4   https://www.thetimes.co.uk/edition/news/research-into-rise-of-girl-gender-referrals-w6b5v6fx5 (2020).

5   https://www.theguardian.com/society/2016/jul/10/transgender-clinic-waiting-times-patient-numbers-soar-gender-identity-services (2020).

I don't know how many referrals annually the Leeds GIC received when I passed through their care in the mid-eighties, but I was one of only three to complete treatment in my year. Besides questions as to the causes of the immense rise, there must also be concerns that screening and treatment will inevitably suffer due to the sheer number of applicants processed. How can they effectively select which patients would most benefit from medical treatment? How to best screen out those to whom this would not be appropriate? How to determine who has a psychiatric condition, such as a Munchausen type syndrome?

Gender Theorists argue that seeking to be selective in diagnosis is only an artefact of the way Western society constructs gender and of the medicalised treatment pathways which have arisen over the last century or so, resulting from the work of the likes of Dr Magnus Hirschfeld and Harry Benjamin. But just as the former had come to believe that homosexuality was an innate disposition, so the latter came to hold that psychoanalytic treatment of transsexuals was ineffective in removing the preoccupation, and that medically altering the individual so that they were able to live as they imagined themselves was a route worth considering in reducing their existential stress. The fact that those who were able to successfully pass as women expressed satisfaction with the process led him to consolidate his concept of transsexualism, as detailed in his 1966 book *The Transsexual Phenomenon.*[6] The triage and selection of patients who are more likely to pass physically has long been criticised as privileged and elitist by those who wish to destroy conventional concepts of gender, but there is much anecdotal evidence, not least from transsexuals themselves, that the better one passes, then the more likely one is to adapt and assimilate to society post-transition. I have seen comments by those who have chosen not to transition because they did not feel they could pass in their desired gender, from both sides. While it is remarkable what can actually be achieved, nonetheless one can sympathise with

---

6   Benjamin, H. *The Transsexual Phenomenon.* The Julian Press Inc.; First Edition (1966).

those who feel that to live a life in which one is obvious and sticks out like a sore thumb could be even worse than the original sense of dysphoria.

Comparable cultures have arisen in other, very different societies around the world, with very different historical roots.

The two principal examples which come to mind are the hijra of India, and the kathoey of South East Asia, expressions of the trans spectrum which correlate closely with Western transsexuals. The Native American Two Spirit term is only a recent invention and is so involved with ethnic identity issues that it should not be compared to the long-standing cultures of hijra and kathoey.

Members of these two groups frequently seek transsexual medical treatment and see themselves as fitting that paradigm. Indeed, the paradigm has become so well accepted in some places that Thailand, the home of the kathoey — ladyboys —, has developed both entertainment and medical tourism industries around this culture. It is perhaps no coincidence that the phenotypic differences between male and female are less marked in people of Thai ethnicity, allowing a more relaxed attitude to a gender-bending culture; definite divisions between categories still exist nonetheless, with some ladyboys only engaging in what might be termed recreational or temporary transgenderism, whilst others pursue full medical reassignment.

The subculture of the hijra, with its crude methods of total castration, surely only continues to exist because its members are unable to afford or gain access to the medical procedures available in the West, or indeed Thailand. Jan Morris in her *Conundrum* had said that if she hadn't been able to find a surgeon who would do it, she would have taken a knife and 'done it myself'. This is how desperate it can become. To argue that hijra and transsexuals are merely similar due to social construction is to ignore the deep underlying similarities, probable causes and profound motivation that would drive someone to such extreme measures.

I would further add that the convergence of techne, skill or control, of techniques that produce the desired result for those seeking them, is what we see taking place here, rather than entirely different constructs which merely have some appearances in common, as the deconstructionists would have it. Probabilistic functionalism in both its perceptual and practical application. One is more likely to realistically be able to perceive oneself, be perceived by others and to function in one's desired gender if one has undergone these procedures.

I have heard it proposed by some as long ago as the early 2000s that if we were to be accepted as the social gender of our wishes, surgeries would become unnecessary. I didn't believe these people were serious at the time, although with the proposed change to Gender Declaration it seems that they are trying to make it so.

Clearly there are populations which have certain key characteristics in common and which fit the endogenous hypothesis of atypical neural differentiation, for which there is now plentiful evidence. Gender theorists have yet to demonstrate that transsexualism is socially caused, while the Reimer case provides strong evidence to the contrary.

A highly controversial hypothesis was put forward in the late nineteen-eighties by psychiatrist Ray Blanchard[7] who argued for two classes of transsexual: HSTS (Homosexual Transsexual) and AGP (Autogynephilic), reverting to the type of sexual orientation categories for MtF transsexuals that had formerly been used in Benjamin's six or seven stages. The HSTS were supposedly feminine homosexuals who sought a female identity and were less interested in physically congruent female morphology. My friend who detransitioned and had little interest in reassignment surgery might have been classified in this group under this way of thinking, despite not pursuing reassignment in the end. I have known other gay transvestites who have had no interest in physical reassignment. The AGP group, it was claimed,

---

7 https://en.wikipedia.org/wiki/Blanchard%27s_transsexualism_typology (2020).

had acquired their bodily sense as a paraphilia, as transvestites do sometimes from becoming aroused by female apparel and advancing to sexual gratification whilst wearing it and progressing eventually to a complete fantasy of oneself as a woman, which must be physically realised.

While such individuals can and perhaps do exist, to build the entire structure of trans identities around either externally motivated sexual attractions or an acquired paraphilia is surely putting the cart before the horse. Most of whom Blanchard would probably call Autogynephiliacs have clear memories from early childhood of the kind I have described, an awakening to the incongruence of our bodies, and to label us as having an acquired paraphilia is not merely insulting, but without basis.

Curiously, Dr Blanchard takes the view that both these groups may benefit from medical reassignment, including reconstructive surgeries. He was recently interviewed about current developments in the world of trans[8] and he discussed the different usage of the terms transgender and transsexual, the latter having become unpopular in certain quarters.

The somewhat vaguer term Gender Dysphoria has now replaced the former category of Gender Identity Disorder in the Diagnostic and Statistical Manual 5 (DSM-5),[9] the manual used by the American Psychiatric Association, and whilst many of us might welcome the kinder tone of the term, long established as a concept, it has not come without a price.

In the interview, Dr Blanchard critiques the fact that the term transgender, the much wider umbrella, has put transsexual into

---

8　'Meet the Bold Sexologist Questioning Transgender Orthodoxy' By Madeleine Kearns.　https://www.nationalreview.com/2019/05/ray-blanchard-transgender-orthodoxy/?fbclid=IwAR2zcQlkZbB9D38GBxVKVtX2R_78p3aveIDyb3jKpGs8JRRWO8yRLz7n41A (2020).

9　https://www.theravive.com/therapedia/gender-dysphoria-dsm--5-302.85-(f64.9) (2020).

disfavour with trans activists in the wider discourse, who critique us as medicalising what they claim is a perfectly ordinary social choice. He goes on to say that consequently he uses transsexual whenever he gets the chance, specifically referring to those of us who may, or already have, indeed benefitted by full reassignment. Putting aside my personal feelings about his ideas on the aetiology of transsexualism, I am pleased to see this.

Gender Dysphoria seems to be in a category of its own in the DSM-5. I would prefer to see it listed under Neurological Disorders, since I believe that it is hardwired and for the experience of Gender Dysphoria to be required to have been experienced for rather longer than the six months stipulated in order for medical treatment to be initiated; we need to be looking at those people who have the firmest and most unremitting dysphoria rather than including all and sundry who may have transient experiences, or indeed those who say, 'you don't have to have gender dysphoria to be trans', whatever that might mean!

Dr Ken Zucker of the University of Toronto, himself a somewhat controversial figure in this field, wrote about the changes to the classifications in the DSM: 'Many transgendered activists and some clinicians certainly wanted the disorder to be removed, arguing that GID was not a mental disorder, and wanted its removal for reasons similar to the removal of homosexuality from DSM-III in 1973: transsexualism was nothing more than a normal variant of gender identity, that its classification as a mental disorder contributed to stigma, and that there was nothing inherently "wrong" with a gender identity that was incongruent with one's biological sex.'[10]

In reply to the trans activists who criticise this as medicalisation of something which should not be treated as such, I can only reply that something which causes great continuous distress, which can only be alleviated by medical, even surgical interventions, must surely be seen

---

10 https://www.researchgate.net/publication/296700032_The_DSM-5_ Diagnostic_Criteria_for_Gender_Dysphoria [2020].

as some kind of disorder or atypical condition, whether psychiatric, psychodynamic or simply neurological. To argue that such a view is problematic is in itself problematic to people like me!

Removing gender dysphoria, gender identity disorder or trans-sexualism from a medical diagnosis entirely would have serious consequences for those seeking treatment under insurance plans, or indeed legal recognition in our desired gender, as it would reduce the entire experience and process to one of mere cosmetic procedures. Whereas those who have no dysphoria and merely identify as the opposite sex have no need of any medical treatment, but are in danger of interfering with the processes of those who do.

Back in the day, Gender Dysphoria was a term which those such as myself took to mean a total dysphoria: of which the dysphoria about one's body was the principal factor around which everything else fitted and thereby made sense.

The new criteria in the DSM-5, detailed by Ken Zucker, included eight factors of which at least six had to have been present for a mere six months,[11] of which only two related to dislike of one's sexual anatomy or a desire for that of the opposite sex, the others principally constellating around social behaviours; only the principal A1 factor of a strong desire to be of the opposite sex being considered absolutely necessary. How one can have a strong desire to be of the opposite sex and yet not wish to change one's sexual anatomy to conform to that is a mystery many of us have yet to comprehend.

I do not rule out behavioural factors as contributing to the overall picture, but I do believe that the weighting of six to two is an imbalance which favours social gender determinism overmuch.

In addition, such a transient state as is demonstrated by a six-month spell of social dysphoria compared to a life of years in which this had presumably not been experienced seems to me to be a flimsy basis on which to form a firm diagnosis. Zucker himself said that

11   Ibid.

one of the faults of the earlier DSM-IV diagnosis was that supposed cross-gender behaviour could lead to a diagnosis of Gender Identity Disorder, as it was then called, without a strong desire to be of the opposite sex, either physically or socially.

Humans are a very adaptable species with a great deal of overlap of skills between genders, despite the specialisations, and it is entirely possible that some of those with forms of apparent cross-gendered behaviour are merely from that overlap.

The psychodynamic or learning theory hypothesis of transsexualism is based on the assumption of the brain and thus mind as largely a tabula rasa which receives all inputs equally and constructs its gender archetypes afresh with each individual, or at least that inherited archetypes and drives are easily overwritten. This is the weak point where Blanchard's hypothesis becomes vulnerable to postmodern relativism.

On the contrary, various research efforts have indicated that there are substantive brain differences between the sexes which may cause the experience of transsexualism, or at least gender dysphoria; for instance, the work by Zhou et al[12] on such structures as the central subdivision of the bed nucleus of the stria terminalis (BSTc) with respect to its size, which has been found to be female like in MtF transsexuals. Although only a small sample, due to the difficulty of sourcing brains of deceased transsexuals for forensic examination, the results were of an extremely low probability due to chance alone, at the $p = <0.05$ level. A paper which has generated much discussion.

This study was supported by further work on the presence of female neuron numbers found in the limbic nuclei of MtF transsexuals.[13]

---

12   Zhou J. N., Hofman M. A., Gooren L. J., Swaab D. F. 'A sex difference in the human brain and its relation to transsexuality'. Nature, 1995;378:68–70. https://www.ncbi.nlm.nih.gov/pubmed/7477289 (2020).

13   Kruijver F. P., Zhou J. N., Pool C. W., Hofman M. A., Gooren L. J., Swaab D. F. 'Male-to-female transsexuals have female neuron numbers in a limbic nucleus'. J.Clin Endocrinol Metab 2000 May;85(5):2034–41. https://academic.oup.com/jcem/article/85/5/2034/2660626 [2020].

This is a brain structure involved in sexual function, and thus potentially implicated in sexual identity.

The results may not be considered definitive, in that the samples are small and replication is needed, nonetheless a testable hypothesis has been presented and results produced which are encouraging for further work.

Other physiological evidence has continued to accrue. Dr Milton Diamond, who has had a long research history with transsexualism, found in 2013 that there was a much higher correlation in transsexual transition amongst monozygotic twins than between dizygotic, thus strongly implicating some genetic inheritance.[14]

There were even found to be monozygotic MtF twins who were separated at or not long after birth and still transitioned, thus minimising social influences.

We must remember that the genetic foundation is not the completed phenotype, that there are obviously many other influences, and the *in utero* endocrinological environment contains many of these so that the genetic factors may not completely dominate, one way or the other. Dr Diamond has gone so far as to argue that transsexualism will eventually come to be seen as 'an intersex variation due to brain (nervous system) intersexuality'.[15] A view which I endorse most wholeheartedly. While he has elsewhere argued that intersex in itself is only a natural variation and should not be considered to be a disorder, I would argue that transsexualism, being a condition which affects subjective experience so negatively, should be considered to be beyond the limits of functional adaptive variation, and thus a condition or disorder.

---

14   Milton Diamond, PhD. 'Transsexuality Amongst Twins: Identity Concordance, Transition, Rearing and Orientation.' *International Journal of Transgenderism*, 14:1, May 2013, pp. 24–38. https://www.hawaii.edu/PCSS/biblio/articles/2010to2014/2013-transsexuality.html (2020).

15   Ibid.

It seems probable that a number of different brain structures may be implicated in neurologically caused gender dysphoria and VS Ramachandran, Professor of Neuropsychology at University of Los Angeles, San Diego, has provided evidence that there are those which may cause the sense of bodily dysmorphia. His study focusses primarily on FtM transsexuals who had the sense of a phantom penis.[16] He explains how early descriptions of the phantom limb phenomenon were not taken seriously, but were eventually understood to be the result of brain structures which mapped the lost limbs. Phantom penises are apparently not that uncommon in FtM transsexuals and so we must consider the possibility that they may have neural structures which developed to map body parts which did not themselves develop. Surely this should not be considered normal, or at least not optimal.

He proposes exactly the model that I have previously mentioned as implicated, that the body image is hardwired during gestation dependent upon the hormonal influences, whether it remains a female phenotype or is converted to a male phenotype through the influence of testosterone. It is also suggestive of Sheldrake's Morphogenetic Field, to which I shall return.

An immense amount of research has gone into this subject in the last generation or so, and an entire book could be written on that subject alone. But it is my firm conviction that Professor Melissa Hines of the Department of Psychology at Cambridge University was correct in her 2010 paper 'Sex-related variation in human behaviour and the brain',[17] in which she examines much of the evidence around this

---

16   V. S. Ramachandran and Paul D. McGeoch. 'Phantom Penises In Transsexuals: Evidence of an Innate Gender-Specific Body Image in the Brain'. *Journal of Consciousness Studies*, 15, No. 1, 2008, pp. 5–16. Abstract at http://www.ingentaconnect.com/content/imp/jcs/2008/00000015/00000001/art00001 (2020).

17   Professor Melissa Hines, 'Sex-related variation in human behavior and the brain'; *Trends in Cognitive Sciences*, 2010 Oct; 14(10): 448–456. https://www.ncbi.nlm.nih.gov/pmc/articles/PMC2951011/ (2020).

subject from Darwin to the present day and concludes that the degree of virilisation of the nervous system is strongly influenced by the levels of testosterone it is exposed to during pregnancy, and this is the basis of different behavioural tendencies between the sexes. Interestingly, she unearths evidence that 'watching objects move in space may be more attractive to a testosterone-exposed brains' and suggests that this may influence toy preferences. I would add that this is survival adaptive in the primitive environment where males principally hunt and guard the clan, and is characterised by C. S. Lewis in his description of the male or masculine archetype from his *Perelandra* that I reference later.

This all fits the neurological concept of gender dysphoria, and thus transsexualism, which I support.

There is a rare type of intersex which gives extraordinary insight into the neurology of gender identity. It is known as 5 α-Reductase Deficiency[18] and is a genetic condition which produces a deficiency of 5 α-Reductase, the enzyme responsible for converting ordinary testosterone into dihydro-testosterone (DHT), a more powerful virilising agent than its precursor. Children who have XY chromosomes and are born with this condition often appear morphologically female at birth, but develop male genitalia at puberty, and in some communities where this happens, such as the Dominican Republic, it is a cause of celebration as the child assumes a male identity, which apparently often they had always felt anyway or at least had no difficulty adapting to. In a somewhat in-bred society where this was not uncommon, it is easily accepted, although in the Papuan culture it is less so apparently.

This condition is like a halfway house to AIS, since presumably the neurological components of gender identity seem to have been affected by the testosterone present *in utero* even though it was insufficient to trigger genital differentiation on its own without the DHT.

---

18   https://ghr.nlm.nih.gov/condition/5-alpha-reductase-deficiency#genes (2020).

The point being that the physical gender identity was not dependent on the genitalia one was born with, something we also see in transsexuals, where the preference is clear. This strongly supports my hypothesis that gender identity is neurologically based, especially as these 5 α-Reductase-deficient children are often brought up as girls, a close analogue with David Reimer.

The recent paper by Foreman et al, 'Genetic Link Between Gender Dysphoria and Sex Hormone Signaling', stated that '...*the results of our study of transgender women support the hypothesis that gender dysphoria has a polygenic basis, involving interactions among multiple genes and polymorphisms that may alter the sexual differentiation of the brain* in utero, *contributing to the development of gender dysphoria in transgender women.*'[19]

I recall that as early as the nineteen-eighties my own consultant Dr Philip Snaith had been researching correlations with certain genes.

Everywhere you look the evidence racks up, pointing to a neuro-developmental basis for gender identity.

If gender identity were entirely dependent on social role modelling, we would probably see a much higher prevalence of transsexualism; but transsexualism is not only about social role, it is even more about physical self-perception, and this is where the gender activists cause division and confusion. The recent spike in supposed childhood FtM applications could well be the result of social modelling from media coverage, and I would suggest that these cases could show a high proportion of pseudo-transsexuals, in other words girls who have become entrained on the social desire to engage in competition with men as has become so encouraged by feminism, which also treats

---

19   Foreman, M., Hare, L., York, K., Balakrishnan, K., Sánchez, F. J., Harte, F., Erasmus, J., Vilain, E., Harley, V. R. 'Genetic Link Between Gender Dysphoria and Sex Hormone Signaling'. *The Journal of Clinical Endocrinology & Metabolism*, Volume 104, Issue 2, February 2019, Pages 390–396, https://doi.org/10.1210/jc.2018-01105 (2020), https://academic.oup.com/jcem/article/104/2/390/5104458 (2020).

bearing children as if it were some dreadful, oppressive imposition which gets in the way of their self-actualisation, whilst at the same time latching onto the latest rebellious fad promoted by the media.

This sharp rise does, and should, cause concern but it must not be used to build up the idea that all transsexuals have simply learned inappropriate identifications.

The 0.2 or 0.3% or so suggested by Conway's analysis existed before the current promotion, and indeed came from a time when social stigma was still attached to the concept of trans identity. Indeed, if one looks beyond the media promotion, it widely still does. We must then face facts, that we are a real population, one which exists with only superficial differences between separate cultures despite the overlay of the new trans trender population, which is causing confusion and conflation.

The palaeo-ultra conservatives and radical feminists who abuse us and say that transsexualism is a mental illness need to understand that we exist and will probably continue to do so for the foreseeable future until medical science is able to isolate the precise causes and offer successful antenatal prophylactic interventions.

Neurologically based transsexualism is no more a mental illness than Huntingdon's Chorea or Parkinson's Disease, which are neurological conditions but which may cause psychiatric symptoms as they progress, although in the case of transsexuals these are probably caused by social stress rather than neural decay.

One aspect of the Conway material which I must address and about which I have come to no firm conclusion is the fact that there is a certain proportion of transgender people (I use the term advisedly) who never seek physical reassignment surgeries. Some of these may not do so simply for practical reasons; they live in countries where they would need to fund treatment themselves, for instance, and they cannot afford the medical costs, but there does seem to be a proportion who have no interest in being congruent with the phenotype.

This is the only category to which I feel it is worth applying a new term, but only as intergender, the term I suggested to Dr Hines when I first met her. Just as intersex have physical characteristics intermediate between male and female, so it seems that the intergender people have psychological characteristics between the two genders. They apparently wish to present socially and interact as one gender, whilst being happy to engage sexually as the other. Some have already taken the appellation genderqueer to themselves.

I am quite undecided and still a little confused as to where such people fit in. The Concern Vultures will doubtlessly insist that they don't need to fit in, and the Libertarian in me understands the need for freedom of expression, but the Pragmatist alongside is concerned about how society will function with those who do not fit the age-old categories, which still mostly exist. Nature may be harsh in its unyielding demands but these categories are as they are for good reasons of survival adaptation. We should not forget that billions in both our own and other cultures would only accept intergenders at the most marginal level.

All identity is a negotiation between the self and the world. On the recent *Genderquake* debate held on Channel 4, one of the participants claimed that they did not see themselves in any relation to gender, that they saw themselves in some kind of abstract relation to their body that excluded that. This is even further out than intergender. I think it is an unrealistic position to hold since we all have some relation to our bodies, but if someone wants to construct their identity along such lines then I would not seek to prevent them, although it seems to me to be an attitude of dissociation more than anything else, and thus maladaptive. It reminds me of Dr Halberstam's refusal to engage with the world and reality. All I would say is that the rest of humanity should not be held to blame if they find that they do not fit in, or are treated as the gender they most obviously resemble. We must remember that survival of the fittest is not just physical fitness, but the best fit to the environment one finds oneself in. Since some 99.7% or so of the population are gender normative in their self-perception, and most of the remaining 0.2 or 0.3% seek to be, or to present as such, even if they are intergender, then those who define themselves as 'without gender' or agendered are in an almost vanishingly small group.

I have seen presentations in which intersex and genderqueer, or what I might call intergender, individuals rail against the normative assumptions of society as if they were purposely intended as an oppressive persecution of themselves, personally. We should surely seek to become individuals who are whole, and integrated, not only within ourselves, but with society and the world to some degree.

We must understand that we are very largely breaking new ground here. Too much deviation from the survival adaptive norm has tended to become taboo, and in some cultures this is still the case. We in the West are rushing into the understanding that like Russell's table that is made up of trillions of molecules, gender is a gestalt indicated by a trillion subtle factors and cues, but are too easily forgetting that the table is still a table, and gender is still the archetypal function that it was intended to be by nature, evolution and psychology.

Perhaps that is why those intergender people who don't seek reassignment surgeries still seek to present in a gender normative manner. They know that we all have perceptual presets which like to be able to categorise people into the archetypal categories of male or female, and so they conform to those, partly I suppose because it is convenient, and partly because they like it, perhaps.

I would strongly assert, however, that such folk must be distinguished from transsexuals who seek bodily congruity, and those intergender or genderqueer individuals who argue that they are no different from us or that we are just genital fetishists are missing the point. We see two different categories with only superficial similarities, while they argue that those similarities are what matters and that the differences are of no import (while condemning them as medicalised fetishism).

I'm particularly concerned with how we define legal status and the pragmatic decisions that must be made in deciding where gender boundaries are drawn, as drawn they must be, in a society which wishes to allow women-only spaces, principally, but also those for men. Postmodern gender theorists want to deconstruct the idea of physically based gender so completely that they would cease to be recognised, like the Emperor's New Clothes. They want it to be banished as a concept.

This inevitably impacts on the issue of public toilet facilities. We hear from the genderqueer that no one sees what one has in one's knickers and so it doesn't matter. This is like saying it doesn't matter if you are only speaking to an AI bot and not a human if you can't exercise a Turing Test and distinguish that it is so. A particular group of trans trenders who have come to be known as traps are known for dating heterosexual men and then when it comes to the point and the guy freaks out when he realises that his date has male sexual anatomy, will complain that he is transphobic because he won't have what to him amounts to gay sex. As if sexual anatomy was of no importance in the game of sexual attraction and mating!

Which is not to suggest that all intergender or transgender people would be likely to do this of course, but it is the progressive drive from the few who would that is causing the change in the assumptions, the deliberate moving of the Overton window of what we are allowed to accept or reject, that is really causing the disquiet of the silent majority about this.

It is all stuff which many find hard to get to grips with. There are those transsexuals among us, with whom I am in agreement, who hold that if someone says they want to be a woman, or feel that they are but their body is wrong, or whatever way in which you wish to put it, then surely they must want to inhabit a body which has that sexual anatomy.

A new term that has arisen lately from the trenders for those of us who feel that we define our identities in such a way is Truscum, a term of abuse for those of us they previously called Transmedicalists who fit the Harry Benjamin Syndrome profile.

The person who says that they are 'happy with their female penis' may be comfortable with having a penis, but it is not, and never can be, female in any meaningful way. And yet many will claim to be transgender or even transsexual, arguing that physical dysphoria is of minor importance.

How we deal with this issue in its relation to public toilets is a matter which must be fully debated in the court of public opinion and not simply conceded to vocal lobbies.

There are numerous positions vying for dominance.

The Radical Feminists would have it that anyone who ever had a penis should never be allowed into a women's toilet, but then some of them would like to extend this to Y-chromosome-bearing morphological females with AIS. Ironically, the ultra-conservative palaeo Right have a similar position in many cases.

My understanding is that many laypeople are happy to accept the low-resolution understanding that existed before the Corbett vs Corbett verdict was reached: that MtF transsexuals who have had reassignment surgery should be regarded legally as women, at least so long as they also present socially as such. Certainly, there seems to be much more acceptance of, and much less resistance to, what fits this somewhat vernacular impression of gender than those intergenders who don't, and purposely so.

The only thing that will not do is to revert to a position wherein genetic sex is the only, unchangeable and fixed gender status that a person can have. While at the same time we should respect the order which Nature has laid down for us.

Nature runs on instinct, what has been learnt through countless generations of what works and survives; but human rationality can fine tune this, tweak it to overcome anomalies, so we should use the natural order as the template, but accept that there is fine detail which needs to be accommodated.

It may be that a majority of people don't care if intergender individuals who pass as women but don't have anatomical congruity use the female toilets so long as it is not made apparent. It is certainly the case that what we don't know about is unlikely to worry us. On the other hand, those who haven't gone through any process of transformation at all, and don't really attempt to pass socially as women but insist on claiming that they are, through the proposed institution of Gender Declaration, are likely to cause some disquiet amongst the normative population of women. (I dislike using the term cis as it plays into the Gender Studies narrative.)

Surely, if intergender and genderqueer people with male anatomy were not at this present time attempting to force their way into women's spaces on the basis of legal loopholes created almost specifically for this purpose, as with the 2010 Equalities Act, we would see a great deal less pushback from the TERFs and probably from the archaeo-conservatives as well. For instance, self-identified transgender people have been allowed to work in women's refuges about which there has been a large furore; but I would venture that if it were established that the only trans people who would be employed would have had full medical reassignment and all that this entails, including legal recognition, most, not all perhaps, but most women in the refuges movement would be satisfied.

Indeed, far beyond this we are now hearing reports of untransitioned male-bodied people being allowed to stay in women's refuges, and rape victims have been obliged on occasion to share rooms with these people. The removal of sex or at least morphological conditions for entry into dedicated private women's spaces such as these are putting women at risk, and fully transitioned transsexuals are being conflated with these.

Again, all this needs to be debated in the public forum. All that can really be established firmly at this stage is that tyrannical enforcement of politically correct codes of speech and behaviour around this important topic will only lead to conflict and backlash. Shielding trans people, or those who claim to be, and treating them as special and above criticism will do no good.

The importance of the Lynn Conway paper is that it established an evidential basis for the existence of transsexuals as a legitimate class, and one which is clearly neither going away, nor is it going to go away without either a huge advance in medical prophylaxis or a seriously repressive crackdown from those who deny reality and the right to freedom of expression.

We are Social and Phenotypical Women and Men. A looser category than genetic or biological sex, but one which is still relevant, that should seek to base itself around the precursor patterns found in nature. Our gestalt is such that we need legal status as that which we have become.

In terms of practical day to day psychology, phenotype is archetype.

English Common Law, based as it is on the dictum Do no harm, has become the basis for legal systems in a number of major nations, and the First Amendment to the Constitution of the United States, enshrining as it does the right to freedom of speech and expression, reinforces the concept of freedom to do as one chooses, so long as it does no harm to others or their property.

It must be decided whether intergender use of women's facilities is considered harmful to the women there. It has been claimed that there has never been an abuse of what might be called transgender privilege by intergender people, that no one claiming to be transgender has ever exposed themselves, or molested women in the female toilets.

This is a highly questionable assertion. I recently came across a story of a sex offender who was probably mentally ill[20] who did just this and one can surely be certain that if mere declaration allows access to such spaces, then this will happen. As I pointed out with

20   https://www.thecourier.co.uk/fp/news/local/fife/819644/mum-of-super-market-toilet-sex-assault-victim-warns-freed-attacker-could-strike-again/ (2020).

the Parliamentary debate on the Gender Recognition Bill in 2004, the function of a law is to correctly identify and frame the possible offences which may be carried out in a given situation, so as to be clear as to what it is that is forbidden, not to avoid such clarity on the basis that the offence is supposed to not have previously occurred, and therefore never will.

Laws are legislated for the protection of the people in the future, not for judgements on the past. New circumstances allow for new possibilities.

It would probably be wildly impractical to legislate against those who pass as women but have male sexual anatomy from using women's toilets simply because it would be so invasive. But this is obviously not the case with those genderqueer individuals who demand to use these facilities. I have known some who have deliberately engaged in what has become known as genderf***, the deliberate messing with the perceptions of the person on the street by purposely putting out conflicting and confusing cues as to what gender one belongs to.

Doing this on the street or in a public space is one thing, and might be classified as freedom of expression but doing so in what is understood as a women's space is surely intrusive. Is intrusion the same as harm? Or would it merely be subjectively perceived offence? The distinctions are now becoming important with recent new laws establishing that to cause someone to be offended is now a criminal offence in its own right, as opposed to the English Common Law harm.

I am inclined to the belief that intrusion is closer to harm than it is to offence, since it is akin to trespass into a private space rather than a mere offending which might be entirely subjective. Although intrusion and trespass will doubtless cause offence in their own right, but this is in addition to the harm of intrusion.

Whatever conclusion we may come to, and which may pass into being a social standard, or even into statute, we should ensure that it is clear and is understood and accepted by as large a proportion of the people as possible.

And while we must evolve beyond a strict genetic reductionism which fails to account for anomalies, we must respect that gender expression arises out of that biological division of the sexes, so we must use that as the basic template even where anomalies are found which do not fit exactly on one side or the other. Those true intersex and hermaphroditic individuals who genuinely are so much in the middle as to be unsure what they feel in themselves should not be coerced into a particular identity, but neither should the overwhelming majority be forced to abandon their own well-established and conventional notions of gender to satisfy a politically motivated minority of genderqueer activists who are largely motivated by Cultural Marxism and the gender theorists who stoke their discontent, exploiting both intersex and transsexuals for political ends.

CHAPTER 14

THE JEREMY CLARKSON POSTULATE

I N T H E P A S T, trans identity was something on the edge, something which was beyond the limit of most people's experience. And why should it have been anything else?

As this phenomenon gradually climbed over the horizon of common awareness, those who found the easiest acceptance were those who, whether through good fortune from nature, or through greater diligence, have fitted best into the conventional world.

I knew that the more I put into it, the more I would get out.

Today, however, we have devolved to a point where the mere claiming of an identity is supposed to command respect.

This is why I put forward what I call the Jeremy Clarkson Postulate.

Gender theorists argue that there are no essential qualities to gender, that chromosomes, gonads, hormones, morphology, neurology and reproduction are not what it is about. These are irrelevant. What is really going on is that society is constructing the concepts around certain stereotyped notions of what masculine and feminine qualities are and that these are merely performative displays to fit the desired role.

Since even this has now been deconstructed to the point where the only required performative act to qualify in a particular gender is to claim that one is of that gender, and by implication, sex, we are left with my Jeremy Clarkson Postulate. Jeremy Clarkson, as most of my British readers will know, is a particularly outspoken and politically incorrect television presenter on that most mannish of subjects, cars. He is also a reputed to be a male chauvinist pig, and would probably be proud of it, I believe. If it is otherwise, I apologise to him. I have no particular objection to Jeremy Clarkson; I find him quite amusing and he adds variety to our existence. I intend him no disrespect and merely take him as an example.

The thing I wish to postulate about Jeremy Clarkson is whether, should he one day suddenly pronounce that he was a woman deep inside and that he had only hidden from saying it for so long because of embarrassment, we must be bound to accept what he says simply on the basis that he said it?

This is a serious philosophical question, which the modern LGBT Cultural Marxist lobby hasn't properly dealt with.

In the realm of epistemology, we usually require reasons for believing that such and such a matter is the case.

The contemporary descent into unreason, which has currently possessed both the academic and political Lefts, allows that in certain circumstances no evidence other than an unsubstantiated claim is considered sufficient to engender belief, whereas in others, no evidence of any kind at all could ever be enough.

My own take on this is that extraordinary claims require extraordinary evidence, but that there may be conditions in which such claims can be substantiated if such evidence can be produced.

So, if Jeremy Clarkson continued to appear and act in the same way as we are accustomed to seeing him appear and act, should we believe his claim that he is really a woman, or that he is a transsexual who at least wants to become a woman insofar as that is medically possible?

If his behaviour and appearance remain the same, then I put it to you that we should not believe him. We should conclude that he is either joking with us in a manner which should not surprise us, or that perhaps this is a passing whim. If he had never shown any indications of gender confusion, had never tried to feminise his appearance and never behaved any differently than the typically masculine way in which he has always behaved, then we should say that at most this is some idea which lurked at the back of his mind, but which had never been strong enough to find its way into any actual form or manifestation in his life; that more was required than the mere assertion that he is a woman, when all evidence appears to the contrary.

This is probably a convenient point at which to introduce my own way of understanding sex and gender that I develop in later chapters. I shall make reference to Dr Jason Reza Jorjani's concept of the spectral, but I think my core theory is only expanded by that.

Dr Jorjani has argued persuasively for the existence of what he terms a *Spectral Realm*[1] from the analytic efforts of Descartes, Kant and others, and I think that this may be only one of several, or many, layers of preceding metaphysical levels and structures between us and the *Absolute Ground of Existence*. Thought, consciousness, imagination, possibility, memory, but also parapsychic experiences and more all exist in the *Spectral dimension*. I find this an immensely helpful conceptual advance in category distinctions of the phenomenal world. I cannot here recapitulate the entire history of Western Philosophy in order to demonstrate that there must be something behind the experiential world of the senses, which, though we have come to understand some of it, also clearly has some extremely evasive, but persistent, qualities and features; however, I would simply argue that we must find some way to reassimilate *consciousness* into our structural ontology of the world — and *gender*.

I earlier referred to my spectral sense of self, the ghostly haunting by my potential self which sought to manifest itself in my material

---

1   Jorjani, Jason Reza, PhD, *Prometheus and Atlas*. Arktos Books (2016), https://www.amazon.co.uk/Prometheus-Atlas-Jason-Reza-Jorjani/dp/1910524611 (2020).

existence. But spectres are merely ghostly images that haunt us unless they can find some purchase in materiality to affect or become real.

Existence is a confluence of uncountable influences, which may vary from one moment to the next. Our own stream of consciousness is the nexus of our immutable past with the external influences of the present, which we may project into the future through our choices. I would suggest that the spectral sense is a type of latent morphogenetic field, such as has been proposed by Dr Rupert Sheldrake, on which I shall elaborate later; an influence of formative causation, as he describes it. The actual mechanisms would be the brain structures which tend to resonate with existing stable patterns and so produce certain subjective experiences of self.

As I have mentioned, *techne* in the Ancient Greek has the meaning of control or skill from which we get technology and so, by extension, it can be a useful notion when applied to survival adaptation. The techne of the genome of a species would include the specific adaptations which enhance its success in survival, such as petals that attract bees, scents that attract mates, and so forth. This is not techne in its fullest sense as an agent of conscious intent, but neither is it simple physis, the mechanical workings of the unconscious material world. It is the emergent expression of the drive within the Universe to know itself.

On a more macro scale, male and female are a dynamic which enhance survival adaptation by allowing for exchange of genes. The qualities of the principles masculine and feminine were known to the ancient Chinese as Yang and Yin, the Great and the Small.

The expansive, the contracting. Day and Night. Up and Down. And so on and so on.

Male and female are the expressions in biology of these principles. Just as they are demonstrated in the Law of Motion that 'for every action there is an equal and opposite reaction': meta-level principles are expressed through physical laws.

Gender is the driver of one's inner make-up. If the only expression is the obvious, we must say that it is what it appears to be.

In the court of public perception, our hypothetical Jeremy Clarkson must do more than simply claim, he must at the least act in some way as to demonstrate his conviction. His Spectral Self must show itself to the world and establish itself in some way or else it remains no more than an unproved ghostly imagining.

The danger we face today is that we may encourage what in previous epochs might be seen as mass possession by these ghosts, copycat psychoses promoted by a media hungry for the latest thrill.

How may we distinguish between those anomalous individuals who are so hardwired that they cannot escape the resonance of their Spectral Self and those who merely adopt this sense through social entrainment as the girls at a school where seventeen of them are receiving various degrees of treatment seem to have done?[2]

It is commonly said that if it looks like a duck, walks like a duck and quacks like a duck, it probably is a duck. This is probabilistic functionalism as applied to perception. You cannot be making conscious judgements on every perceived detail of reality every moment. Assumptions have to be made on the basis of past experience and inherited archetypal templates.

There is a curious subgroup within the trans community who in some ways embody the hypothetical situation of Mr Clarkson. Claiming to be male to female transsexuals, they then, rather than sorting out some facial hair removal, or even just shaving and using a concealer, actually allow their beards to grow. When questioned about the apparent incongruity with their claimed identity, they answer that some women have facial hair, so why shouldn't they?

And it is, of course, true that some women have facial hair. I don't mean a little down on their upper lip or the odd coarse hair on their chin, but a stronger and more widespread pattern of growth, more

---

2   https://www.dailymail.co.uk/news/article-6401593/Whistleblower-teacher-makes-shocking-claim-autistic.html (2020).

akin to the male pattern. And this is the point. While these women have all, or most, of the other characteristics which identify them as female, and thus override an interpretation of them as male, these supposed 'male to female transsexuals' who let their beards grow rarely have any, if at all. The beard is an evolutionary adaptive signal demonstrating male fertility. Why would you choose to present this signal if you want to be taken as a female?

Perception is a stable hallucination projected on the basis of external sensory data, which is filtered and interpreted in the light of both learned experience and inherited unconscious material, which hopefully has enough verisimilitude to be probabilistically functional. The postmodernists might say it is a construct, but they are so profligate with their use of this term that it becomes meaningless. Every detail of every aspect of human life is a construct in their view, whereas in a world in which consciousness takes centre stage we must think more in terms of meaning, interpretation, intentionality.

So, when we ask what does it mean to conceive of oneself as a woman, we are to some extent asking how that conception might be brought to fruition, indeed how should one birth this self-concept into materiality?

How is the Spectral Self to be expressed in one's life?

Fitting into perceptual archetypes so that one may more seamlessly interface with society seems to be the logical thing to do, for most. Tens of thousands of transsexuals have done this over the last seventy years or more with a reasonable degree of success, and without seriously challenging these perceptual archetypes.

If someone comes along and claims to be transsexual, or more likely transgender these days, and not only retains their hidden male characteristics, but also those which are most visible, the strongest signals of male virility, a display conceptually not unrelated to the colour of the male stickleback's belly, surely we must have some doubts in our mind as to whether this is serious?

Should we accept that this is simply another way of constructing gender? Should we accept Jeremy Clarkson if he said that he identified as a woman but made no indicative changes to his presentation?

If I had declared in my early twenties that I actually *was* from another planet as I had playfully fantasised, would that have made me an alien from another world? Of course not!

Identification is a two-way street. One may identify oneself as anything one likes in one's imagination. People need to be able to identify you for themselves, and we need to have our laws based on the collective sum of how these identifications are made.

So long as what people self-identify as only affects themselves, their close family or community, it is of little consequence to the wider world and there is usually little need to legislate or interfere in such matters. But when demands are made for acceptance as something which is counter-intuitive to our perception and understanding of the world, it must at least be examined.

Postmodernism demands that everything it doesn't like must be questioned and deconstructed, while at the same time refusing to question the outcomes of their own assumptions, which lead to a formless chaos untethered to any basic evidential reality. Instead claiming rights to a freedom that is in effect a tyranny over the freedom of others.

The fact is that reality itself is oppressive in the sense that it is unavoidable, that existence itself makes demands on us if we are to survive, to advance, to prosper. We all experience Martin Heidegger's *thrownness*, we find ourselves thrown into a life which we (apparently) had no hand in making. Other people will always impose some limits on our behaviours because it is necessary on the basis of 'Don't tread on me'.

But like gravity, these limitations give us form and structure, which have been built up over countless generations. We may adjust these as we go and improve them, but to dig out their foundations is foolhardy without a tested replacement. I would suggest that post-modern Gender Theory is not that replacement.

While we may accommodate postmodernism to the extent of acknowledging that there are grey areas which don't precisely fit into exact and firmly delineated categories, this should only be taken as a spur to further elaboration of our epistemological and ontological understanding of the world.

We need to make ad hoc judgements on an ongoing basis. Course corrections are inevitable on any journey. Nothing is ever going to be completely defined. Reality goes on forever into infinity.

The philosopher who imagines that they have finally climbed up the last ladder and understood and explained it all ends up sliding down the snake to a new beginning like Lord Kelvin who in 1900 declared that science had basically got it taped but for a few details that were left to be worked out. Within a decade Einstein had come along with Relativity and Planck with the beginnings of Quantum Theory.

But we are still left with our inherited archetypal perceptual reality, which is based on the material world, and most especially human society. It did not evolve for the purpose of examining the workings of the atomic levels of existence, either in matter, or in our psychology. Postmodern deconstruction reminds us, like the slave who whispered 'Memento mori'[3] into the ear of Marcus Aurelius, that we should understand our theories are not perfect, nor we immortal, that we will be superseded, the world will go on without us. We need the world more than the world needs us. But we should not be confused and let the whisperings of critique become the Emperor, for there needs to be a logos. All that postmodernism should amount to is a formalisation of the need to look at where things are imperfect and where they can be improved. But it has become an all-consuming cancer which seeks to destroy everything and leave nothing in its wake. Nothing is True…

---

3   'Remember you will die'.

The irony should not be lost that in critiquing to destruction the historical process which has bootstrapped the human race, or at least some parts of it, out of the mud, rising from brutality, slavery and the rest to our present, perhaps over-cultured society, postmodernism has, throwing the baby out with the bathwater, replaced it with absolute subjectivity, absolute relativism (are such things even possible?) and an infinity of competing narratives with little basis in objective, or even shared, realities.

If one such as the postulated Jeremy Clarkson cannot implement the adaptation, the expression of what they claim, through some techne — the skill of demonstrating what they believe, does not even want to try but merely base their claims on a spectral sense, which may in itself have been acquired and adopted from others through passive social modelling, then I suggest that such assertions should not be taken seriously. If a scientist can have their theory rejected because it has failed to produce the evidence it claims exists, the same should apply to those people who make extraordinary claims about themselves which they expect to be recognised by others. These claims remain in the spectral realm of infinite possibility and the imagination but fail to firmly and conclusively enter into the world of material and consensus reality.

Butler's assertion that there is a performative element to gender is not really controversial. Of course there are performative differences. This so easily slips into it being no more than performative. But I would turn this round and say that the performance is demonstrative. It demonstrates the presence of the inner reality and manifests it outwardly. Mere performance on its own is simply a shell, like an AI bot imitating human language, pretending to be conscious. For Butler and her acolytes there is nothing inside; it is hollow.

The Spectral Self must be demonstrated before we can accept it. If our hypothetical incarnation of Jeremy Clarkson is unable to demonstrate his inner feminine through behaviour, or changed appearance both in dress and physical presence, then on what basis are we expected to believe that he really feels himself to have a feminine inner being, or however it may be expressed, that he wants us to believe in?

Is the mere performative act of claiming to be a woman sufficient to create a reality?

Hopefully Mr Clarkson has no such conflict between his inner and outer selves, for if he did, or at least claimed to have, then we should surely wish to critique his claims in good postmodernist style.

Regrettably, in the present climate it seems to be the case that the mere questioning of claims, the felt need to see evidence in the long term, is deemed transphobic. On the contrary, we are expected to extend affirmation on the basis of mere unsupported claims.

This is why someone such as myself has to stick their head above the parapet and cry 'Stop!'

CHAPTER 15

WHERE ARE WE NOW?

THE CURRENT WAVE of liberal obsession with exploiting transgenderism has deep roots but has come out into the open in recent times.

The Caitlyn Jenner affair seems to have been the starting gun for what has happened since. This media personality has been lionised by the media for transitioning in public and was awarded a 'Woman of the Year' award by *Glamour* magazine in 2015 at the age of 66 as well as various other awards. Jenner, who it is rumoured had earlier abandoned attempts at transition behind her, came to prominence as an athlete in the nineteen-seventies and had remained in the public eye not least because of her relationship to the reality show media family the Kardashians.

The very public manner in which her social transition took place was capitalised on by the media for promoting transgenderism, even at such a late age.

Gender reassignment is a technical and medical intervention which should be intended to aid in developmental individuation, and as such is likely to be most successful in aiding that development if done at a stage when the person is old enough to understand what they are doing and take responsibility for the consequences of their choice, while still young enough for their appearance to be malleable by treatment, as well as for them to have enough of their life ahead of them that there is a reasonable prospect they will adapt their personality and live out as full a life as possible afterwards.

Gender theoreticians, such as I have referenced, are critical of what they see as pandering to a heteronormative, cis-gendered hegemony by trans people such as myself who have sought (at least until now) to avoid drawing attention to ourselves, and thus see no problem with someone like Jenner having a public male identity until their mid-sixties, and then living out the latter third of their life in their acquired gender.

Certainly, the media won't let Caitlyn Jenner forget her previous identity, and this is the very same reason for my reluctance in coming to write this book myself.

However, I have one big advantage, which is that I don't have the millstone weight of a public persona on record for the last forty years for people to refer to; my pre-transition life is so remote in the past that only a few close friends and family can recall it. And in those intervening decades of half of my life and now more, I and those like myself have been afforded the space to find ourselves through society and work in ways that must be entirely impossible for Caitlyn Jenner, surrounded as she is by the clamour of the media and having put it off all this time so that there will inevitably be a large backlog of unprocessed emotions and self images, not to mention the social inertia of the established persona.

This was when the concern vultures gathered to feed on and exploit us to the hilt, reinforcing non-normative gender expressions, media pundits calling them 'brave' and helping to enforce the new laws which had come in around the subject.

In Britain, the 2010 Equalities Act had effectively allowed anyone who claimed a particular identity, if it was one of the 'protected groups', to demand special treatment. In the case of individuals claiming to be transgender, this allowed them the rights and privileges associated with their desired gender, even if they had not qualified for a Gender Recognition Certificate, had had no treatment to modify their gendered appearance and had not even been diagnosed with gender dysphoria.

This allowed the now infamous Lily Madigan to sue her school and force them to let her use the girls' toilets. I have encountered this young person through her comments on my video blogs on YouTube and she does not seem to acknowledge that transsexuals need to negotiate their identities with society in the sense of establishing an identity de facto before seeking to have it confirmed de jure — something I believe to be extremely important.

Lily Madigan has also stood for election as a Women's Officer for the local Labour Party in Rochester and Strood, campaigning heavily on the Anti-Transphobia ticket and seemingly calling anyone who didn't think she was a suitable candidate a TERF. Subsequently she was elected. One suspects that this was due to the local party members either being hoodwinked by the identitarian claims, or simply afraid to be branded Transphobes. This is obviously contentious and pushing boundaries. Despite the fact that many of us have achieved social passing and legal recognition, we should still be sensitive to the fact that there are certain aspects of women's issues of which we have no experience and therefore cannot fully engage with. Indeed, how can one represent a group when one has barely even established oneself as belonging to it?

If Lily were to be put forward as a candidate on the recommendation of her peers based on a record of good work, then that would be one thing; but to press forward and challenge existing members on the basis of promoting trans rights and almost purposely create conflict and division with feminists in that forum is, I believe, perverse.

Radical Feminists have long been hostile to the presence of transsexual women, but where my own tack since my early experiences has been to seek to avoid sensitive situations wherever possible, preferring to establish my identity and carry on with my life in stealth mode, folk such as Lily seek deliberate confrontation which promotes antagonism, without having prepared the ground. The term TERFs — Trans

Excluding Radical Feminists — has been used by Lily and other radical trans activists who push against anyone who has the slightest difficulty coming to terms with the existence of trans people or even just certain trans individuals; reifying this term as a full-blown identity in the same way that radical gender deconstructionists reify each of the newly invented genders with the various terms non-binary, pangendered and so on.

I had written to Germaine Greer in the late nineties criticising her use of the title 'Pantomime Dames' for her chapter on transsexualism in her book *The Whole Woman*.[1] I did receive a reply, but only to say that she didn't have time to read my fairly lengthy missive; however, she suggested instead that I read her entire book!

My criticism had been that her stereotyping of this caricature was not only unkind, it was untrue. She focussed exclusively on the type of trans person who is a late transitioner that had built a masculine persona over years and had probably been in a marriage, or the rather stereotyped image of a Beaumont Society transvestite. Someone whose earlier choices had made them less flexible to transition. Perhaps someone like Caitlyn Jenner. I make no criticism of Jenner for transitioning, but surely the weight of a lifetime's habitual way of being must tell, both on her and how she is perceived.

Of course, Greer will have noticed those who are visible, but refuses to acknowledge those who succeed in passing into invisibility. I was amused at my own memory of feeling like the Principal Boy in Aladdin while she projected onto me as Widow Twanky! Her refusal to engage in any dialogue but rather to pontificate on the basis of her flawed understanding of developmental biology and false stereotyping of transsexuals was simply a mirror image reflection of the patriarchy of which she complained.

---

1   Greer, Germaine. *The Whole Woman*. Doubleday (1999).

But now the likes of Lily Madigan are forcing situations which would doubtless provoke the TERFs — giving them a certain amount of reason to push back.

Recently, a confrontation developed at Hyde Park Speakers' Corner in which a trans activist was later convicted of assaulting a TERF.[2] Some of the radical trans activists claiming to be trans women did not appear to have modified their appearance or behaviour in order to appear more like women, and were behaving in a most masculine manner,[3] charging at the TERFs like wild animals and clearly giving them justification in saying that they were not women!

This kind of thing is entirely unhelpful, playing as it does into narratives such as that of Germaine Greer.

The invisible bulk of the trans population remains misrepresented, and there is little we can do to counter that misrepresentation from both sides, the trans trenders or the radfems, other than to behave with as much dignity as is left to us.

Nevertheless, like it or not, we have to accept that however much we manage to successfully pass as social females through physical changes and social readjustment, we grew up with some aspects of male biology and socialisation, albeit often extremely androgynously, even if we do now more resemble a sort of feminised intersex. Issues of social integration do exist for FtM men but do not seem to be so severe. I have not seen any Trans Excluding Radical Men's Rights groups going around protesting about trans men invading their spaces although I recently came across a report about a gay men's bathhouse where users complained about the presence of a 'woman' who was a transman. Allowing himself to be seen naked and expecting no

2   https://www.standard.co.uk/news/crime/transgender-activist-tara-wolf-fined-150-for-assaulting-exclusionary-radical-feminist-in-hyde-park-a3813856.html (2020).

3   '*CLEAR FOOTAGE* Assault on a Woman by Transgender Activists', Speakers' Corner, London 13/9/17 https://www.youtube.com/watch?v=8snmtpi89hw (2020).

comment was surely another example of wantonly pressing boundaries and expecting no pushback, so perhaps the TERMR activists are not so far away after all.

I disagree with those conservatives who say that we merely disguise ourselves; I believe the process is much deeper than that, but we can never be fully as female or male as we would like. There are limitations of which any transsexual will know in their own body. But this flawed, limited process is so much better than the alternative we are leaving behind that those limitations are of little consequence to the transitioner. The accident victim does not complain about the limitations of their robotic prosthesis, rather they marvel and are grateful. We may have some aspects of male biology, but we are not men.

Nonetheless, these limitations exist, and one's past exists, even if it isn't public. This is not the place to argue the details of exactly where the boundaries should be set, and they may be nuanced depending on the individual, but if incompletely transformed trans people make too many demands, they will be the less respected for it, and the pushback has already begun.

We need to have some legal status in the social world, but that must be purchased by us at the cost of some basic recognition of the values of the world that we are in. Carte blanche to do as we wish without any consequences because we are a protected category will not do.

However, larger bodies and forces have now come into play following the fallout from the 2010 law in this country, and more widely in the Anglophone world.

In 2017, the Church of England declared that transgendered children at all their schools should be allowed to dress as they preferred and were to be addressed by their preferred gender pronoun.

A teacher has been suspended and is likely to have his career ruined because he called a pupil who claimed to be transgender by their 'old' gender.

The Arch Concern Vultures reside in the ivory towers of the Church of England and the world of academia and they are becoming the new Thought Police. Colleges are now proscribing the use of terms such as 'mother' and 'father', 'boy' and 'girl'.

In Canada, a new law, C-16, has potentially made it a criminal offence to address someone by other than their preferred gender pronoun. This doesn't just mean he or she but one of any of a newly created list of pronouns several dozen long, some of which you may see represented by symbols on the front cover of this book. It has been said by some that this law does not mandate the use of such pronouns, but legal interpretation is causing concern that the law might be stretched to that.

Psychologist Dr Jordan B Peterson has risked censure in saying that he will not comply with being forced to use particular words. He has been criticised by some on the Right for speaking to Theryn Meyer, a moderate Canadian trans rights activist, but this criticism is invalid.

He did not say that he would refuse to speak to trans people or address them as they preferred as a courtesy; he had said that it was the use of invented pronouns to which he objected, and the legal threat of sanction on those who refused to use them, that being the opposite of freedom of speech in that it was enforcement of speech. Indeed, he has said that the best way to approach this is to refer to an individual one is addressing by the gendered pronoun appropriate to their presentation.[4]

I made a short video blog on this subject.[5]

I'm not entirely certain that Dr Peterson is fully up to speed on the neurodevelopmental side of all this, and he is by no means the most

---

4   https://www.lbc.co.uk/radio/presenters/maajid-nawaz/jordan-peterson-why-i-refuse-to-use-special-pronou/ (2020).

5   'Mark Collett Misquotes Jordan Peterson' https://www.youtube.com/watch?v=F-WgQ7VyN7s (2020).

pro-trans academic on the planet, but at least he is prepared to give us a modicum of respect.

The suppression of free academic discussion of these topics was highlighted in the Laurier University scandal in the autumn of 2017 in which teaching assistant Lindsay Shepherd was summoned to what amounted to a Star Chamber hearing and told that an undisclosed number of complaints had been made by students about a five-minute video clip of Dr Peterson she had shown in class discussing the use of the pronoun *they* as a non-gendered pronoun in the singular. Incidentally, I mostly agree with Dr Peterson, but not entirely; I think there are a limited number of linguistic circumstances in which *they* can be used as a singular pronoun, mostly when there is an element of vagueness or uncertainty, but these should not be used as an excuse for the wholesale implementation of the word as a replacement for gendered *hes* and *shes* in common parlance, or to allow people to demand to be called by non-gendered, non-binary or pan-gendered terms.

These are the real constructs, invented categories which bear no real relation to actuality, the made-up pronouns as Dr Peterson calls them, there being no objective correlates to these words, which are merely subjectively generated labels. Thus, transsexualism is used as a means of breaking down traditional gender concepts, despite the fact that those of us who fit the HBS profile seek to fit into them and want clearly defined laws to govern recognition, access to spaces and so on.

It transpired that no actual complaints had been made against Ms Shepherd, and that the entire Star Chamber episode had been created by the staff member who interrogated her. This is literal policing of language.

Various episodes have occurred in which people have been penalised for refusing to comply with this policing of language. In the UK, recently a doctor was fired for saying that he would not in principle, hypothetically, refer to a bearded man as *she*[6] — on the basis that this was unlawful discrimination or harassment under the Equalities Act 2010.

One is reminded of the words of Lynne Jones, MP, one of the sponsors of the GRA, in debate in the Commons in 2004:

'LJ: To be candid, if the hon. Gentleman is suggesting that someone who sports a full beard would have their application for a gender recognition certificate granted, I wonder what world he is living in.'[7]

… and one realises how far the Overton window of acceptability has moved.

I may not agree entirely with all the views expressed by *The Conservative Woman* on the subject, but who can blame them for pointing out such egregious nonsense? Other similar examples are now coming thick and fast, too fast to fully record, besides which to give too much detail might expose me to litigation for even daring to mention certain legal cases.

I myself, as we have seen, was shut down through the powers of the Centre for Interdisciplinary Gender Studies when I was scheduled to give a preview of the material in this book at the local literature festival. If this phenomenon is to be above examination by the very people who have experienced it, and the academics are to be empowered to silence those of us with whom they disagree in order to promote their own version, then we are truly in Chapel Perilous[8] and the Church of Postmodern Gender has taken control.

---

6   https://www.conservativewoman.co.uk/the-transgender-faith-beats-christianity-and-common-sense/(2020).

7   See Appendix B *Commons Debate on the GRB* 25 May 2004 Hansard.

8   A metaphor derived from Malory's *Le Morte d'Arthur* meaning an especially intense form of cognitive dissonance that is difficult to resolve.

CHAPTER 16

CHILDREN AND SOCIETY

THIS HAS BECOME A QUAGMIRE, and one into which children, amongst the most vulnerable members of our society, are being thrown.

I recently received an email circular from the LGBT hub of Leeds City Council announcing the creation of a position at £24,000 pa for an officer to run a local Mermaids group.

Mermaids is a nationwide group for younger people who may be trans. I have been aware of this group for more than a decade, and at first thought it was a good idea. At the time I believe it was self-funded through donations and worked at the level of a social network, like SHAFT in the eighties. Local government-funded officers pulling big money salaries from local councils was certainly not the picture back then.

However, now it appears to have become a major lobbying group, and it has allegedly facilitated the controversial medical treatment of minors with puberty-blocking hormones, according to *The Times of London*.[1]

---

1   https://www.thetimes.co.uk/article/mermaids-uk-charity-ban-as-boy-forced-to-live-as-girl-dvx3j99cn (2020).

Unfortunately, I am reluctant to even discuss this group beyond a simple introduction as there is so much litigation around people associated with it that I fear to comment further.

I recently saw an interview with Erika Ervin,[2] the actress known as *Amazon Eve*, who is transsexual, talking about many of the issues between *transsexualism* and *transgenderism* which I discuss, and it was not until about half an hour in that she mentioned that she was six foot eight! On the screen she had looked to me like a normal woman, and my teedar[3] is pretty good. But this impressed mightily on me several things.

Firstly, how utterly motivated she must have been to transition, knowing that she would always stand out and draw attention, however well she might pass. And secondly, that if she had been able to have some earlier treatment, she might have been spared this. Perhaps she doesn't mind at all, even enjoys it for the professional edge it gives her, or perhaps she is so used to it now that she doesn't feel it anymore, just like I forget my own disfigurement most of the time.

The question, though, is how to select those adolescents who genuinely have irreversible gender dysphoria from those who are merely gender non-conforming. For myself, I believe that remission of my dysphoria was impossible, and psychiatrists have often commented that full-blown gender dysphoria is often entirely resistant to remission despite all the conscious desires and intentions of the victim.

I cannot say that it would *always* be *completely* wrong to treat an adolescent going through a difficult puberty, since I think back to how some medical intervention could have saved me the physical pain of my cystic acne, the permanent damage it caused and the concomitant social abuse I received; or of Erika Ervin who might have been spared growing to a height unusual even for a man; or others who might have unusual physical conditions accompanying unremitting dysphoria.

---

2   https://www.youtube.com/watch?v=eZhEexgbFaA&t=7s (2020).

3   My own trans version of *Gaydar* — Trans Radar.

However, we are on very thin ice with this subject, and if other medical interventions could be found that would prevent these serious, and permanent, outcomes which would be problems regardless of the gender issues, then these should be taken in preference surely? If there are no accompanying physical pathologies, why intervene medically?

How can one determine the mind of a child for certain?

There is some hope of narrowing down selection in this field with the evidence provided by such as Professor Julie Bakker[4,5] of the University of Liege in Belgium, who presented evidence in 2018 from her analysis of MRI scans of 160 individuals at the European Society of Endocrinology annual meeting in Barcelona which indicated that those who were gender dysphoric had cross-sex brain structures and neural activity; however, sufficient scientific blunders and errors (such as those of Dr Money) have taken place in the past that we should exercise the greatest caution even in such cases and take the widest possible account of the various aspects of any case before anyone makes any decisions, especially in the case of children, whose brains are not fully developed and whose MRI scans may develop over the years. I am brought to mind of the extraordinary 5 α-Reductase Deficiency children who may experience an apparent morphological sex change at puberty and seem to entirely accept it.

The Standards of Care of the World Professional Association for Transgender Health[6] (WPATH), formerly the Harry Benjamin International Gender Dysphoria Association (HBIGDA), recognise that there is a difference between gender nonconformity and gender dysphoria. Early play in infants may explore a wide variety of expressions, some of which might be considered gender inappropriate, but the child itself may not develop a sense of its own gender until some

---

4   https://www.telegraph.co.uk/news/2018/05/22/transgender-brain-scans-promised-study-shows-structural-differences/ (2020).

5   https://www.newsweek.com/transgender-people-brains-wired-those-gender-they-identify-new-study-shows-939504 (2020).

6   https://wpath.org/publications/soc (2020).

time later. Nonconformity and dysphoria do not always coexist, and may change, disappear or become more severe during adolescence.

One might think then that to wait and see would be the best course of action in the event a child demonstrates any of the features of concern.

There has been no controlled study of minors who have received early medical treatments, while the WPATH Standards of Care cites some studies on gender non-conforming children which have shown that a high proportion come to terms with their birth sex, or are of a homosexual orientation when they become adults. Other researchers have suggested that these studies are flawed in that they do not sufficiently examine the differences between those who become gender accepting and those who don't. A small population remain nonconforming or declare themselves to be *genderqueer* or some other self-identified category. We should remember that such labels are a recent invention and are subjectively applied, often with political intent and often have little or no relation on the individual's biology, or even their presentation.

Policy attitudes amongst professional bodies seem to have subtly shifted in recent years. The HBIGDA itself has been influential in the trend away from using the term *transsexual*, preferring to use the term *transgender* in its new title. As we have seen, this is an umbrella term which has been used by some against actual transsexuals who seek full medical reassignment. The argument is often made that requiring sex reassignment surgery before at least MtF trans women can be legally recognised is discriminatory against those who would like to have it but so far have been unable to source the treatment due to financial circumstances. But those making this argument are often what I would call socially transitioned *intergenders,* who themselves have no desire or intention to have reassignment surgery and would appear to be promoting this as worthy of legal gender recognition, rather than merely defending the position of financially challenged transsexuals.

A private source who has had long term involvement with the HBIGDA (now WPATH) alleged to me that there is (or was) at least one highly placed medically qualified individual (who could obviously pay for any treatment if she had wanted it) in that organisation who fitted this description. That person was not Professor Stephen Whittle (who is a legal scholar and sometime President of the WPATH), whom I had known when he was first transitioning back in 1975, but I can't help remembering how he too as far back as the early 2000s had been lobbying for a Gender Recognition Act which did not require reassignment surgery, even for MtF trans people.

Now, after all these years, I am reminded of the brief period of intimacy we shared back then, and how in retrospect, things he said privately to me or did at the time can be seen to hold the seed of his later lobbying of this position not to require reassignment surgery, not just for FtM transmen, but for MtF transwomen as well, although at the time that position may have been less popular than my own. Remember that in late 2005 or early 2006 Professor Whittle and his colleague Lewis Turner had written:

> ...for the purposes of the gender recognition act, "changing sex" was never about changing biology but about changing legal definitions of what gender recognition/legal sex was.

> We share Sandland's (2005) view that as we can now have men with vaginas and women with penises, the act does undermine the binary of two morphologically distinct sexes.[7]

I don't wish to try to prevent people living as what I call *intergender*, but I observe the drift away from the focus on *transsexuals* in the WPATH towards a wider concern with umbrella *transgender diversity*. Unfortunately, this can lead some to exclude and demonise the *transsexual founder population* as *privileged* and *elitist*. But circumstances differ around the globe. Some countries have relatively easy access to socialised medical treatment. Others have complicated insurance schemes and others have none. Professionals on good incomes complaining about the circumstances of others which they do not share sound disingenuous.

The WPATH seems to be much more about *gender diversity* and *gender expression* these days than when it was the HBIGDA, which is doubtless why many transsexuals have taken the term *Harry Benjamin Syndrome* to themselves, seeking to distance themselves from the move to the *open-ended category without a core* that seems to now be the ideology of transgender.

Subtle changes to the criteria in the Diagnostic and Statistical Manual 5 (DSM-5)[8, 9] also took place a few years after the WPATH was reconfigured, as I have mentioned in a previous chapter. Some of these were helpful, and others perhaps less so.

The former diagnosis of *Gender Identity Disorder* (GID) was an unpopular term and was replaced with the term *Gender Dysphoria* (GD), which had long been used by transsexuals. Many welcomed the removal of the diagnosis from the categories of sexual dysfunction and sexual paraphilias, which was motivated by the desire to remove the stigma of a mental disorder in the same way that homosexuality had been taken out of the earlier DSM-II in 1973. However, I am not alone in suggesting that to designate it as nothing more than natural variation in the way that homosexuality is, takes this too far.

Anomalous gender identity was not considered problematic except in cases in which it caused actual *Dysphoria*. I presume this was retained so that those whom I would call transsexual could still qualify for medical treatment. One serious problem I find with this is that one only has to have experienced gender dysphoria for as little as *six months* for this diagnosis. This would seem to be providing the

---

8   https://www.researchgate.net/publication/296700032_The_DSM5_Diagnostic_Criteria_for_Gender_Dysphoria (2020).

9   https://www.huffpost.com/entry/gender-dysphoria-dsm-5_n_3385287 (2020).

premise on which so called *Rapid Onset Gender Dysphoria* (ROGD)[10] is based. This phenomenon, almost exclusively found in teenage girls, makes the preposterous claim that these girls who had never had any experience of gender dysphoria while growing up suddenly develop it to such a degree that they are demanding to be allowed to take male hormones after this incredibly short period of time, some examples of which I examine later. How this can be allowed as a legitimate reason for reassignment treatment, especially in minors, rather than a longer term and more persistent experience of dysphoria is beyond my comprehension. I would suggest that the widening of the catchment demographic by the likes of the WPATH to *gender diversity* rather than being tightly confined to the issue of transsexualism and the simultaneous promotion of concepts such as female penises and men with vaginas may have contributed somewhat to this mess. *Assessment* and *affirmation* are two entirely different things. To be afraid to even question is a cowardly and dangerous path.

At least the A1 diagnostic criterion for children to be diagnosed with GD has been tightened up, requiring that they had expressed a strong desire to be of the opposite sex, rather than merely being observed to engage in gender non-conforming or atypical behaviour. It is quite extraordinary to me that anyone would consider diagnosing a child with GD without that child having expressed a desire to be of the opposite sex, persistently.

Without the kind of hardwiring of the body map that Professor Ramachandran has produced some evidence for, it may be possible that those with only partially cross-sexed brains could develop social self concepts within their physical birth sex. While there is strong evidence from primates that males statistically engage in rough and tumble play and females in grooming, it doesn't mean that we should be limited to those tendencies. Having an archetype of men as strong

---

10 https://www.theamericanconservative.com/dreher/rapid-onset-gender-dysphoria-hell/ (2020).

and independent doesn't mean that there can't be variation around the edges. That is what all evolution is about.

The current preoccupation with gender seems to be a heady concoction brewed first from feminism and then LGBT ideology. The early (and I believe legitimate) moves to forms of legal recognition for our adapted statuses have been seen and then weaponised to other ends, so that we are raddled with discontent, but without knowing what we really want. This is *Cultural Marxism* in the raw: destroy the basis of your identity but offer no replacement other than chaos. If someone expresses negative feelings about their gender for as little as six months, they can change it. The Butlerites would even say that merely to say that you are of a certain sex is *performative* of it.

With the sudden rise in referrals to Gender Identity Clinics in recent years, one can't help wondering if parents are referring their children because they have rigid social expectations of them which they aren't fulfilling. Gender nonconforming behaviour without a strong and persistent desire to be a member of the opposite sex does not make a transsexual, and that child doesn't need any special treatment other than to let him or her find their own way without interference.

As far back as 2015, the Gender Identity Research & Education Society[11] (GIRES) was reported to be advocating teaching transgender issues to children as young as three.[12] Speaking for myself, I had no conscious concept of gender at that age, but when I did awaken to the sense of my own gendered body I didn't need anyone to explain it to me. I would agree with Dr Joanna Williams, author of *Women vs Feminism*, that schools are merely sowing confusion[13] about gender identity, and a comment of hers that I particularly took to was 'that

---

11   https://www.gires.org.uk/ (2020).

12   https://www.breitbart.com/europe/2015/09/22/gender-fluidity-promoted-children-young-three-educators-still-want-go/ (2020).

13   https://www.telegraph.co.uk/education/2017/06/23/schools-accused-sowing-confusion-childrens-minds-over-promoting/ (2020).

teachers are now "urged to see trans children as an opportunity to enrich the school community."'

No clearer description of what I call *transploitation* could be given. They want to use us for their own political agendas. The *Weaponisation of Trans*.

I shall not take a final view on the details of how apparently trans adolescents should be treated, as that is not my main focus, and needs to be the subject of open debate in both medical ethics and the public fora.

That main focus which I must return to is the deconstruction and destruction of all past notions of gender. It is this that I believe is the real danger which children are being exposed to and the cause behind the sudden rise in referrals for treatment. Simple gender nonconformity is being weaponised by exposure to unnecessary ideas that children aren't ready for. Combined with this, there is a sudden fad for drag queens to read to pre-school children in libraries.[14] Some may say this is no different from Widow Twanky in *Aladdin*, but it is. Besides the context — a weekly event to normalise it rather than a special annual holiday outing — the drag queens are all trying to look glamourous, something that could never be said of Widow Twanky! And then the children are asked if they want to be drag queens them-selves, entraining them into a kind of groupthink.

Who cares? one may say. This is all about *transgression*, right? I would venture that pre-school infants need to be learning more about boundaries than *transgression*. Like musical scales, you need to learn boundaries and rules before you can understand how and when it is all right to break them. Children are purposely having a mixed-up set of influences fed to them just for the hell of it. And if some of the children who don't have an actual inner conflict pick it up and run with it, the work of the chaos makers will have been successful.

---

14 https://www.lifesitenews.com/blogs/drag-queens-at-public-libraries-the-new-strategy-to-indoctrinate-kids-and-s (2020).

It is still early days for the research work of those, such as Professor Julie Bakker, whose results demonstrated structural differences in the brains of transsexual people; however, it gives the hope that we should at least be able to screen out from medical treatments those who only appear to have gender nonconforming traits, who may imagine that they would prefer to be of the opposite sex through social programming of the sorts described but don't actually have a dysphoric neurology; while those who have still need to be cross-confirmed with other psychometric and behavioural diagnostic tools.

A further important aspect to this work I would suggest is that it would seem to support the neuro-psychological roots of this phenomenon rather than the social constructionist claims, which I greatly appreciate.

Those involved with the nurture of such children should take care to observe the difference between *social behaviour* and *physical gender dysphoria*. Social misidentification without the physical experience of dysphoria is much more likely to remit through adaptation than strong physical dysphoria, however the child may adapt socially.

Later stage *Reparative treatment* for transsexualism is a controversial subject. Forcing something on someone rarely works. We don't want to go back to the kind of aversion therapy models that were still present in the nineteen sixties in which people were subjected to strong negative reinforcers associated with their homosexuality, transvestism or transsexualism in order to suppress these inclinations.

But at the same time, we should seek to avoid seeding the minds of impressionable children with inappropriate ideas. Affirmation of everything a child says is a poor way of bringing it up.

It would be much more fruitful to understand the phenomenon better, and thereby distinguish the different taxonomic classes of trans people and the sub-type of gender into which they best fit. The current fashion is going far too fast and heavily into undifferentiated promotion of transgender as one big fuzzy ball that no one must criticise or examine too closely.

I claim my *Positionality*, as some might call it, to challenge this. If everyone is afraid of saying obvious things about how the Emperor is naked because they are afraid of being called *Transphobic*, then it is left to someone like me who is impervious to these darts. I know what the LGBT lobby and genderqueer demographic think of me because I have already experienced it, but I know also that in many ways I represent the intuitive feelings of the ordinary person who has been willing to accept a few passing trannies over the years when we are invisible anyway and don't cause offence, but who has seen the explosion in the last few years and is becoming uncomfortable because of its massive diversification.

This situation must be examined without the fear of causing offence.

In online images from the 2017 Leeds Pride march, there was a contingent from the Trans Leeds group holding amongst others a sign reading **'There will be more of us'**. Elsewhere I have seen placards claiming **'Trans is Beautiful'**. No, it isn't. It's a bloody nuisance to have to deal with, and anyone who thinks otherwise is mad. *I* know!

This is the nightmare scenario. They make it sound like it is desirable. I would not wish physical gender dysphoria on anyone, and to suggest that it is in any way a good thing is bizarre.

There probably *will* be more of us, due to hormone-disrupting chemicals in the water and so forth, but we should be doing everything in our power to limit those chemicals, to find ways of preventing children from having their nervous systems influenced by them, or even ways of helping to correct the neurodevelopment *in utero* of vulnerable babies, and definitely **not** promoting it as some kind of wonderful panacea to life's problems on the social level.

Celebrating transgenderism by declaring that 'There will be more of us' is no different in my eyes to celebrating say, Cerebral Palsy. We should of course do all that we can to support those who suffer with this affliction, but to suggest that it is a perfectly good thing would be just plain silly. It is a disability which causes some impairment of function, and the same is the case with gender identity problems which are sufficiently serious to require medical interventions.

Furthermore, parading down main street with green hair and facial piercings whilst having done little to modify their gender presentation will do little to change the average person's concept of gender.

Certainly, people should be allowed to present as they see fit; as an art therapist I of course recognise the therapeutic value of experimental expression in processing long repressed feelings, but this does not mean such behaviour should be normalised and promoted. Indeed, radical trans activists would probably rebel against any such normalisation and only develop some even more unusual form of behavioural display.

We should remember that it has been found that gender equality in more developed countries favours the expression of gender differences,[15] supporting from the other end the evidence of primate rough and tumble or grooming behaviour.

The conventional pathway of transsexual self-referral, diagnosis, treatment in parallel with social transitioning over time and successful passing culminating in confirmation surgery is a Rite of Passage which gives some sense of a change of state, a movement into a new dimension of life which mere 'declaration' cannot by itself achieve.

Any change of state of an object, whether it be a material melting from solid into liquid, a caterpillar mutating inside its chrysalis, or a child becoming an adult, involves the input of energy. Even a refrigerator which makes things cold needs to put in energy to achieve this.

The change of state from one sex or gender to the other is such a profound transformation that surely it must require some immense input of energy in order to achieve the necessary internal reorganisation, the reversing of the energy spin, the emergence of the archetype,

---

15   Falk, Armin; Hermle, Johannes. 'Relationship of gender differences in preferences to economic development and gender equality'. *Science*, 19 Oct 2018: Vol. 362, Issue 6412, https://science.sciencemag.org/content/362/6412/eaas9899 (2020).

or whatever it takes to be able to present the desired perceptual gestalt to the world and have it accepted.

To reduce this to a simple statement that one 'identifies' with this gender and have that accepted is ludicrous.

While one can be certain that in most parts of the world outside of Western culture — Asia, Africa, the Far East — none of this Gender Studies theory has any effect, is at best considered irrelevant, is ignored or probably laughed at. Transvestites and transsexuals exist in these places, and deal with their difficulties as best they can, but they are not trying to deconstruct the biological and social expressions of gender; they are trying to fit in, just as most of us have tried to for many decades.

The example of Thailand is instructive. Their culture allows cross-gender expression in children as a form of play or social experimentation. Many *Ladyboys* will end up marrying and having children. One is again reminded of the 5 α-Reductase Deficiency population groups which develop at puberty, and these boys apparently show no physical gender dysphoria. The achievement of a masculine persona seems to be a natural thing for these groups, while for other *Ladyboys* and transsexuals it is not.

Trans identities are emergent phenomena, and the advice of Jan Morris to me that I should take my time seems to be the most valuable thing that could be passed on to any child who faces a gender conundrum within themselves. And yet something so delicate and spectral is being promoted as if it were the next best thing after sliced bread.

A recent scandal to burst is what I will call the Daily Mail Seventeen, which I mentioned earlier in the chapter about the Jeremy Clarkson Postulate.

It has recently been disclosed by a teacher[16] that seventeen girls at the school where she teaches are in the process of receiving gender treatment, many with puberty-blocking hormones and one

16 https://www.dailymail.co.uk/news/article-6401593/Whistleblower-teacher-makes-shocking-claim-autistic.html (2020).

even apparently planning a mastectomy. There appears to have been deliberate concealing of what was going on with the girls from the parents of other children as a matter of policy. Several of the girls were apparently recognised to have strong autistic tendencies, and there is a large amount of what I would identify as fashion imitation in which apparently, they imitate certain hair styles and manners. Such social imitation is not uncommon in adolescent girls, especially when coupled with an element of what might be seen as edgy rebellion, in other words, pushing boundaries.

To any external observer, even without experience of the world of mental health, surely it must be obvious that this is a social contagion. Perhaps one child to start with had some issue, but the ultra politically correct attitude of the staff being such that they were unwilling to test this in any way would have reinforced it and encouraged it to go viral.

Trans activists argue that the only course to take with someone who expresses claims of transgenderism is affirmation. I would suggest that unqualified affirmation is dangerous, and that a neutral response is the only responsible attitude to take, at least in the early stages.

It beggars belief that supposedly responsible teachers would let this get so far. Surely too, the deliberate concealing of what is happening from parents and guardians of other children must be extremely concerning when such a large cluster exists. This is not one isolated child being assessed.

Unquestionably, we can expect some serious law suits a few years down the line.

Trans activist Julia Serano has argued that contagion is a concept which is inappropriate to attach to this phenomenon, claiming that it only arose recently through the blogging of anti-trans parents.[17] It may have gained some currency due to their online material, but to suggest that they invented the idea is ludicrous. It seemed obvious to

---

17   https://juliaserano.blogspot.com/2019/02/origins-of-social-contagion-and-rapid.html (2020).

me the first time I came across the cluster, before I researched material on the subject. And more clusters have been quick to emerge, such as the coolest state secondary in town[18] where there is a cluster of forty children claiming not to identify with their birth gender.

Serano also attacks the criticism of Rapid Onset Gender Dysphoria made by these writers, claiming that

'[w]ithin trans health circles, it's been well established that trans people may become gender dysphoric and/or come out about being transgender at any age.'[19]

Coming out is one thing, but becoming gender dysphoric? If one can become gender dysphoric, one can surely unbecome it?

Are we not talking about transitory social developmental problems that young people are having rather than deep-rooted neurological facts?

The Tavistock Institute has been running a clinic for 'transgender' children which has seen something like a fifty-fold increase in referrals over the twelve years to 2018,[20] which has led to some five clinicians resigning over concerns that children were being treated at too young an age, and apparently as many as eighteen staff resigning in the previous three years over related concerns.[21]

The Times of London spoke to these five clinicians, who said that the clinic was risking a 'live experiment' in prescribing life-changing drugs on the basis of insufficient evidence. They said that some gay

18   https://www.theargus.co.uk/news/17255829.dorothy-stringer-school-has-40-children-who-dont-identify-with-their-gender/ (2020).

19   https://medium.com/@juliaserano/everything-you-need-to-know-about-rapid-onset-gender-dysphoria-1940b8afdeba (2020).

20   https://www.medscape.com/viewarticle/911736 (2020).

21   https://www.dailymail.co.uk/news/article-6897269/Workers-transgender-clinic-quit-concerns-unregulated-live-experiments-children.html (2020).

children might be misdiagnosed, raising the concern over what I had seen even for an adult as long ago as 1986.[22]

In early 2019, one of the directors of the Tavistock Foundation resigned over concerns that trans identification in children could often be the result of other conditions such as autism, or a reaction to child abuse.[23] My detransitioned friend had been introduced to gay sex as a minor and I had always wondered how much that had influenced both his gender identity confusion as well as his sexual orientation.

Clearly there are massive issues around this, which cannot be dismissed as mere transphobia as many try to do. This has become nothing more than a weaponised term intended to shut down legitimate examination of what is going on, something we see as endemic in the postmodern academic world. Whether it is intentional, or simply naïve blundering on the part of well-meaning idiots is almost irrelevant. The danger is there, and much damage has already probably been done.

A new balance is needed. A recognition of reality. A map which encompasses a true intersectionality — the intersection of biology, developmental neurology, perception, psychological archetypes and instincts, along with the recognition that we are all expressions of the fractal pattern generation of an actively growing ecosystem that has practised the binary for some billion years or so at the level of the DNA code of life, and is likely to continue to do so well into perpetuity.

Transsexuals will be most successful in their life path and in the expression of their potential if they tap back into a spiritual sense of the archetypes and seek to resonate with it.

But what we see at present is nothing short of a collective psychosis. Irrational ideas unsupported by evidence are being spread on claims of social justice. A small hegemonic class have claimed ownership of

22   https://www.thetimes.co.uk/article/calls-to-end-transgender-experiment-on-children-k792rfj7d (2020).

23   https://www.theguardian.com/society/2019/feb/23/child-transgender-service-governor-quits-chaos (2020).

this and are preventing those in their sphere of influence from challenging these radical social and political ideas, thereby encouraging
the grass roots in what should otherwise be seen as simply the kind
of fashion craze that all children go through at some time, whether it
be conkers or hula hoops or fidget spinners or the latest fashion hair
style.

Instead, children too young to legally smoke are being encouraged
into medical treatment that will have lifelong consequences.

It is perhaps the case that there are some small number of adolescents for whom this might be appropriate; for myself it would have
saved me a lot of physical pain, and lifelong scarring. But I am unwilling to use my own bad experience to promote treatments for minors.
To do so would only be to project my feelings onto a mass of children,
each a unique case, and inevitably some would get drawn in unnecessarily. Until there are reliable diagnostic tools which can assess which
category of gender atypical syndrome the child is experiencing, it is
simply too dangerous to engage in physical treatments.

Research studies vary tremendously in their results for the progress and outcomes with young people who have been identified as
being gender dysphoric or atypical, and this is why we should be cautious. Well-intentioned but naïve concern vultures, such as the staff at
the school of the Daily Mail Seventeen, can too easily push children
in directions that they would not take left to themselves because they
think it is the politically correct way to proceed, or just fail to ensure
the kind of boundaries that adults should.

One very important point which I have never seen raised is
whether children who have been given puberty-delaying hormones
and then receive genital reassignment surgery at an early age are able
to experience full sexual arousal. I think it is entirely possible that
many would not. In which case such children would not only be unable to have children themselves but would not even be able to enjoy
the sexual act. This is surely a matter which must raise concern.

The rush to normalise early treatments seems to be a function of political agendas, agendas which we are being radically discouraged from questioning, and have more to do with creating certain effects on society than with helping adolescents come to terms with their sense of gender identity.

Our Western civilisation is at a crossroads with respect to its understanding of gender.

At one and the same time we are being indoctrinated with ideas of gender deconstruction, which seek to break down all traditional notions of gender and even take down the established paradigm of gender reassignment established over the last seven decades, while we are also finding that there are those who wish to push that paradigm beyond acceptable limits with interventions to children not yet fully competent to make life-changing decisions.

Is it any surprise that socially conservative elements are pushing back on this, attacking the whole concept of transsexualism and transgender, calling all trans women 'men who have cut off their *****'?

I don't like it, but I understand why it is happening. When April Ashley became known in the media, no one was saying that of her. When Caroline Cossey was outed after it became known she was trans and had her sequence trimmed from the Bond movie, no one said 'That's just a bloke', they all went 'Phwoar!' instead. Even Jan Morris, hardly a pin-up girl and transitioning at the end of her thirties after a public male identity, didn't cause too much outcry because of her discreet manners and demure persona.

But now, no one is expected to do anything other than make a claim as to their gender identity and they can gain access to gendered spaces or even demand permanent surgeries, and the world has to concede to them, even if they are still only children.

CHAPTER 17

POLITICAL POLARITIES: THE WEAPONISATION OF GENDER

WILL LEAVE ASIDE the larger political situation in the West as being outside my remit for this book, but the promotion of all varieties of transgenderism, conflating all variant or atypical gender and sexuality types is definitely a tool of the international Left because it fits perfectly with their desire to break down all the institutions of our society in order to be able to manipulate populations who have been deracinated.

This following excerpt[1] details the techniques of Saul Alinsky, author of *Rules for Radicals*[2] and a hardcore Communist.

...The push for homosexuality is also a goal of the communist party. Referring back to Cleon Skousen's "The Naked Communist" and the 45 declared goals-

---

1   https://freedomoutpost.com/alinsky-rules-communist-goals-and-the-silence-of-disapproval/ (2020).

2   Alinsky, Saul. *Rules for Radicals: A Pragmatic Primer for Realistic Radicals.* Random House, 1971 https://archive.org/details/RulesForRadicals/page/n1 (2020).

25. Break down cultural standards of morality by promoting pornography and obscenity in books, magazines, motion pictures, radio and T.V.

26. Present homosexuality, degeneracy and promiscuity as "normal, natural and healthy..."

By today's standards and parlance, Alinsky, darling of the activist far Left, would be considered homophobic (as was Che Guevara, another communist icon) in the way that he associates homosexuality with degeneracy and promiscuity.

I would briefly distinguish between homosexual attractions and behaviour and the culture which is often associated with them. It is not unknown for some socially conservative gay commentators to criticise aspects of popular gay culture as promiscuous and degenerate.

Homosexuality has existed since the beginning of recorded history and there is evidence of it amongst other mammals. Taking a proscriptive attitude to it is counterproductive. However, we must understand that it has been socialised in different ways in different cultures.

What really matters is the manner in which this socialisation takes place. Clearly Alinsky and his cohorts did all that they could to turn homosexual subcultures into the direction of their choice.

This is Cultural Marxism in action. Take something that exists in its own right, but is perhaps somewhat marginal, colonise it, pump it up as something that has been oppressed and victimised and then piggyback your new chaotic agenda on it. It isn't about whether being gay or trans are legitimate psychological tendencies, but rather about exploiting them for their chaos value.

So just as homosexuality has been endlessly promoted in recent times to the point where it is more culturally prominent than the proportion of homosexuals in our society would predict, so it is the case with transgenderism. The BBC has now implemented a goal of increasing the number of LGBT employees to a level way beyond our actual statistical representation[3] in the population, just as it has previously removed some white men from their programming[4] simply for being white men, and has actually posted adverts for jobs which are exclusively for non-whites.[5] In 2018 there were 417 transgender employees at the BBC, four times the proportion in the population. And it wants more. It probably has them by now. I don't suppose they'd offer me a job, with my problematic views! Affirmative Action is being applied and staff are being recruited on the basis of their sexual or gender identity rather than on their job skills.

And not only the BBC is at this; Channel 4 has run several trans-themed programmes, hosted by such well-known leftist and feminist icons as Cathy Newman. It is now almost a weekly, or even daily occurrence to see new discussion programmes on the subject of controversial trans stories in the news. It has become the flavour of the month or even decade for the concern vultures.

The far-left string-pullers aren't interested in helping trans people with their personal choices; we are merely cannon fodder for their agenda. They don't care if pseudo-transsexuals are left as damaged wrecks and the general population turns against us for this collateral damage from their agenda to create chaos and confusion that they can exploit.

It is hard to find figures for the number or percentage of trans people who regret surgeries, but stories emerge, and these could be just the tip of the iceberg. It has been some years now since some regretters and concerned specialists caused a big fuss and as a result standards of treatment should have been tightened up but the opposite seems to have happened in some areas.

---

3   https://www.express.co.uk/news/uk/982116/bbc-transgender-staff-survey-lesbian-gay-bisexual-lgbt-diversity-uk-news (2020).

4   https://www.dailymail.co.uk/news/article-3817609/BBC-sacked-white-man-Radio-4-comic-told-need-women-minorities.html (2020).

5   https://theduran.com/whites-need-not-apply-bbc-still-advertising-positions-exclude-white-people/ (2020).

Dr Russell Reid had for many years been the entry point for many transsexual people into treatment. But after he left the Charing Cross GIC in 1990[6] to go into private practice, it appears that he had perhaps been making referrals for hormones and surgeries a little bit more eagerly than he might have and was found guilty of serious professional misconduct in 2007[7] by the General Medical Council of the UK, only being allowed to return to practice under supervision after a year's suspension. Combine this with a patient who de- and re-transitioned because they regretted and became confused about what they really wanted, and you have a perfect storm. More rigorous standards for access to what is, after all, serious medical treatment would surely have gone a long way to prevent such awful situations and damaged lives.

I recently saw a story on social media in which a young person said that he 'missed his penis'. That is really sad, and clearly he had not had the lifelong sense of bodily dysphoria that actual transsexuals describe, but had somehow been allowed or encouraged to get to the point where he had irreversible surgeries.

This is not a unique situation. A former soldier by the name of Peter Benjamin[8] has recently come forward and admitted his mistake in transitioning and having reassignment surgery. These tragedies occur because no one dares to question or challenge anyone around these issues. When I had to go through a rigorous assessment, I had plenty of time to reconsider and back out. Not so today, apparently it's the modern panacea.

This kind of thing can only produce pushback, and so it should, but it should not end up being about damning trans people who have

---

6   https://www.gendergp.com/trans-healthcare-who-takes-responsibility/ (2021).

7   https://www.theguardian.com/society/2007/may/25/health.medicineand-health2 (2020).

8   https://www.thetimes.co.uk/article/gender-reassignment-im-man-enough-to-admit-that-it-was-a-mistake-g2nn79j9j (2020).

made quiet successful transitions and are now passing in stealth in their new lives, or indeed criticising gay people for their relationships.

Rather it is about the politically motivated exploitation of genuine people who deviate from the statistical norm, but who have no axe to grind on the political front.

We have two factors at work here.

Firstly, the Gender Studies deconstruction has been going on for some three decades now, since Judith Butler published her unreadable treatises:

Gender Trouble: Feminism and the Subversion of Gender Identity[9, 10] (1990) and *Bodies That Matter: On the Discursive Limits of Sex* (1993).

In these she argues for performativity rather than phenotypes as the basis of gender distinctions.

This was the modern starting point for the total deconstruction of traditional concepts of gender and on which all the ideological developments in Queer Theory and so forth rest.

I have heard some say that Butler is a transperson who rather than take the medical route explained her feelings away in terms of language and behaviour. This may or may not be true, but I certainly found that what I managed to read of her work did not explain or even properly describe my own experience.

Other ideologies, such as Foucauldian concepts of power, intersect with this to produce the modern gender fluid or gender non-binary world, which is being inflicted on us in this new millennium as a supposed response to the oppressive standards of patriarchal gender normativity.

The conclusion that many will draw from this is that we are supposed to believe that your gender is pretty much anything you want it to be. I am reminded of Terence Trent D'Arby who, when he was asked

---

9   Judith Butler. *Gender Trouble: Feminism and the Subversion of Gender Identity.* Routledge, 1990.

10 https://selforganizedseminar.files.wordpress.com/2011/07/butler-gender_ trouble.pdf (2020).

by Jools Holland on The Tube in 1987 'What is Art?', replied 'Whatever you can get away with'.

The second factor is like a mutated and weaponised version of the first.

There has been an immense assault by the cultural Left to introduce ever younger children to concepts of atypical sexuality and to question their own gender identity.

Children are being introduced to gender anormativity in kindergarten, being asked to reflect on their gender and whether they are happy with it, even to question it or would they like to be the opposite; in some schools they are being taught about anal sex and child drag queens are being encouraged at Gay Pride parades. Impressionable young minds are being influenced in ways they are not ready to understand, when the example of gender-balanced societies is that children will find their own level in their own time.

All this plays into the sexualisation of children and thus the attendant proclivities of paedophiles.

And as we have seen, gender reassignment treatments are being begun at ever earlier ages and children who are not old enough to make legal decisions are being begun on treatments that could have lifelong impacts and outcomes.

While the Left have done what in my view amounts to promoting mental illness in those who do not actually have full-blown gender dysphoria and Benjamin's transsexual syndrome, there are those on the Right who conflate a wide variety of conditions and disorders under that very same heading of mental illness.

It is not my wish to insult those readers to whom this is no mystery and who understand that these irregularities can occur at different levels within our beings — bodily, neurologically and psychologically. These may interpenetrate in their influence. But I probably have to labour this point a little as there seems to be much confusion about this.

Let me begin with an example of misunderstanding.

Germany recently passed into law that a *third gender* could be adopted onto birth certificates, besides male and female, to cover intersex births. It's not really a third gender, more like an in between, as the prefix *inter-* denotes, but it is reasonable to treat it as such for legal and linguistic purposes.

I saw this posted on social media with the comment attached which asserted that 'Intersex is a mental illness'.

When challenging this with the straightforward fact that *Intersex* is a physical condition, I was hit back with the assertion that there are only two genders (a fact with which I agree) and that they are *solely* determined by having an *x* or *y* chromosome (an assertion with which I do **not** agree). Even should this be the case, it would be illogical to assert that the physical condition of a child when born could in any way be described as a *mental illness.*

Those who hold views such as this are either just ignorant of the material facts of the science, or are so entrenched in their belief system that they don't care about facts.

In some primitive societies, if identified, such children might be stifled at birth or be left to die of exposure; in others, they might be venerated as some kind of avatar or divine being, while in more recent times, attempts were often made to 'correct' the anatomy from a well-intentioned but clumsily effected desire for the child to fit in.

Attitudes and medical policies to intersex changed towards the end of the twentieth century after intersex people got together and argued against early medical interventions. Many were unhappy about what they saw as mutilation and considered that they had been wrongly treated.

The general policy, as I now understand it, is that interventions are only made if medically necessary, such as urethral hypospadias, the malformation of the urethra, which apparently is as common as 1 in 250 for the male population alone, as a form of developmental malformation which would not be so severe as to be considered *intersex.*

So, children are allowed to grow up with their birth anatomy and while they are brought up in what seems the most likely gender role, are not forced if they should behave or choose differently, and are offered plastic reconstruction at puberty if this seems to be the case.

It is well understood that some physical intersex conditions are influenced or caused by hormonal interruptions during pregnancy, as I have previously detailed. Intersex children may not grow up to have the gender identity of their genetic sex, or this may be a mosaic, a mixture, which obviously adds complications.

My own view is that *Intersex*, being a condition of being *between* the sexes (or genders) is not a *third gender* as such, but rather an *Intermediate* condition between those two. The *I* should also be understood to mean *Indeterminate* or *Indistinct* at birth and should not be reified as a third gender. A similar rationale could be applied to those born with *hermaphroditic* conditions, although perhaps they are the only group who really do qualify as a *Third Gender*, containing both within themselves, as compared to those *intersex* who are simply in between them.

In the same time frame as Judith Butler was deconstructing gender socially and behaviourally, researcher Anne Fausto-Sterling[11] suggested that there were actually *five* sexes,[12] including what she called *herms* (true hermaphrodites with both sets of gonads), *merms* who have testes and some feminisation of genitals, and *ferms*, with ovaries and some male characteristics. She later apparently withdrew from this position, saying that it had been somewhat tongue in cheek, but has continued to argue for a spectrum of genders.

I have no problem accepting *sub-genders* within the greater scheme of the binary, as that is how nature works and I develop this a little later, but we should not reify endless subdivisions as separate

---

11   http://www.annefaustosterling.com/fields-of-inquiry/gender/ (2020).

12   Fausto-Sterling, Anne. 'The Five Sexes: Why Male and Female Are Not Enough'. *The Sciences*, March/April 1993, p. 20–24, https://nyaspubs.onlinelibrary.wiley. com/doi/abs/10.1002/j.2326-1951.1993.tb03081.x.

classes in themselves when what we have is an overarching structure into which they fit.

It is only a small step from developmental physiology to developmental neurology.

Let me repeat the syllogism I suggested in the Introduction.

Major Proposition:

Men and women are not only different in the obvious physical characteristics, but in other less obvious ways to do with thought, feeling and behaviour, which are the result of differing developmental pathways *in utero* and childhood, which affect neurological and endocrine development so as to cause these differences.

Minor Proposition:

Sexual differentiation of the nervous system and the genitals *in utero* take place at different stages of pregnancy; the hormones triggering these developments can be interrupted, causing there to be incomplete development of one or both, and thus potentially a mismatch between the brain and the body in one or more of morphological mapping, sexual orientation or emotionality; or in the event of a genetic influence, which inclines the brain to one gendered phenotype or the other.

Ergo: It is at least a logical possibility that some transsexuals have brain-body incongruity.

Having established that this is at least a logical possibility, I argue against the Gender Studies model in that it fails to distinguish between the neurologically influenced transsexual identity and the socially acquired model that they promote, since they deny the existence of the former. Thus, it seems clear to me that they are, if not promoting, at the least failing to critique what is to many mental illness, or at best maladaptive behaviour.

Bearing in mind Dr Milton Diamond's contention that transsexualism will be seen as an intersex variation, there will be those who do not experience full-blown Harry Benjamin's Syndrome (HBS), but at the same time have some atypical feminisation or virilisation of their neurology. Such people are probably mostly gay. If they don't experience what I would call *Ramachandran's Syndrome*, a hardwired internal body map that is contradictory to the physical body, then medical interventions shouldn't be necessary. I would suggest that this is possibly the deciding factor in whether HBS is present and crystallised. This may or may not be fully developed at birth. The neonate's brain is not fully formed at this time, and some functions, such as walking and talking, arise spontaneously as the brain structures responsible develop. This could well be the case with Ramachandran's Syndrome. I think it unlikely that this would be influenced by social factors in early development. If one doesn't feel that sense of bodily disjunction, why would one need to change things? My friend who detransitioned was quite feminine in many ways, but in the end was not at odds with his gendered body. However feminine a man like him might be, would it be appropriate to allow him to use a women's public toilet? I would say not.

We have in recent years expanded our concepts to the degree where homosexuals and lesbians are accepted without needing to revise our judgement as to whether they are male or female; we need to have a broader concept of what it is to be a man or a woman, without at the same time eviscerating their cores.

What the Alinskyite Left has done is to make us think that simply because we need a wider understanding of what can be included in *male* or *female,* we should abandon these concepts entirely and either institute an infinite number of newly invented terms or refuse to engage with any categories at all.

The latest thing as I write is the *Trans Trenders* who have been associated with *Non-Binary,* a concept I addressed earlier. *Trenders* seem to have jumped on the bandwagon for the political fashion statement it embodies, often claiming 'you don't have to have gender dysphoria to be trans', an assertion that many I know would find self-contradictory. While *traps* take *genderf**** to a new level.

My view of this is dismissed as *problematic* in some LGBT circles since they ask why would anyone put themselves through the social ostracism and general difficulties that are associated with gender transition if they didn't really have gender dysphoria?

I would make so bold as to suggest that those who hold such a view are naïve in their assumption. I have known more than one person who transitioned and then de-transitioned when they realised it was not the best path for them. And this was long before it became fashionable. In the present wave of political gender anarchy, which is sweeping academia and the politically correct social Left, an element of *gender norm transgression* is almost becoming *de rigueur*, and there is a competitive angle to this, what is basically adolescent rebellion, in some circles.

It is clear to me, as I have detailed elsewhere, that the promotion of Gender Theory encourages such wrong ideas about gender that there are indeed people who, having problems of their own, see these as answers to those problems, when they are not.

People who would otherwise not even consider their gender are being encouraged to question it and see it as a problem, to decide that they are *non-binary* or *agendered* simply because they don't fit what they consider to be a rigid stereotype of social and behavioural gender.

If they have other problems, it is easy to palm these off on a gender issue and invent an identity as a symbolic or metaphorical outgrowth of this. It is ironic that in modern Western society, which is probably the most liberal that has ever existed, the concepts of male and female are considered oppressive.

Since the 2010 *Equalities Act,* almost anything is possible on the grounds of *equal treatment.* One will not be surprised if *Otherkin* are included in legal identities before long!

In the face of such chaos, it doesn't surprise me that there are those on the conservative end of the political spectrum who think this has all gone too far, and is mental illness. There is certainly irrationality, and some mentally ill people mixed into it all, but it is my conviction that the core feelings of strong gender dysphoria are derived from one's neurological structures and how they have developed, and so cannot be called a *mental illness* since there is no psychodynamic element involved in the originating cause; with the recent evidence that even genetics may be implicated in some ways supporting the notion that this is a far more deeply rooted experience than the superficial social explanations of postmodern gender theorists.

The error that these conservatives make is to conflate all the different taxonomic categories of atypical gender identity under one heading (as does Gender Studies but with a different interpretation) — *Mental Illness* — when they have different aetiologies, some organic, some acquired through social experience, sexual abuse or maladaptation.

I am often quite alarmed at the extreme hostility which seems to be aroused in those projecting their own interpretations.

One claim which deserves singling out is the assertion that this must be a mental illness because it is, to quote the words of one critic, *extreme and dysfunctional*. These people rarely seem to have a basis in logic or reason, for the most superficial consideration will reveal that for a behaviour to be extreme is no cause for it to be considered *mentally ill*.

Some may consider mountain climbing a little mad, and there are many other more extreme sports these days for the thrill-seeking adrenaline junkie, but no one says that engaging in them is a sign of mental illness. Perhaps if someone repeatedly received injuries from these activities we might consider them a danger to themselves or others, but the simple action of participating cannot be defined as mental illness.

Similarly, this critic was making assumptions about what is dysfunctional. He merely thinks that seeking gender reassignment is dysfunctional, without understanding that the individual is seeking a better function than they already have. Being a transsexual is not the most optimal evolutionary adaptation, but successfully transitioning is less dysfunctional than committing suicide in despair or mutilating oneself, so long as one genuinely fits the profile.

The Catch-22 for both sides of this debate, the pothole into which they both stumble, but from different sides, is that there *must* be a difference between male and female neurologies to account for the differences in behaviour that we see in all mammalian species, and to assert that the most differentiated nervous system of all mammals, that of humans, is not differentiated at all, is absurd.

The sociological understanding of gender imagines that the entire brain is a blank slate, that everything is learned, and that there are no pre-sets or innate tropisms. I would say in the past to students of Gender Studies that I couldn't believe that after a billion years or so of the sexual reproduction of life on our planet, organisms wouldn't have developed some internal mechanisms of gendered behaviour, and sense of what they were.

But it is only in humans that we see serious confusion. Granted, homosexuality is observed in animals under certain conditions, and inner transsexual/cross-sex neurology would probably largely display as such if and when it occurs. The actual confusion that is experienced arises, I believe, from two main factors.

Firstly, through the highly elaborated nervous system with which humans are endowed we are able to explore our own inner worlds in conscious self-reflection and analysis, which we believe is not developed in such a way in other species, even primates, such that we can *interpret* our inner world, *construe* it, make some sense of why it is that we have these persistent feelings, these inner images that haunt us, like hunger or thirst.

Secondly, this has led us to evolve the capacity to have abstract thoughts and ideas detached from our physical experience, and it is due to this that we have been able to consider ourselves in such ways and construe our self-gestalt. And it is the nature of humans to solve problems, to apply solutions to problems; thus the medical *construc-tion* that the radical trans activists complain about is only a means of *techne* to solve that problem if no other means can be found.

So, it is possible to have such thoughts in a mistaken way or for them to be reflections of the emergent material of our unconscious minds deriving from our organic nature. To what extent is the self-perception veridical? Does it have some probabilistic functionality? On what is it based?

For example, I tell my gay friend who detransitioned as an instance of mistaken understanding, but which was corrected either through reason or from urgent messages erupting from his unconscious that this was not what it wanted, that he had misinterpreted its earlier signals and he should reconsider. While in my own case it seems to me likely that at that early stage, when I had only an embryonic sense of myself, I recognised an image from my unconscious in the external perception of our neighbour's daughter.

A hostile critic once claimed that my story could be one of some type of imprinting, but he didn't give any sufficient reason why this should happen. Probably the most common reaction amongst most little boys would be to notice that he had something she did not and be pleased with it. Sometimes young boys will be frightened or upset when they see a girl naked for the first time because her shape seems unfamiliar or mutilated. There is little anecdotal evidence or otherwise for little boys suddenly and irreversibly acquiring a lifelong and irreversible self-image without any other contributory cause than simple imprinting as happens say with ducks when they hatch. And of course, while this may have been at a young age, I was well past being a neonate when such imprinting might be likely.

The regressive ultra-Right and the authoritarian Radical Feminists, such as Janice Raymond, would seek to abolish transsexualism: to 'morally mandate it out of existence'. I have had Tweets addressed to me in which outspoken rightists declared that while they realise that people with gender issues may not be to blame for their conditions, that they should nonetheless be suppressed for the good of society.

I shall call this gentleman *PalaeoHominid* since his attitudes are prehistoric.

This is to go way beyond the social conservatism of hegemonic heteronormative gender values, and to regress to a time when attic children were kept hidden in lofts as if they were *The Picture of Dorian Gray.*

It is one thing to reject the reversal of values in which minorities are given privilege and dominion while the majority are *accused* of it because of their numerical position, but it is another to go so far that those minorities should be made to not exist.

What would that mean?

Probably a lot more than suspension of medical support systems for trans people. Surely it would involve some sort of persecution, because there is an existing population who are not going to vanish overnight. And many of us are stealth. How would they deal with that?

Not to mention, of course, that this is now a worldwide phenomenon, a convergent evolution of *techne* which seems to respond to the needs of a certain particular element in society.

Searching down people from ancient medical records or rescinding legal recognition (the 2004 Act is greatly flawed, but is not entirely without merit, and while needing amendment should not simply be abolished) would be reminiscent of Soviet regimes and is an utterly abhorrent notion. Meanwhile the West is embedded with tens of thousands of jihadist sleeper cells, which are surely a higher priority than gender nonconformists.

The practical implications of such a repressive ideology would be extensive.

I would refer back to Lynn Conway's foundational paper on *Prevalence.* We exist, and in fairly large numbers, but thinly dispersed throughout the population and only as a very small percentage of that entire population. Many of us live in *stealth* or something closely approximating it, and cause little or no social friction, while contributing more to society than we would have done had we remained in our previous conflicted state.

On the other hand, there are those who make a show of being visible, of saying that they don't mind the obvious markers of their abandoned gender and promote postmodern notions of gender deconstruction; some might be called *trans trenders* rather than actual transsexuals.

And there are those who regret and detransition, who don't fit either group.

While the Left seeks to falsely conflate these and other categories under one category (so as to exploit them for their own purposes), the Right falls into this trap and believes that it is so, and then carries on to see us all as mentally ill or even agents of the *progressive Left* who want to level our entire society and remove all differences.

My correspondent on Twitter, *PalaeoHominid,* expressed a fear of *dicks under dresses.* His aversion is such that he doesn't even want to know that in many cases that wouldn't be the case, and that often he wouldn't even know if someone was transsexual.

His reply was that our invisibility was something that he also found disturbing. Basically, he doesn't want us to exist and wishes that we could be suppressed for the good of society, indeed thinks that we *should be suppressed.*

This response is actually almost the same as that of the so-called *triggered snowflake,* who seeks their *safe space* because they have encountered something that is outside of their expectation system. Or the *Radical Feminist,* who seeks to deny us the rights to treatment or self-presentation as we see fit. One may allow them their space for their future shock reaction, but to take a permanent posture of resistance to our existence is mere denial of reality.

The Universe is not only stranger than we imagine, but stranger than we *can* imagine.

To suppress or prohibit transsexuals would be impossible in the modern world.

One may be able to hold the line against new understandings of reality for a while, but it is better to engage with those realities in order to be a contributor to their understanding. Ideas should compete on their value, their *probabilistic functionality*. Ultimately, we should be concerned with *what works*.

My Palaeolithic Twitter correspondent simply could not get his head round our existence; he thinks we are all just the same as the *trans trenders* who don't mind their visible markers, who flaunt them, who say that they are *happy with their female penis* and do their best to be *genderqueer* and engage in *genderf****.

I would argue that he doesn't need to get his head round our existence, for numerous reasons. Or at least not the existence of folk like myself. For instance, we are not trying to impact on him or change his life in any way. For another, there are many obscure and occult aspects of reality which none of us understand and yet we don't spend time endlessly puzzling over them, thinking that they shouldn't exist because they don't fit our model of reality (unless perhaps we are quantum physicists).

It is this endless conflation of different groups that *both* sides engage in which is the downfall of their approaches.

He has bought the postmodern propaganda and imagines that we are what *they* say we are, and what the *trans trenders, gender queer activists* and *fashion icons* have turned this thing into in the popular imagination. He is concerned about those who are in his face as it were, and I don't blame that, it is rather understandable. But to be labelled as if we were all the same is mistaken.

It is well known that if you say a lie often enough, people may start to believe it is the truth.

The capstone on Mr Hominid's failed approach to this was his refusal to engage in any discussion beyond a very few exchanges on Twitter, a format extremely limited and not given to subtlety. Indeed, he said that he was tired of nuance and that this was a subject on which he sought clear lines. I understand, for that is a part of perception, the desire for the absence of ambiguity, but I shall shortly explore how smooth and sharp boundary conditions are hard to find in nature.

Refusal may have a place in certain circumstances, but in this instance it has more in common with that of Judith Halberstam discussed above in the chapter on Gender Studies than with a legal case where a retrial is refused because of a lack of new evidence. I offer plenty of evidence, which I am fairly certain is new to him and many others (although much of it has been around for decades), but his refusal is made on the grounds of this evidence being perceived as a threat to his worldview.

Confident thinkers do not behave like this; it is the defensive posture of one who can see that their position is untenable, and who thus takes the advice of Sun Tzu and avoids engagement because they know they cannot win.

I had done this myself in resiling from my proposed entry into the Department of Gender Studies, but in that case it had been the entire edifice of the Department, its staff, the course curriculum, the prevailing hegemonic ideology and not least my prospective fellow students, with which I had felt unable to engage in battle singlehandedly; so I had gone away to consider how I might fight my corner, which I now return to do. On the other hand, my more recent opponent had shied away after a few short sentences.

I should say that we, as transsexuals simply trying to find a more tolerable relation with our own bodies, seeking to find a way of being which fits more comfortably with the society in which we find ourselves, should not be persecuted simply for having atypical feelings about our bodies. It is how we actualise those feelings in our lives and in the world that is the standard by which we should be judged.

To be made into weapons for the Alinskyite Left, which then leads to our demonisation by the Right, will not do. We are people, not political projectiles.

CHAPTER 18

SOCIAL ENTRAINMENT OF GENDER

I AM CONCERNED THAT most commentary which I read on the current development of ideas around gender and transsexual issues seems to come from young people. As I have advanced in years I have come to see how poor my understanding of the world was when I was younger. Young people's political and ethical ideas are often highly coloured by a lack of personal development or maturity, while at the same time being much more prone to influence from group attitudes rather than by thinking independently.

Older, more mature people of the transsexual experience seem to take a back seat and rarely contribute to the fray. 'The current fashion sets the pace, lose your step, fall out of grace', as John Perry Barlow once said.[1] And it's true.

But I'm used to being sharply out of step with the rank and file and I'm not afraid to fight my corner, now and on my own terms, rather than in the conceptual prison which would have been provided by the Leeds University Centre for Interdisciplinary Gender Studies.

Strong gender dysphoria is not simply a phenomenon caused by inadequate social role models in which to find a place. It is a psychic

---

1   Barlow, J. P. and Weir, R. *Throwing Stones* (1982).

phenomenon deeply rooted through innate neurology to instinc-tual patterns of perceptual functioning and archetypal forces which in themselves are expressions of the cosmic or divine forces that sustain and drive our existence.

Heidegger raised the point that technology changes our view of the world; it extends our influence and allows things to come about which were not possible before.

Like everything, this can be good or bad.

We can use the technology to alleviate distress and assist func-tional integration, or we can use it to create a transhumanist future like that envisioned by C. S. Lewis in his *The Abolition of Man*, which I will come to later.

I have placed myself against that school which claims that *Gender is **merely** a social construct*, but its *expression* clearly does have some influence from culture and society.

How to arrange the relationship between these two so as to be most functional is surely the challenge which we face.

Nature provides us with our starting point as always, despite those feminists reviewed by Diane Elam in her *Feminism and Deconstruction: Ms En Abyme*[2] who argue that recourse to Nature only leads to an infinite regress. But this is a regress into forces which are beyond social influence, eternal, and thus finds causes and roots of the society which Feminism critiques in a different category of things, which is surely one way of understanding what science does. Explain things, not just complain about things.

Once we are able to explain why things are the way they are from the point of view of Nature, not just to look at our society, decide what you don't like and seek to replace the whole thing lock, stock and bar-rel according to some idealised template that has never been properly tested, then we are in a better position to know how to improve upon it.

---

2   Elam, Diane. *Feminism and Deconstruction: Ms En Abyme.* Routledge (1994).

This will be most effective if it draws out existing patterns and tendencies.

We are presently in the throes of a revolution in ideas about sex and gender, which are entirely different to what has been accepted almost universally throughout the history of mankind. In fact, they are almost entirely *opposite* to those conventional and traditional concepts.

The deconstruction of gender leaves nothing behind but arbitrary social constructs, which have little or no basis in Nature.

It also combines with Intersectional Feminism to fragment society into warring factions worse than the old class system ever did.

Anomalies exist, but they should not dominate the majority. The social system of a society should be geared towards the survival of that majority, whilst at the same time allowing the presence of anomalous minorities which have arisen endogenously, so long as they do not threaten or destabilise that system.

As diversity increases in all dimensions and demographics, this becomes an ever more fraught balance to achieve. It is not only gender anomalous populations who are seeking space, but other populations who would oppose their very existence.

These conflicts and confusions will not go away unless we take a position that can survive the turmoil and overcome. That position must be based on natural reality, while allowing freedom of expression within that framework.

Presently, there is a cultural trend towards absolute *diversity of genders* but these do not have survival adaptive niches and are mere self-applied labels that do not connect with external factors the way that *synthetic a priori* understanding does.

Children are very flexible, and even throughout our lives we can remain *neuroplastic* to some degree. But however you may train a tree, an oak remains an oak, and a willow a willow.

Gender role modelling is decried as *stereotyping* and *oppressive* but this is to presuppose a kind of *Noble Savage* concept of development in which all enculturation is declared to be evil. This is in denial of the fact that social reinforcement of natural tendencies was survival adaptive in a world before contraception and white goods; and while their arrival may have opened up possibilities and opportunities for women in those societies where such things can be afforded, it takes a lot longer than a couple of generations for the deeper adaptive tendencies and tropisms to be bred out of our biological drives.

Should such a view be conceded, we are left with a world in which there is nothing but raw power. This appears to be the Foucauldian deconstruction.

Certainly, there is always power, but it does not always have to be despotic, selfish and tyrannical. A stable and cohesive society may have benefits that spread beyond the dominant elite, such as protection from outside predation, economic development and so on. All, or at least most, can benefit.

The French philosopher and feminist Simone de Beauvoir said, 'One is not born, but rather becomes a woman.' This is presumably intended to mean that women, or rather *females*, are entrained into their roles and identities by outside forces, presumably men. But more importantly, it implies that these roles are entirely artificial, arbitrary, and thus, dare I say, *oppressive*, rather than arising out of natural conditions that are merely modulated and adapted to some degree by circumstances.

She was highly influenced by her rigid Catholic upbringing, but she generalised her experience to the whole world. Part of her reaction to this was to criticise monogamy, failing to accept that stable relationships with men who are the father of their children is usually the best way to live if the opportunity is available, dividing the labour according to the available skills. Not all fathers and husbands are abusive controllers.

She seems to have suffered from boundless *ennui* and offers little in the way of resolving the problems she claims to identify, other than the kind of *brotherhood* (interesting use of the word) promised by the

Soviets but never delivered. The absolute failure of Communism must bear on her ambition to some degree. You cannot implement a system that is built on false premises. You cannot force *equality* in a world where people are different.

This claim of hers may be taken with her contention that the human standard is seen as male and that when women act in larger society they are seen as imitating men. The advent of labour-saving devices in the home, birth control and the proliferation of employment in service industries in the West has led to an explosion of opportunities for women no longer chained to the drudgery of housekeeping but these very recent developments have not changed the nature of women any more than heavy machinery has changed the nature of men. They have merely demonstrated that the human species is very adaptable, able to generalise skills that had once been the exclusive territory of one or other gender. But we still see a massive preponderance of men in construction, sanitation and the more dangerous, dirty employment, while women are dominant in teaching, healthcare and professions which involve a lot of human interaction. Which conforms to the expectations that one has from the neonate studies, showing male children more interested in objects and females in people.

The structuring of society and its propagation through the principles on which it is founded will determine the efficacy of its survival adaptation. Men and women should not compete *against* each other, but should compete against members of their own groups for the best of the opposite group, in order to then co-operate in mating. This is what happens in nature, and what has happened throughout human history. Feminists like de Beauvoir detach themselves from our historical origins and posit male and female as *tabulae rasae* in all but brute strength and reproductive capacities, which is applied oppressively by males to mould females to their wishes. Apparently, in this vision females have no agency or interests of their own. One may read the interpretation that the mere possession of the ability to bear children is *oppressive*, while some of us might consider it a great gift. Obviously, different conditions impose different limitations, but men have their own burdens to bear, and the wear and tear they experience leads to an earlier grave statistically speaking.

We should bear in mind that the social mores of the modern West are extremely new and are quite localised.

In those societies which have more rigid gender expectations, these expectations have arisen out of past survival choices, however much we might think of them now as versions cramped and distorted by religious or social dogma, or having gone down a destructive path.

Even today, there are many cultures where it is necessary for men to protect their women (from other men mostly). In evolutionary time, this was an acquired necessity, and is represented in countless myths and fairy tales

Cultures and civilisations vary, but the archetypal foundations of those which succeed and prosper are not mere chance happenstance or nothing more than brute power, as the postmodernists might suggest.

For instance, despite various interruptions due to climate disasters and migratory invasions, the civilisation of ancient Egypt lasted some three thousand years or so. It had an archetypal religious belief system which was based on masculine and feminine divine principles, and although there were one or two possibly trans pharaohs in that im-mensely long period of time, this did nothing to change their cosmo-logical structure. Trans or gender-changing gods, such as Loki, occur in some pantheons, but are *Trickster* gods, indicating indeterminacy, uncertainty. The twilight zone. In some cultures, hermaphrodites and transsexuals are regarded as shamanic beings of another world.

I believe we should critique why it is that a civilisation that had supposedly *stereotyped* and *oppressive* gender role models could have been so successful as the Egyptians to survive for so long and create such lasting monuments, while our own present culture has only presented its modern ideas on the subject for a few decades, but is considered to be at a higher level of understanding.

Feminism has claimed the term *toxic masculinity* recently, which it has then gone on to apply to all forms of male behaviour. But when we examine the strands of male culture running through history, we see again and again the entrainment of masculine energy to deeds which would often have been impossible to women, or at least to which women would not be inclined to give their energies. And the reverse is true. This is not oppression but simple survival adaptation and specialisation.

Cultures need to promote aspects of themselves which enable survival adaptation, and the most effective way to do this is to capitalise on its assets. You do not send young girls into battle if you have strong young men who can do the job. Evolutionary adaptation determines that the sex which bears the young will be the most efficient in caring for them sensitively and have adapted a psychology to manage hearth and home. Hestia, the Goddess of the Hearth, was female, or rather a feminine deity and archetype. Men are physically adapted to the hunt and the more robust psychology needed for that. Of course, as always, these are statistical statements. But *Phenotype is Archetype*.

Our societies are no longer dominated by agriculture and martial tradition in the way that they used to be; however, they should have values which are able to employ and adapt those drives and skills for which our ancestors were selected by their survival over hundreds of thousands of years.

Social entrainment has created a politically correct culture, in which men are prevented from properly expressing their natural drives. Gender Studies preaches that these are bad, and promotes a *gender fluid* world, in which transgenderism is seen as just another option, and anyone can be anything, regardless of its suitability or appropriateness.

It was my sense of wanting to fit into a gender normative structure that drove me. I never sought to deconstruct that normative structure, and it is now clear to me that it is in large part responsible for the success of Western civilisation, while its destruction seems to be leading to its decline, not least in the important dimension of birthrates, in the face of alien cultures, which nonetheless have maintained some tether to Nature, while ours is rapidly drifting off into the ionosphere.

CHAPTER 19

PROBLEMATICS...

THERE ARE ASPECTS TO this that have come up while researching and writing this book which I did not like at first but have been forced to accept. For instance, that there are trans people who have sufficiently transformed themselves through hormones, hair removal and facial feminisation surgeries that they are completely able to pass as women but have no intention of becoming genitally congruent as female.

Realising from the Lynn Conway evidence that there were not just a few people like this, but a fair number, has been something of a challenge for me in developing my approach.

But far more problematic in the greater scheme is surely the prospect that people who *have not* gone to these or any other serious lengths to make themselves pass as women are now demanding to be allowed to use women's toilet facilities and other spaces.

A man who described himself as 'trans feminine' recently caused uproar in a women's changing room at a Top Shop clothing store. The picture I saw showed him as physically quite masculine with strong facial and body hair showing.

If such occurrences can become acceptable and widespread, the entire concept of even social gender will become meaningless.

In fact, perhaps it already has. I have just seen a news item on how trans women are to be sent appointments for cervical screening so as not to 'offend' them. I myself had such an appointment sent to me accidentally some years ago, simply because I had reached the age where such things are routine health checks for women, and my GP had forgotten to opt me out of the automatic list processing. I immediately called the clinic to explain that I wouldn't need this check-up, and why, requesting that I be removed from their lists so as not to waste the time and resources of the Health Service in future. This was a few years before the current craze set in, and I had merely slipped through the system because there were so few trans women around that no administrative option to exclude us from this had been set up.

As usual, postmodernism reverses normal reality. Instead of the trans person opting herself out for practical reasons, the NHS administration is expected to include people who would never, *could* never, need this examination or any treatment of this kind, in order to avoid *offending* them.

Some years ago, I had an ultrasound examination for a problem I was having with a hip joint. The radiologist said, 'I can't find your uterus but you don't have an hysterectomy scar.' To which I replied that I had previously had gender reassignment and I had neglected to mention it simply because it hadn't occurred to me to do so, presuming it not to be relevant to the examination. Her response was, 'No one tells us anything!', in a joking kind of way — a perfectly reasonable response from someone who needs to know practical details. I certainly didn't find it *offensive*! Today, she might feel inhibited from even mentioning her technical observations in the examination for fear of the potential reprisals if she suspected the person might be trans.

One can't help suspecting that many of those *declaring* their gender without actually having had any medical reassignment treatment would be at the front of the queue for their imaginary cervical screening examinations. I'm reminded of my former client who had apparently falsely told the radical feminists that her surgeon had found female internal reproductive organs when operating on her in order to gain entry to their circle.

There was recently the almost incredible story of how a woman admitted to hospital in the UK had asked to be examined by a female doctor. When a doctor who was obviously male in appearance came into the examination room, the patient complained. Fortunately, the hospital administration apologised to the patient, because if they hadn't, but had chosen to take a different route, they apparently could have legally sued the female patient for *transphobic* behaviour under the Equalities Act, since apparently this male-appearing doctor was claiming female identity under the conditions of that law, despite as yet having had no treatment that was visible in his appearance nor was there any apparent change in his dress presentation or behavioural manner! Perhaps this doctor had heard about the case of the other doctor[1] who was fired for refusing to (even hypothetically) refer to an apparent bearded man as *she* and decided to exploit the entry point.

I purposely do not give the reference to this case so as to avoid possible legal repercussions myself as I don't wish to be prosecuted for failing to respect the declared gender of the doctor in question. Surely someone in a position of responsibility, such as a doctor, should be expected to present in as congruent a manner as possible and not claim to be something that on first impression they are not? Or am I alone on an island adrift in the past?

However, with the sudden (and to my mind suspicious) rise in both the presence of and publicity about trans people, we have to address issues such as this, and we shouldn't let our common sense be abducted by the fear of causing 'offence'. Dr Jordan Peterson managed to bring Channel 4 News presenter Cathy Newman to a condition of speechlessness when he made the, to my mind obvious, statement that we should not censor ourselves for fear of causing offence in response to her asking why his right to 'cause offence' should outweigh the 'right' of a trans person not to be offended; which he supported by saying that he was himself being put in an uncomfortable position

---

1   https://www.conservativewoman.co.uk/the-transgender-faith-beats-christianity-and-common-sense/(2020).

where his interviewer was being slightly offensive in her challenging of his position about trans pronouns, and that such challenging could be a good thing. How else can we find truth if we don't challenge and test assertions? The *right not to be offended* is an invention of the post-modern Left, although they seem to think it is fine to offend anyone who holds conventional views — which is likely to be the majority of the population.

When Lily Madigan took issue with my views again on a YouTube vlog,[2] in which I expressed the opinion that people will find that they are accepted in society much better if they are more gender congruent, she complained of my *beauty standards*. However, while this is about appearance, it is not about *beauty*, although it is about *standards*.

Back in the days when this first drew media attention with the likes of Christine Jorgensen and April Ashley in the fifties and sixties and up to and beyond Jan Morris and Caroline Cossey in the seventies and eighties, there was the implicit understanding that one had to *pass* as a woman to be accepted as one.

This was not some bigoted, transphobic prejudice; it was simply the way people have always taken gender to be at an archetypal level of perception. The journalist Mark Steyn expressed this understanding in an address he made in late 2017, seeming to allow that in the past transsexuals who had transitioned and passed as women (few really seem to care about whether men are offended at FtM transsexuals who pass as men and enter their space so long as they do not show themselves fully naked) were accepted because they passed and they fitted into society; but now he was baffled because none of that seemed to hold anymore. And I'm inclined to agree with him. The current craze for deconstruction by Gender Studies is by no means what I signed up for, and trans people who flaunt their status contradict the very starting point of what this is all about for those of us in my particular group.

---

2   'Justine Greening/Tories "Gender Declaration"' Proposal, https://www.you-tube.com/watch?v=ymXwDN_WH1o (2020).

Transitioning should be, I believe, about sufficiently expressing the archetype of the gender one feels oneself to be through physical appearance, clothing, manners and presentation in the context of the culture in which one finds oneself that one is accepted as such. It should not be about trying to change the assumptions of society about these things in order to minimise, or even avoid, making any changes in one's own presentation, while demanding special legal protection for one's unsupported claims.

Perhaps the most troubling and problematic development arising as I am finalising this book is the presence of physically intact male-bodied prisoners being allowed into female prisons and who have engaged in rape of their fellow prisoners. Even some as notorious as actual rapists have claimed to be transgender, presumably in anticipation that under the 2010 Act they will be allowed to be placed in female prisons.

There can be little doubt in the minds of most people that these are scams, but the consequences of these instances are already becoming apparent. For example, internet commentator Carl Benjamin (Sargon of Akkad), who used to take a laissez-faire attitude to trans people, has now moved to a position in which he argues that trans women who still have intact male anatomy and have been given a custodial sentence should be placed in special *Trans Units* so as to protect women prisoners. (Fortunately, he has also begun to distinguish those trans women who have completed a medical transition from those who have not even yet begun it.)

This is the kind of pushback which is entirely to be expected. As the deconstruction of gender pushes forwards apace, anyone who is seen to fit into this *open-ended category without a core* will be associated in the mind of the populace with rapists and child murderers, due to this rampant abuse of political correctness and the 2010 Equalities Act.

Technically speaking, a trans woman who has successfully completed her medical transition and received a GRC and who has been handed down a custodial sentence should be placed in a women's prison. However, if the moral panic goes too far, even those who have only been convicted of white-collar crimes and have no record of sexual offences could now be put in danger of being placed in men's prisons, where they would surely be at risk of being sexually assaulted themselves, if the knee-jerk response to the scammers is not moderated.

In 2004, David Lammy, MP, claimed in the House of Commons that it was wrong to suggest that trans people would abuse their legal position should they gain a GRC without having completed a medical transition. And yet now, due to the excesses of the 2010 Act, not only are such people protected, but even those who have never spoken to a psychotherapist or counsellor about their sense of gender identity, let alone completed medical reassignment.

I was very relieved that the case of Freddy McConnell, a transman who gave birth but wanted to be known as the 'father', was rejected by the High Court in 2020.[3] He had Gender Recognition as a man but had suspended hormones in order to become pregnant. Presumably, fertilisation with sperm from a male was required for this, and bearing a child is the function of a mother. A child deserves both a mother and a father. To bring the child up with two legal fathers and no mother is an absurdity, but the leftist media was outraged at this recourse to biological precedent. Renee Richards, on the other hand, the transsexual tennis star, had famously not objected to her son calling her 'Dad' after her transition. We must respect that there are others involved in this with whom we have immutable biological relations.

One of the latest developments is for cross-gender *identifying* people (obviously all male-bodied) to take part in sports events of their *self-identified gender* rather than of their physical birth sex. A number of such athletes who have now been participating in this way have won due to the mechanical advantage of their virilised physiques

---

3   https://www.theguardian.com/society/2020/nov/16/trans-man-loses-uk-legal-battle-to-register-as-his-childs-father (2020).

and this has led to some complaints by female contenders. These are not medically reassigned MtF transsexuals, like Richards, who have been considered borderline in the past due to no longer having the boost of male hormone, but fully male-bodied people who simply declare themselves to be female by taking oestrogen. We appear to have reached *peak insanity* at the same moment as *peak trans*.

People become uneasy and confused when there are no clear boundaries in a field, especially one which is quite novel and where unconventional behaviours are being displayed. This is one where, it seems to me, liberties are being taken under the guise of being in a *Protected Group*. To have a protected status is the very definition of *Privilege*, a term which is usually negatively applied to *heteronormative males*, but now is turned around and given to anyone who doesn't wish to be part of a normative reality. Classic Alinskyite divide and conquer, aimed at those souls who are in the vast majority in our world, whose simple view of gender is the target that has to be deconstructed and destroyed.

It is not my place here to define precisely the parameters and details of exactly how society may recognise a person's gender, their rights and obligations as such, both legally and socially, but only to clear the ground in order that gender itself may be recognised as an objective principle underlying our lives, how we express ourselves, and how we are perceived.

CHAPTER 20

WHAT ARE WE?

THERE IS MUCH HEAT generated as to whether transsexuals are *real* women or men on both sides of the aisle and the different threads in this need to be teased out.

The LGBT lobby has, on the one hand, become so *progressive* that it is becoming common to argue that merely a claim that one has some subjective sense of being of a different gender is enough to qualify one for all the rights and privileges of that gender; that conventional notions of gender are oppressive and must be deconstructed, even destroyed for the sake of social justice, so that we can all express ourselves without constraint. Even that we should be empowered to create entirely new, previously unimagined genders for ourselves with specific names and novel gender pronouns that we can demand people apply to us on pain of criminal prosecution should they be unwilling to do so.

Not only are there those who wish to dissolve all gender and attempt to universalise the trans phenomenon, there are, on the other hand, those who want to deny the existence of trans altogether, to put us all back in the box, since some social conservatives argue that gender is absolutely fixed in our genes and cannot change under any circumstances.

Here we go from one extreme to the other.

It is part of the greater battle of our time which is being fought over who should determine reality, the postmodernists who believe in nothing but raw power and subjectivism, the palaeo-conservatives who fear anything new or those of us who yearn to restore some balance and objectivity into our shared reality.

This is the central axis on which the purpose of this book pivots.

Is there any reality to the concept of gender in terms of some form of anchor in the world, or is it merely a subjective assertion that anyone can make, and which requires no objective evidence? Or if it does exist, should it be destroyed because it is oppressive?

Reality is guided by universal principles, but they are often imperfectly translated into the world of manifestation, and it is the imperfection of our world which is the ontological basis of my own understanding of the trans phenomenon.

I have had a number of online discussions in which I have found my antagonists seeking to too narrowly explain the phenomenon of transsexualism. But I do understand that it is a challenging phenomenon at first, and that is why I disagree with the aggressive approach of the LGBT lobby in seeking to guilt trip everyone who has any reservations with accusations of *transphobia*.

But at the same time, the conservatives need to understand that this *is* a real phenomenon, although they have my sympathy in their response to the ultra-liberal LGBTIQXYZ lobby; however, to refuse to allow any accommodations is unrealistic, in view of the mass of data such as the Conway statistics and the material evidence which has begun to accrue.

The Pope's recent educational document *Male and Female He created them*[1] has signally failed to grasp the most basic of nuance and distinctions in this, attacking *Gender Theory* legitimately because of the way it presents male and female 'as merely the product of historical and cultural conditioning' (Introduction para 1) and 'denies

---

1   https://thepopespeaks.org/male-and-female-he-created-them/ (2020).

the difference and reciprocity in nature of a man and a woman and envisages a society without sexual differences, thereby eliminating the anthropological basis of the family' (Introduction para 2), with which I have no problem, but then fails to understand that transsexualism has almost nothing to do with *Gender Theory* and everything to do with developmental neurology. An office that has nearly unlimited resources seems to lack the basic will to even research intersex conditions.

'Efforts to go beyond the constitutive male-female sexual difference, such as the ideas of "intersex" or "transgender", lead to a masculinity or femininity that is ambiguous, even though (in a self-contradictory way), these concepts themselves actually presuppose the very sexual difference that they propose to negate or supersede.' (Reasoning: Rational Arguments point 2)[2]

This demonstrates the same kind of ignorance displayed by my social media contact who thought that intersex was a mental illness. And to conceptually conflate intersex with transgender, while making no mention of the term transsexual in the entire piece, shows their absence of familiarity with the field. It is almost humorous that a document aimed at *education* should include such uninformed ignorance. Although, ironically, they do reach some truth with remarks that 'these concepts themselves actually presuppose the very sexual difference that they propose to negate or supersede'.

Where I would seek to balance between the two is as follows.

The position of the far Left with regard to absolute self-definition is ultimately untenable since it leads to an inevitable and complete dissociation between the archetypal functions of the sexes and their characteristic genders, while that of the ultra-conservative wing fails because it insists on ignoring facts of objective and logical variation.

The LGBT lobby must accept that there are objective distinctions in the world, that evolutionary psychology plays a part in this, that it

---

2   Ibid.

is not all arbitrary social constructions, that there is a law-driven reality of which we are part, but which we can probably never completely describe and that there are pragmatic means whereby our survival has been secured through adaptation.

The views of the traditionalists are based in history and what has worked in the past, but often refuse to acknowledge or integrate challenging new phenomena or data. There may be various reasons for this, which we shall explore. But to simply ignore the evidence will not do.

I would propose that we do employ objectively determined categories, in defiance of the postmodernists, but that also we allow for the existence of anomalies. The world of manifestation is, as I have suggested above, imperfect.

A further point to add to this is that in the sense of Heidegger's *Being in Time* and of *techne*, now that scientific investigation and medical intervention into the phenomenon has taken place, and many thousands have pursued the medical *techne* to modify their bodies and their lives, who are we to say that in itself this is wrong?

This is not to say, I must hasten to add, that we should rush to the usage of such medical technologies at the first impulse, but merely to acknowledge that those who seek to reduce the experience of stress in their lives through this path have the right to try it. As Hippocrates, the Father of Medicine said, 'Extreme diseases may require extreme remedies', an earlier form of Guy Fawkes' 'a desperate disease requires a dangerous remedy'.

The further purpose of this work, after establishing parameters for the understanding of the nature of gender, is to seek to deter and prevent those who would redefine their gender on a whim, influenced by the current craze for transgenderism, which seems to be sweeping the West these days, the seeming *trans trenders* who apparently have no physical gender dysphoria, but nonetheless claim to be *transgender*. That craze is affecting not only the lives of the individuals who are obsessed with it but is an attack on the very basis of our society and the way ordinary people think of themselves: The War on Gender.

There are endless clamouring voices claiming to know the causes, why it should be encouraged at the earliest of ages, why it is morally wrong, why it should not be allowed under any circumstances, why all claims to be transgender should be respected and not questioned, why those who experience these feelings should be subjected to medical and psychological treatments to cure them of their preoccupations, why it is a delusion caused by trauma at the earliest stages of life, why it is an innate condition, why it is a sexual perversion, why most of those who experience it grow out of it, why there is a high or low suicide rate amongst pre- or non-transitioned transsexuals, why there is a higher or lower suicide rate amongst post-transitioned and post-operative transsexuals and so on and so forth.

We have the two sides of this reality.

The biological construction of our material beings, and the archetypal construction of our psyches, both of which must find ways of interfacing.

It is a postulate held by the Jungian school, and which is supported by experimental evidence (such as Fantz, 1961,[3] etc.) that we are born with perceptual presets. This is found to be the case with depth perception, tropism towards features resembling faces, fear of creepy crawlies and so forth.

By extension, we can infer that the larger part of the structure of the world that we perceive has been categorised through evolutionary experience and thus saves us the trouble of having to relearn everything anew which our ancestors survived over millions of years — instincts and the associated archetypal recognition patterns.

Male and Female then are not merely empirically derived categories, which we all have to learn from scratch, but are *a priori* categories of neurological discrimination *with which we are born*. A billion years

---

3   Fantz, Robert. 'The Origin of Form Perception'. *Scientific American*, 1961 May, 204:66–72.

of sexual reproduction has hardwired this into the brains of all our vertebrate cousins in the same way as gravity, up and down.

Sex is the particular expression, the noun if you like, of gender, the quality.

However, material anomalies exist. But their presence doesn't disprove the existence of pattern in the web of life. They only demonstrate that there is some randomness, struggle and uncertainty in the material expression of the underlying noumenal drives of the *Thing in Itself* as it comes into being.

Much of nature produces itself through fractal patterns. Fractals are patterns which repeat endlessly, always basically the same, but always different and varied. Postmodernists don't understand that variety within a pattern doesn't negate the existence of that pattern. All life proceeds through fractal patterns — the growth of trees, spiral shells, ferns, cell division, the Fibonacci sequence and on and on.

What I believe we are exploring here is the expression of the great dynamics of nature, the manifestation of Yin and Yang, the archetypes of the Feminine and the Masculine. These are not mere categories, descriptions, but rather principles and metaphysical forces in their own right.

It should not surprise us that embryonic development unfolds according to fractal principles. This can be seen symbolised in the Yin and Yang image of the Tao:

Both dark and light literally hold the seed of the other within themselves, although there is also a clear division between them. If we use our imaginations to visualise the sorts of more developed fractal we see on the borders between, say, cloud striations on Jupiter, or at the Equator on Earth, we can suggest that this could be a model for a new explanatory diagram of gender distinction.

The cloud striations remain perpetually distinct. And yet at the border between them, they are perpetually mixing, and we see the fractal eddies and flows bearing a remarkable similarity to the vortex spiral of the symbol of the Tao. The vortex is one of the most basic principles of energy flow and propagation in all of creation, and we might think of this mixing as representative of the fusing of gametes, a function necessary to all sexual reproduction, an uncomfortable fact for some.

What the postmodern Gender Theorists are seeking to do is to deny the existence of these parallel streams that have fractal interaction. To implement this then creates chaotic and turbulent flows between the two that destroy their functionality. They think this is a good idea, promoting 'equality', but it's not.

What it actually does is make humans less survival adaptive through creating so much turbulence at a meta-level that both streams are turned into a kind of emulsified foam, where each is so broken down and mixed up with the other that they have ceased to have any distinct form or qualities, and are thus unable to function archetypically in terms of masculine and feminine, male and female, at all.

Due to the laws of nature, winds start to spiral in opposite directions in the opposite hemispheres on a planet, the planet being a whole made of complementary parts. Sex and gender are the same in the sense that the complete organism is a combination of the male and the female, since only by that combination can life be generated; in some philosophic systems, the male and female energies, or *chakras* of the body, are considered to spin in opposite directions and at different vibrational frequencies.

We cannot prevent nature having its turbulence and fractal variations. But we may consider that vortical ingressions across the boundary limitations of the polar streams, the Equator, which neither fuse and blend as in sexual fertilisation, nor conform to the direction of spin in that hemisphere as a fully reassigned person might hope to do, as being like politically motivated *progressive trenders*, who see this as an opportunity to infiltrate and destabilise the natural order (which they consider oppressive); but in actuality they can do nothing to change the dominant natural pattern of the whole. All they can do is create storms.

Transsexuals would seem to me to be like vortex spirals of weather which, finding themselves spinning in the reverse direction to that in which they were apparently born, have crossed the Equatorial boundary, and fit in with the opposite hemisphere flow and spin. While the trans trender seeks to bring the Northern Hemisphere spin to the South, claiming it is oppressive not to allow it there!

At a psychical or cosmic level perhaps, the crossing of gender boundaries serves some function in helping balance the *Tao* in our world. As I have observed, the first medically reassigned MtF transsexuals emerged in the 1920s, at exactly the same time as women were getting the vote and engaging *en masse* in the world of men in ways they had not done before.

The natural order is the basic template for life, certainly as we know it, and so should be the template or at least starting point for the expression of gender in the human world.

Subdivisions within the sexes are apparent in other phyla of life, so why should we not acknowledge this within our own species? Queens and workers, kings and soldiers, these are subdivisions of the sexes in the insect world, we can think of as alphas and betas. It doesn't mean that sex or gender does not exist in the world of ants, bees, wasps or termites; it just means that they have a more *differentiated*, or at least more *obvious*, set of sexual *structures* by which it is expressed than we have at present realised in our own human race.

But I am cautious and wish to argue that a man is still a man, whether an Alpha, Beta or Gamma. *Male* and *Female* are *gestalts*. Wholes which are more than the sum of their parts. An AIS individual may technically be a biological male, but to all intents and purposes she appears and functions as a female, both socially and even sexually. To insist, as some do, or perhaps would if they knew of this anomaly, that this AIS woman is in fact *Male* and by extension a *Man* is quite clearly preposterous. *I* may have some aspects of male biology, but I am not a *man*. So, we must see the categorisation differently.

I must say that at this point that I am not seeking to conflate AIS and Transsexualism. Clearly there are some significant differences. My main purpose in repeatedly drawing attention to the AIS condition is to demonstrate that a rigid and sharp genetic or biological reductionism in categorisation of the sexes is not absolutely definitive and only produces problems for our perceptual and social world despite the fact that these factors are strongly influential on developmental gender and usually indicative of it.

We need to understand this differently. Our world of experience is filtered through the inherited perceptual presets of evolutionary adaptation and we interpret the appearance and dynamics of our experience on this basis. We should categorise people on the basis of the dimension in which this category is relevant.

An AIS individual is only *Male* in ways which are not only invisible to the world, but invisible even to herself until she is put under forensic medical examination.

The eminent Oxford philosopher Sir Peter Strawson argued for a theory of personhood or identity in which parts were not separated away from each other.[4] This was originally intended to be applied to the work of René Descartes who had separated Mind and Body entirely, arguing that the separated parts could not be considered to be personalities on their own, but need to be considered as a whole.

I would posit that this could also be applied to the gender of anomalous individuals, such as those with AIS, or indeed transsexuals who have undergone medical reassignment, in that the *whole person*

---

4   Strawson, P. F. *Individuals.* London: Methuen & Co Ltd (1959).

is seeking congruence with the universal archetypes in our collective unconscious. The transgender person who is only socially defined remains in a conflicted state about this.

As an example of this, I recall a tale which a friend related to me. A married person whose spouse was unwilling to consent to them socially transitioning or having reassignment surgery apparently wished to gain recognition in the opposite sex to that in which they were born but could not do so unless they presented as a woman *full-time*, to fulfil the conditions of the 2004 Act to gain a GRC. My friend asked me why such a person shouldn't be able to gain recognition in a simplified version of the GRC procedure.

My response was that not only had they failed to achieve physical congruence, a condition that many like myself would prefer as a requirement, but that this person was still living in the social role as a man for most of the time with their spouse.

In no sense, surely, could they be said to have achieved a unity of personhood within their own personality and identity, but were still in a divided, or at least incomplete state. Like a water molecule that is trying to boil off the surface but hasn't reached the necessary energy level to do so. It could aspire to be a steam molecule all it liked, could claim as much to be the case, but until it has enough energy to reach that escape velocity and achieve the gaseous state, it remains just plain old liquid water. A certain minimum amount of energy must be put in so as to be able to change state, to transform from one to the other.

To achieve optimum function we need to be *whole*, *undivided* and an integrated *gestalt*, and hopefully not ending up with a *multiple personality disorder*.

We are not living in Flatland, but in a world through which multiple different sections can be taken, each of which can become a Flatland of its own. The perceptual gestalt is a whole arrived at largely in an unconscious manner due to our inherited presets. Only when someone has incongruity do the conscious cognitive processes of construing and construction take place.

What this amounts to in the end is that the gestalt of sex, and by extension gender, is construed on the basis of what we might consider as some kind of percentage scale, but perhaps with some *sine qua non* factors.

To be a Man or a Woman then is a combination of the various factors influencing how they function and are perceived, *in toto*. People can still be anomalous, indistinct, indeterminate; but our neurology demands functional judgements in perception which will match our instinctual templates. Transgenders who pass socially but are still intact in their natal sex must understand that to expose themselves in changing rooms, or even for people to simply know that this is the case, would change the perceptual gestalt. This is not oppressive or transphobic, it is simply a recognition of nature.

The sexual differentiation of hive insects is a lot more rigid than this, of course, but they can all perform some of the archetypal functions which is the core of what it is to be male or female, although none of them do all. To fertilise and to fight in defence are the masculine, and to be fertilised and to nurture are the feminine. These behaviours are characteristic expressions of the gender, not the gender itself, which is the underlying structure and dynamic.

Returning to the human condition, Jungian psychologists recognise more extended ideas of male archetypes such as the *senex* and *puer* or the female *virgin, mother* and *crone*. These are not different *sexes* or *genders*, but exist on a completely other axis. They are different phases within the dynamic of the expression of the masculine and feminine principles in humans: *Boy* and *Old Man*, just as *Worker* and *Queen* are like *Maiden* and *Matriarch*.

Postmodern Gender Theory does not like taxonomy, because it does not like structure. Structure would suggest function; function suggests purpose, and that, they cannot allow.

But a taxonomy of sexual and gender identity anomalies must surely be helpful in dealing with this thorny subject.

Perception of gender is a complex gestalt of cues. However, you cannot demand that someone see something that they do not see. To insist on this is to become O'Brien holding up four fingers to Winston Smith and demanding that he see five. When at a recent local event I saw someone whom I would otherwise not have thought was trans with a badge saying 'I am Trans' while wearing a tee-shirt with a slogan that read 'Pronouns She/Her', my sense was that this person was being deliberately challenging and confrontational, rather than wishing to fit in, which she otherwise appeared to.

It will not do to say that our perception of gender has only been socially conditioned so that we perceive this particular configuration of physical characteristics and pheromones as female, that it is merely a social construct and that we must accept someone as female simply because they say so.

This is madness.

The very social construct that they refer to is derived from the physical sex and gender that they dismiss as being of no importance.

Even the Pope's education document got this point.

The perception of gender is an *a priori* preset in our ancestral neurological structures and their functioning, and it had to be this way to be survival adaptive. There will always be a few people who don't fit the templates through no fault of their own and not being any sort of trans. But the butchest woman and the most feminine-looking man can demonstrate the *performative* behaviour that the Gender theorists like so much, and thus reinforce their identity, for this is a large part of its actual survival adaptive function.

Men and women have always sought to emphasise and even exaggerate those characteristics which demonstrate their sex, and which the opposite find attractive, in what ethologists would term *display*, just like birds of paradise or peacocks. If the male stickleback could make the colour of his breast stronger in order to more successfully attract a mate, he probably would!

Deliberate *transgression* — a favourite behaviour of the *gender queer* — produces perceptual confusion outside of the adapted presets of our evolutionary history. It is now some years since pop singer and drag queen Conchita Wurst, wearing a beard, won the Eurovision Song Contest. Talk about deliberate trolling! But this is nothing to Alex Drummond, a transgender person who claims to be a woman while eschewing all medical treatments and wearing a full beard.[5] Or Philip Bunce, aka Pippa,[6] who divides their time between their masculine and feminine personae and has received an award as one of the Top 100 *Women in Business*. No wonder we are experiencing pushback!

I cannot repeat enough that the biological templates of a natural male and female appearance and instinctive behaviour should not be considered 'oppressive' as they have an essential survival adaptive purpose for our, or any, species. The vilification of *Cisgendered* people, those who simply fit the successfully adapted norms of probabilistic functionality for survival, is just another trope of the Left which can only lead to conflict.

In a free society, people can present themselves as they like, but they should not complain if not everyone takes to it. We trans folk must find ways of interfacing with society which are more adaptive than shouting *Bigot!* if someone gets our preferred gender pronoun wrong because we are presenting in an ambiguous and indeterminate way.

If you look and act ambiguous and indeterminate, be prepared for people to respond accordingly. Our perceptual processes like to be able to make unconscious judgements on an instinctual level because if we had to process all our perceptions *consciously,* we would never get anything done. This is not prejudice, it is survival adaptation.

---

5 https://www.buzzfeed.com/patrickstrudwick/this-transgender-woman-has-a-full-beard-and-she-couldnt-be-h.

6 https://www.dailymail.co.uk/news/article-6195853/Credit-Suisse-boss-dresses-woman-slammed-appearing-100-women-list.html (2020).

And yet we have seen from the evidence of Gender Studies that they are pushing towards a *gender queer* world, with an infinite multiplication of genders, which ultimately seek to contradict and deny any basis in biology or reproduction, and replace it with a mere socially constructed hierarchy built on the sand of intersectional oppression, privilege and victim narratives.

I would seek to escape from this moral dictatorship and return to both function and form as being the basis on which we may declare the categories of things, and beings, that we experience. We must emphasise that moral imperatives, whether truly or falsely constructed, are not descriptors of what *is*, but only of what some argue *ought* to be the case. So, in effect the postmodernists are arguing that the forms of existence in which we find ourselves are morally wrong and should be abolished, such as the tautological fact that women are able to bear children, which is considered *oppressive*. The means whereby they hope to do this are not clear, since it would involve upending the entire ontological basis of reality and Nature itself.

Clearly this is absurd and we must find other ways to define ourselves, should it be necessary on occasion.

There has of course been much pushback from the other side, with posters declaring for instance 'Woman — noun: Adult female', which has caused no end of fuss on social media platforms.

As someone who acknowledges the anomalous nature of my being, but who is nonetheless entirely confident that I am in some way driven by a *Feminine* archetypal energy, I wish to find some middle way between the left and right factions, the *progressives* who want to abolish everything, and the *reactionaries* who refuse to adapt to any new information of ways of seeing.

We may not entirely fulfil the terms of the dictionary definition as quoted above, but neither do those who may have one of a number of recognised intersex conditions, such as *Androgen Insensitivity*. It would be both absurd and insulting to refuse to accept those with *AIS* being female or women because of their anomalous genetics.

Rather, I think we should have a looser qualification for *legal status* than that strictly demanded by the genetic purists, but at the same time retain the commonsense categories of perceptual recognition for purposes of the law. '*If it looks like a duck, walks like a duck, and quacks like a duck, then it probably is a duck.*'

I would suggest the terms *quasi-female* or *quasi-male*, meaning *appearing to be*. Sort of but not quite. Fitting the profile of the archetype without fulfilling the function. If we are able, or even cannot help, performing and being perceived physically as Social Females and Males, then like the stickleback our display will trigger the archetypal perceptual recognition patterns on a consistent basis and our gestalt is of that gender.

There will always be grey areas in life and our experience of it, and those who find themselves in that territory should not be prevented from locating some conventional niche in which to fit.

But they must fit. Claiming to belong to a round hole, whilst still having a square shape will not do. One must at least make some effort to shave off the square corners, as it were, if one expects to be accepted as such. The mere *Declaration* of one's gender is not a satisfactory measure. If we wish to be recognised as something, we must do more than that and provide demonstrative evidence of pragmatic function at least approximating to the archetype we claim to be expressing.

The demand for *Declaration* to be considered as sufficient for legal *Recognition* will, if ever actioned, become a tool with which the radical gender theorists will seek to actually dismantle and destroy the entire basis of what has been a universally accepted understanding of sex and gender, failing to understand that there will be reaction. The proposed law to support this may have been withdrawn for the time being, but these people do not give up, and new assaults on reality will be made.

CHAPTER 21

METAPHYSICS

Postmodern Gender Theory has it that gender is only a *construct*, a version, that there may be other equally valid *constructions* around the same thing. They point to the superficial cultural differences which we see in gender expression and insist that these are entirely arbitrary or imposed oppressively by dominating males, but deny that there is any underlying strata of drives over which these are laid.

The structure of our minds, which is rooted in the physiological functioning of our brains (although perhaps not entirely limited to it), determines our understanding of metaphysical reality.

This revisits the whole history of ontology and epistemology that Western philosophy has engaged in over the last few hundred years since the Renaissance. The unknowability of *Thing in Itself* is established through the likes of Descartes and Kant but there is much which can be inferred through reason.

Nature is the realisation of the world of metaphysical origins. The Male and the Female are not simply arbitrary functions which have been thrown up by random chance. Rather they are expressions of principles.

But the postmodern Cultural Marxists will have it that Male and Female as reproductive functions are also only *constructs*, overlays of interpretation which are subjective.

College professor Nicholas Matte of the University of Toronto,
lecturer in Transgender Studies in the Department of Sexual Diversity
Studies, recently stated in a televised news discussion, which included
Dr Jordan Peterson, that it had now been established that Male and
Female as such did not exist.[1]

Dr Sally Hines, in whose study on the outcomes of the 2004
Gender Recognition Act I had participated, wrote in an email circulated to the Gender Studies mailing list, to which I was subscribed, in
late 2018, that she held that not only gender, but sex as well are only
constructs. It should be of some concern that a professor in Social
Studies should be expressing such personal opinions without citing
any evidence, especially as I do not believe that she has any qualifications in the biological sciences. We may recall that she promoted the
2015 London Conference workshop, which argued for trans identity as
'an open-ended category without a core', while stating its promotion of
radical trans feminist activism.

Neither she nor the professor who made this claim to Dr Peterson
have produced any evidence in support of this contention. It seems
possible that they were referring to the paper by Whittle and Turner I
referenced earlier, but neither were explicit as to sources. Peterson is a
psychologist with strong leanings towards physiology, while it might
be said that Whittle and Turner's position is a *legal fiction*. I do believe
that we must have legal definitions which can smooth over the complexities of nature, but they must bear *some relation* to nature.

It could be argued that all that we find in Nature is a *construction*
since everything is made of parts which are put together. The evidence
of Fausto-Sterling and others is only a demonstration of how parts
can be put together in jumbled up, random or probabilistically less
functional ways than the statistical norm, which has been demonstrated as the most effective subdivision within Nature over millions

---

1   'Genders, Rights and Freedom of Speech' https://www.youtube.com/
    watch?v=kasiovoytEc Matte, Nicholas Univ. Toronto, 11:20 minutes and Dr
    Peterson's reply 24:10 (2020).

of generations. *Herms*, *merms* and *ferms* are not different sexes or different genders but only anomalous and imperfect mixings that do not disprove the existence of male and female.

As always, postmodernism claims that anomalies disprove the general rule, without understanding the deeper rule-governed reality out of which both normative and anomalous offspring come.

The need for the existence of the sexes can be demonstrated by observing the simple fact that in most vertebrates, and in all mammals, life is procreated by the fusing of the male and female gametes contained in the spermatozoa and ova. Some primitive reptiles and fish can reproduce by parthenogenesis (as we may recall some Radical Feminists would like to do!), in the temporary absence of males, but this is only a stop gap, as it limits genetic variation and adaptability. Multiple or imperfect fusions do happen occasionally, but produce offspring that are atypical and have a reduced chance of surviving and producing viable offspring themselves. One ovum on its own cannot generally produce life, it must have some input from the male.

The level to which the deconstructionists have taken their campaign amounts to a claim that our understanding of the very basis of the generation of life is a mere cognitive invention, which is utterly preposterous.

There is no desire to seek underlying principles, general rules, or governing natural laws. Instead, *Oppression* and *Privilege* theory have become the foundational concepts on which contemporary gender relations are based, thus putting the cart before the horse.

I find it impossible to proceed to the end of this work without having recourse to go beyond both the abstract linguistic fantasies of the postmodern Gender Theorists and the reductionist flatlands of the Neanderthal Right.

We must delve into the spectral realm of archetypes, of the hidden realities of the *Thing in Itself*, and even non-local consciousness. I beg for the indulgence of the reader as I make this brief discursion. But it will return to the path erelong.

Before the so-called *Enlightenment* of the eighteenth century, a belief in some kind of divine spirit that existed throughout Nature, and indeed as a Prime Mover, was near universal in all civilisations and cultures since the earliest recorded times. Only since scientific rationalism has become dominant has this former belief been eclipsed. And yet the success of material science does nothing to prove that belief wrong.

Ever since Descartes hived off the realm of consciousness from that of the material world we have gone further and further down the reductionist route, which, despite producing much mastery of the material world, has ultimately led to the nihilism of postmodernism.

Consciousness, the perceiver in Descartes' *Cogito Ergo Sum*, has been left aside, despite the fact that it is the very thing on which the whole materialist construction of reality depends. For it really is, in this case, a *construction*, simply a mechanism. And along with *consciousness*, the *divine spirit* and any notion of *panpsychism* or *animism* are thrown on the junkheap, or at best considered mere *epiphenomena* arising from our neural structures.

Yet there can be no science, no observation, without an observer. And science has discovered that at the quantum level of reality the observation itself has an effect on the determinacy of a wavicle, whether it remains a wave, or is fixed as a particle.

Dr Rupert Sheldrake has recently suggested that a test for consciousness might be whether an object is self-organising. This would relate loosely to Leibniz' notion of *monads*, points of individual consciousness which reflect or are influenced by the rest of the universe.

This postulate would allow for consciousness to somehow inhere in living organisms, as opposed to Descartes' or Leibniz' beliefs that consciousness and matter were entirely different things and their qualities so utterly different that they could not interact, except by their *deus ex machina* inventions.

This is what is known as *The Hard Problem*, the question of what exactly consciousness *is*. Its very nature is, as the above-mentioned philosophers understood, entirely unmaterial, and yet it experiences the material world.

Epiphenomenalism and *Mind/Brain* identity theory are, in the eyes of many, unsatisfactory explanations since while they appear to explain away the unique experience of consciousness, they do no such thing but rather merely push the problem back one level of description.

Dr Sheldrake has produced evidence for panpsychism with his *Dogs That Know When Their Owners Are Coming Home* experiment,[2] in which he tested the anecdotal observation by many that dogs often know that their masters are coming home even at unexpected times and yet are too far away for the noise of their car to be heard and so on, and found results which support this.

That there may be a realm or dimension of existence in which we are connected, at least to those with whom we have emotional bonds, and that this was a realm of consciousness or panpsychism, is not something that would be considered in the least unusual in most historical cultures or civilisations throughout the history of Mankind.

Sheldrake's postulate on the basis of his evidence, and which is subject to testing, is that consciousness is a *field*, which would account for any self-organising properties, just as a magnetic field organises the magnetisable particles within it, but is perhaps non-local as the experiment with the dogs suggested.

Only in materialist reductionist science is such a notion rejected absolutely. Although it should not by now be surprising that Gender Studies doesn't even allow that the evidence of material science should be entertained when it comes to the physical manifestation of sex and gender, so it should be no surprise that they scorn the meta-inquiry behind it.

---

2   Sheldrake, Rupert, PhD. *Dogs That Know When Their Owners Are Coming Home: And Other Unexplained Powers of Animals.* Crown Pub, 1999. https://www.sheldrake.org/books-by-rupert-sheldrake/dogs-that-know-when-their-owners-are-coming-home (2020).

Instinctual drives and archetypal recognition patterns are what re-ally motivate any organism. These are what the organism *is*.

The *Thing in Itself* is the groundless ground of being and has its own way of expressing itself, the *Tao*. The deep brain drives, which we experience as primal or archetypal feelings, ideas, images, are rooted in that *Tao*. We are constrained by our biology, which manifests in our consciousness and experience. The great archetypal reality which lives through us is structured through polarity and cycles; these are its nature and how it is made manifest. *Non-Binary* could no more be a real category than space could lack extension.

The great dynamic of the masculine is complemented by that of the feminine, receptive and compatible to it, but utterly different. We are all a composite of both, but hopefully in accord with the dominant note within that balance.

We should not be afraid to make comparisons with other scientific fields, and here I am brought to mind of *Cymatics*. This is the study of how standing wave patterns can be induced in loose materials, such as sand, when various frequencies are applied to the surface on which they rest. Such patterns as the Yantra may be produced (a pattern that curiously was known to ancient cultures). These standing waves were identified by Ernst Chladni[3] in 1787,[4] who repeated Robert Hooke's experiments of a century before. Dr Sheldrake has elaborated on this concept and demonstrated how resonance patterns may contribute to morphogenesis rather than DNA-generated proteins alone. It certainly seems likely on a simple basis of parsimony that standing wave patterns could be the basis for morphic patterning of cell structures and even larger collections of cells since they provide a kind of spatial template around which more solid forms can aggregate. His example of standing waves that resemble an insect pupa, given in his lecture to the 2019 Conference on the Physics, Chemistry and Biology of Water,

---

3   https://americanhistory.si.edu/science/chladni.htm (2020).

4   https://en.wikipedia.org/wiki/Ernst_Chladni (2020).

is quite remarkable.[5] By extension we may hypothesise that it is possible that many other structures and functions of organisms may have some correlative resonant factors involved in their existence.

I was initially going to write that I would invite attempts to test whether resonance patterns such as these can be determined to exist which may be different between the sexes, but it seems that this work has already begun, with some success, as I have previously mentioned, in the work of Professor Julie Bakker[6] and her Magnetic Resonance Imaging of brain patterns which show sex differences.

Not only does this support the earlier evidence by Zhou et al and Ramachandran but it also suggests that those neural structures are involved in determining the resonance patterns. This supports my own hypothesis that gender is rooted in the organic organisation and behaviour of the brain. I would postulate that such patterns might be elicited due to resonance with metalevel causes that we may call Yin or Yang, feminine or masculine. The eliciting note causes and maintains the pattern, which shows the form of the field. At the very least, there is some kind of functional patterning going on, which is demonstrated by and arises through the different types of brain organisation and behaviour. Thus we might say that the masculine and the feminine can be experienced as resonance patterns, like musical notes or colours, which both have *frequencies*.

Should we find that we feel that we do not have a balance between these two basic frequencies, that something within our spirit, within our nervous system tells us that we are out of balance within ourselves, that we are upside down and back to front and inside out and that we cannot be comfortable until we have rectified ourselves, then we are

---

5   https://www.youtube.com/watch?v=n9QwUWdASZA *Conference   on   the Physics, Chemistry and Biology of Water* (2020) (originally titled *Dynamic Patterns in Water as Analogue Models*).

6   https://www.telegraph.co.uk/news/2018/05/22/transgender-brain-scans-promised-study-shows-structural-differences/ (2020).

challenged to engage with that which is out of balance and see what we can do to right it.

The externalisation of these deep inner metareasons, causes, vibrations, what you will, is surely the manifestation of our individuality. They set up the field of our being, which can remarkably self-reorganise our manifested material person when allowed to in a properly managed way.

If this reorganisation of self, this *self-organisation* is *construed* from a *living archetype of the self,* it is likely to succeed. But if it is merely *constructed* from an assemblage of acquired ideas that have no actual life or consciousness of their own, it will not.

The work by Professor Bakker gives some hope that we may one day be able to have objective tests with which to properly implement a system of triage and vetting for those seeking medical treatment as transsexuals. I would venture that many of those in the large teenage clusters I have mentioned would be found not to have the cross-sex brain patterns associated with true gender dysphoria. Rather, I would suggest that they have experienced simple *contagion* through adolescent rebellion and the chaotic and maladaptive social forces which that often unleashes.

If we are to engage with the treatment of minors, it must be on the basis of objective medical evidence which gives a very high probability of correct diagnoses, not because we are afraid to examine or challenge a child's motivation in saying that it wants to be of the opposite sex. Indeed, ideally there would surely be a battery of tests both objective and subjective that should all concur and corroborate each other. Suggesting that this is all just some social lifestyle choice, which we must respect because sex and gender are merely arbitrary constructs, is a dangerous path to tread.

Prevention of misdiagnosis and the consequent harm which could ensue should be the highest priority in this matter.

Postmodernism denies any metaphysics, but their own philosophy is a metaphysics of nihilism. Only a metaphysics which relates to our world of the physical in giving an underlying structure, pattern and above all else *meaning* can have any value.

Even in the anomalous brains of those suffering with gender dysphoria we can find these patterns and drives to find personal meaning, which can only be realised if we are able to express that vibration through our material person.

> If you bring forth what is within you, what you bring forth will save you. If you do not bring forth what is within you, what you do not bring forth will destroy you.[7]

But if you bring forth something which was not there to start with, but merely planted by some outside influence, then that itself may destroy you.

The proof is not, as is often said, *in the pudding*, but rather the proof of the pudding *is in the eating* thereof. It has to be tasted, it has to be *tested* before it can be proved.

7   Gospel of Thomas v 70.

CHAPTER 22

THE ABOLITION
OF GENDER

THE AUTHOR, literary scholar and religious philosopher C. S. Lewis had arrived at the same conclusion as I some eighty years previously, that gender is the precursor to sex, a metaphysical force and category from which our experience of sex is derived. In his beautiful work *Perelandra* he describes the encounter of his hero Ransom with the planetary archons,[1] *Oyarseru,* or archangels of the two planets Mars and Venus. These beings seem to be pure *quality* as opposed to the *substance* of sex as we experience it.

Lewis describes Ransom's experience as one of seeing 'the real meaning of gender'.[2]

---

1 *Perelandra* by C. S. Lewis © copyright CS Lewis Pte Ltd 1943. *John Lane (The Bodley Head)* 1943 (Quotes from Pan edition 1983, p. 186).

2 It was with a mixture of amusement and embarrassment during the final corrections for this book that I realised Jan Morris had cited exactly the same passage in the explanation she gives of her feelings of gender in her *Conundrum.* Having read it when it had came out, and then burned it some eight or so years later, I was given a paperback copy in the eighties, but never reread it, and purposely put it aside during the writing of *The War on Gender*, so as not to be overly influenced by it. During the interrupted flow of writing this book, I reread *Perelandra* and came across this passage, that I felt was appropriate to make some commentary on, which I include here. But close to completion

Reflecting on how it is that most languages apply gender even to inanimate objects, he understands that gender is not 'an imaginative extension of sex' but 'the reverse'.

'Sex is... the adaptation to organic life of a fundamental polarity.'

This polarity is shown in the two beings that have no sex but are pure expressions of gender.

The gods in our world's myths and religions are not projections of humans and their qualities magnified into exaggerated proportion, but rather the personalisation of cosmic forces. Gender is a *metaphysical* characteristic of existence, while sex is its material manifestation.

Ransom sees the characters of these beings, and these display the qualities of their genders. The masculine archetypal being he describes as 'in ceaseless vigilance, his eyes ever roaming the ... horizon', which is surely a perfect archetypal match for what Professor Melissa Hines found in her 2004 study[3] that androgenised brains are associated with a greater interest in moving objects. What better way to describe Lewis' *vigilance*?

The feminine archetype, on the other hand, is inward looking to a private world of 'waves and murmurings and wandering airs', which 'splashed on mossy stones' and 'arose sunward in thin-spun delicacy of mist', suggesting a nurturing, embryonic mood, one that is well to be protected by its vigilant partner.

of final corrections to this manuscript, I pulled *Conundrum* off the shelf to remind myself of her journey, when I assumed the danger of being influenced was past and almost immediately found the reference to exactly the same passage which Morris had cited in her own work! So I must ask the reader's indulgence and Jan's forgiveness for making what is essentially the same point, and hope that you will not consider this plagiarism, since I have enlarged on it a little more than she with some science, and near the end of my piece, rather than near the beginning as she did. But I am nonetheless pleased to find that I am in agreement with two of the finest writers in the English language of the twentieth century.

3   Hines, Professor Melissa. 'Sex-related variation in human behavior and the brain'. Trends Cogn Sci. 2010 Oct; 14(10): 448–456. https://www.cell.com/trends/cognitive-sciences/fulltext/S1364-6613(10)00172-5 (2020).

This is the core polarity that postmodernists must destroy, not just in the physical manifestation of *sex* but perhaps even more importantly to them in the metaphysic of *gender* as well, and is one reason why I and many like me have preferred to retain the usage of the term *transsexual* rather than adopt the newer term *transgender*. While it may be the case that sex is generally an expression of genes and hormones, the common perceptual experience of it is as morphology — appearance and behaviour. And there is that inconvenient example of AIS, where the genetics fail to be translated into the associated sexual phenotype. It is that which we are changing; it is that into which we wish to fit. We could no more change our *gender* than we could dematerialise ourselves on a whim. That numinous sense of the indwelling force from which we derive our concept of self is the precursor to sex, not the result of it.

Of course, the materialists will say otherwise, that sex is a mere *statistical phenomenon* and gender *the synthetic interpretation* of its accumulated qualities. But Lewis is more than a poet. He raises real questions about what it is that makes a mountain masculine in our imagination, or perhaps the sea as feminine. More parochially, we think of dogs as masculine ('He's a wolf') and cats as feminine ('She's catty'). These *qualia* are pre-existent, not only to humans, or our imagination, or even all organic life. *Up* and *down*, *in* and *out*, *back* and *forth*, are *a priori* qualities of existence. Indeed, we may say that these qualities are, *must be*, some kind of expression of the fundamental *first* principles, the *metaphysics* of existence, the structure of the world in which we find ourselves.

Unfortunately, the postmodernists won't accept concepts of metaphysics — absolute logic from which laws of nature that exist behind and above material reality are derived. But all they have is *power* and *oppression*, actions which contravene their demand for *equality*. But in a world without metaphysical principles, why should we expect to find a moral law in which *equality* is the first principle?

Indeed, if all descriptions of behaviour and value systems are *equal*, then why should the *polarity* of gender be any less acceptable as a belief system than their own of formless chaos? Their assertion of *power* as being the only social force that should be recognised, and that it is always *oppressive*, can equally be turned back at them. They have the dominant belief system at present, and it *oppresses* those who still believe in traditional concepts of gender expressed through sex, so why shouldn't the traditionalists *transgress* the oppressive hegemonic new belief system and return to what they know?

In his short book *The Abolition of Man* (1942), Lewis percipiently predicted the very position in which we find ourselves today in society.

He argues that there are certain universally shared values between all societies, and these he calls the *Tao*, which we have seen earlier. The reader may be familiar with some of its paradoxical wisdom in the original *Tao Te-Ching* compiled by Lao Tzu about the time of Socrates.

The way of the true Tao cannot be explained.

Or perhaps he might have said…

Always changing, the way remains the same.

He might almost have been talking about fractals. Perhaps he had in mind the way organic life grows, or the habit patterns of life we see all around, which we have inherited.

Gender is like this, the driving force behind nature, which somehow manages to rediscover and reinvent itself anew with every generation, and yet still remain that same thing which it always was.

The very word implies *generation*, the creation and perpetuation of life.

To destroy this, to *deconstruct* it, is to turn it into a machine and seek to make it our servant, rather than accept that it is our master. It is life, it is within us and flows through us.

One consequence of this in the Gender Studies reality would be the eradication of *oppressive gender constructs* and *the abolition of gender itself*. Is not gender an obstacle to universal equality?

For former medical student George Gillett writing in *The New Statesman* in 2014:

'The aim of "gender equality" doesn't go far enough — we need to confront the very concept of gender itself.'[4]

He is so hung up on *stereotyped traits* that he is blind to the existence of gender-specific drives and evolutionary history. However, more ironic to me is that he fails to critique the title of the journal in which he is published — *The New StatesMAN!*

Obviously, one of the principal issues about deconstruction or redefinition of gender is the question of who is allowed to use female-only spaces, a point which Mr Gillett neglects to consider. While a couple of years later, in the pages of the very same august journal, Sarah Dittum raises this most salient of issues[5] and critiques the legitimacy of male-bodied criminals, who still have fully intact male anatomy, claiming a female identity in order to be housed in women's prisons. Such examples, where supposed 'human rights' are exploited at the expense of putting others at risk, only increase the resentment of the general population. The presence of physically intact males in women's sporting events is now proving controversial. Cyclist Dr Rachel McKinnon, became involved in a Twitter storm with world famous lesbian tennis star Martina Navratilova, when she had said that she accepted the likes of Renee Richards who had had full medical reassignment surgeries, but that it was wrong for intact male-bodied athletes to participate as women. Dr McKinnon complained about transphobia coming from a lesbian who had faced much discrimination in her own time. But lesbians aren't male-bodied. To claim that

4   George Gillett. 'We shouldn't fight for "gender equality". We should fight to abolish gender'. *The New Statesman*. 2 October 2014. https://www.newstatesman.com/society/2014/10/we-shouldn-t-fight-gender-equality-we-should-fight-abolish-gender (2020).

5   Sarah Dittum. 'What's missing from the transgender debate? Any discussion of male violence'. *The New Statesman*. 30 November 2016. https://www.newstatesman.com/2016/11/whats-missing-transgender-debate-any-discussion-male-violence (2020).

women just need to train harder to beat her is disingenuous, I would suggest.

Lewis' extrapolation of a transhumanist future is one in which we detach ourselves from our ancestral past, or our controllers do that for us, and all we are left with is the gratification of manufactured desires. He would have been aware of Aleister Crowley as one of his most notorious contemporaries, but he was also friends with Charles Williams, a former member of the Order of the Golden Dawn, of which Crowley had been a member, and so was aware of the source of these dangerous ideas which were percolating through society, and which he parodied in his masterpiece *That Hideous Strength (1945).*

Those manufactured desires and feelings are very largely manipulated in this modern world of advertising hooks and subconscious influence, along with generations of postmodern indoctrination so that the changes that are to be made are merely those desired by the ones conditioning the population to them. *Do What Thou Wilt Shall Be The Whole Of The Law* can be used as a justification of hedonism, under the banner of *Nothing is True, Everything is Permitted.* There is to be no discernment, only transgression. Like rats with electrodes in their pleasure centres, we are to be left repeatedly pressing the stimulus button until we collapse from exhaustion.

Instead of seeking to better understand and express ourselves in the context of society, we are being encouraged to change society to conform around us, our desires and feelings, as we found the research into the GRA outcomes sought to do. Even to destroy it. '*Smash the Patriarchy*' — we hear with no word of what is to replace it.

An interviewer once asked Dr Jordan Peterson why he thought that surnames were passed down the male line and he said he would have to think about it. I can tell him straight away. It is not because of *male oppression*, it is because in the past women needed to belong to a household, a family, a close-knit group that would be able to protect them. The only ones who could protect them from other men were their own men. A simple fact. *Patriarchy* is not built only on *dominance* but as much on *protection*. The destruction of the *Patriarchy* would only be local, and other nearby societies would see that we were no longer being protected by our men. There are indications that this has already been taking place.

This is not to suggest that we should not wish to *improve* society, but that we should do that from *within*, fitting into those habits of life which already exist universally and not seek to reinvent the wheel, but to refine how it works. The history of most revolutions is filled with chaos and death, producing at best a Napoleon, or at worst a Mao or a Pol Pot, but always a megalomaniac.

Lewis explained how the paradigmatic shift from *objective* to *subjective value* was setting us adrift with no mooring, since ultimately the subjective values can be anything depending on who chooses them.

It is a little ironic to me that his title was *The Abolition of Man* since that is almost what we are seeing at the hands of the feminists, while he was simply thinking in the old-fashioned language of Man as we know our species, human beings, the human condition of moral choice, and so on. But ironies are perhaps sometimes the way of the Universe in telling us that something is even more true than we had at first imagined.

And naturally, along with the abolition of *Man* or *men* or *masculinity* we also must have the abolition of *Gender,* which has been proceeding at such a pace in recent times.

Different segments of the agenda are carried out by different sets of useful idiots, who might otherwise be at odds with each other, but they all advance the whole.

It doesn't matter whether one faction or another support transgender or gay rights, or are opposed them, in the end the only thing that matters is to cause chaos and confusion so that the people can be more easily conditioned to new patterns of desire and behaviour, which have been inculcated, and to ditch all that went before, throwing out the baby with the bathwater.

'*Self-declaration*' without any physical, social or behavioural evidence to support it in conventional terms entirely detaches gender identity from all traditional beliefs and expectations about gender and sex. This is justified as being 'fairer', and more respecting of feelings.

Everywhere we look we see traditional structures being dismantled by the postmodern left. C. S. Lewis saw this coming, even though it was only in its early stages when he was writing this in the 1940s. He had himself actually coined the word *trans-sexual* in *Perelandra*, but had given it the meaning of *beyond sex*, applying it to his eldils, the angelic form of consciousness of which the Oyarseru are the leading members. And while they may exhibit *gender*, they do not have *sex* since they are not living organisms of the material world and don't need to reproduce. They are in a sense *universal* beings who do not experience the *particular* as we do. Sex is the particular example of gender in physical living form.

Postmodernism is looking to entrain the powerful energies of desire and gratification associated with sex into drives which they can divert to their own ends while bluffing us that it is merely a construct.

And as we have seen, *transgression* is thought by some to be the way forward, in that it is a major weapon in the attack on conventional values. But when all taboos have been broken, what is there left?

For myself I would say that my own journey has been one which I felt to be a spiritual path of finding myself, finding the truest expression possible of that gender which I felt within me, which was distinct from mere sexual motivation, while it seems that it is now being promoted as some kind of trendy social thing. Or that some are persuading themselves it is. A means to stand out and stand against traditional gender values while at the same time receiving attention.

We are surely in the end game for this, as we must either spiral into that chaos wherein all boundaries and distinctions are dissolved or we are close to that spiritual reawakening culturally, where our alarm bells go off which will bring us back into balance with the natural order of things.

And this is by no means confined to the vexed subject of trans identity but is being applied to the whole concept of traditional values, mostly in Western societies.

All the deep-rooted cultural ways of our peoples, which have evolved gradually over centuries and which make us what we are today, are being attacked. We are being told that it is all evil and oppressive and that we should be ashamed of it and the patriarchal foundation on which it was built.

But the only thing they have to replace it with is their own relative values, which are based simply on the power to enforce those values through the conditioning influence of education and the media.

The war on gender is part of the greater attack not only on concepts of normative gender expression, but on all traditional values, the values which built Western civilisation. Even the very idea of objective value itself. Postmodernism as a culture of critique has nothing to offer but the operating table of the vivisectionist.

'And he that breaks a thing to find out what it is has left the path of wisdom[6]'.

---

6   Tolkien, J. R. R. *The Fellowship of the Ring*, p. 272. George Allen & Unwin (Publishers) Ltd, 1954.

RETURN TO LOGOS

NORMATIVE GENDER VALUES in society should not be imposed too rigidly, but there must be a *logos* of gender, and it must be based in its biological origins, which themselves derive from the logical and metaphysical nature of existence. The archetypes of the Unconscious have emerged from our biology and its survival adaptation. Anomalies like myself exist, and I do not wish to be forced into the kind of rigid roles that palaeo-conservatives would impose, but to make rules out of the anomalies, as the postmodernists seek to do, and ignore the 99.7% is both impractical and unscientific.

Logos is meaning. Logos is law. Logos is what has purpose and what functions. The practical application of Logos is probabilistic functionalism. Logos is the underlying truth, which we may never fully apprehend, but for which we must always strive. The loss of Logos tips us into Chaos, which only favours the powerful. Is it not obvious that postmodernism only serves itself in seeking to take down Logos?

We must find a balance between competing ideologies and acknowledge the origin of bodily gender in biological sex, but allow for social and legal exceptions in grey areas. It is not my purpose in these pages to prescribe a final solution to how we should legitimate gender status, but rather to lay down a pathway in reason and evidence, which may guide us in dealing with a field which encompasses apparent paradoxes and contradictions.

The principal basis on which Gender Studies is founded, that *male and female genders are merely social constructs*, is unsatisfactory, as I have argued.

The basis of gender must be rooted in the archetypal differences which have come down to us through ancestry and survival adaptation, and it can only be in accepting this that we shall be able to find a meaningful and balanced way of dealing with gender in the future.

The archetypes of gender are a part of our innate make-up. Attempting to rewrite or rather *replace* nature is the goal of Gender Studies in this matter. The entire *eradication* of gender itself seems to be where they want to take this.

Universalising from the particular is one of the chief intellectual sins of the postmodern Left. They have universalised transgenderism from small anomalous groups and sought to create an ideology in which gender is merely a choice, thereby both devaluing our own deep experience at the same time as corrupting and undermining the developmental identities of those of our youth who do not have serious gender dysphoria but are merely naïve and suggestible.

We should not delude ourselves into complacency simply because the government in 2019 dropped plans for a Gender Declaration Bill due to pushback and Brexit overload. We may be certain that those advocating such a law will continue to do so and will push ahead hardest just when we think they have gone away. That is the way of the Alinskyite postmodern Cultural Marxist. We have only repelled their first wave, and there will be more, repeatedly, which is why I must put this out regardless.

Transhumanist cyborgs are the future that some see for us, and certainly the eradication of gender as a concept would go a long way to enabling this vision. The indoctrination of pre-school infants with the ideology of gender deconstruction, or the ongoing trend for encouraging ever younger children to transition and even take hormone blockers or actual hormones, is disturbing. There is hope that objective medical tests combined with psychological diagnosis may enable more reliable selection and triage of those who may have genuine and irreversible cross-gender neurology.

But laying out prescriptions as to how exactly to deal with possible trans children is not the purpose of this book. The precise medical, ethical and legal protocols need to be examined and considered far more closely with regards to children than seem to have been so far and is way beyond the scope of my current thesis.

My purpose is rather to protect children, and thus our whole society, from unnecessary confusion induced by false ideologies such as postmodern gender theory by defending the traditional view of a gendered world which includes men and women, boys and girls, the stabilised archetypes of our evolutionary, indeed metaphysical, heritage.

Ordinary male and female are in the attack sights of the progressives, while multiple radical genders proliferate.

This is a revolutionary political agenda which is being inflicted on the West under the guise of social justice when in fact it is eroding the very foundations, not only of our civilisation, but what it is to be human itself.

As I draw to the close of this book, I am minded again of C. S. Lewis' *Abolition of Man,* in which he discusses the problem of the limitations of future genetic manipulations which may be inflicted on the human race. To intervene in the making of a human is also to *limit* their possibilities, even if you have supposedly increased their intelligence or physical prowess. You don't know what has been lost. This also applies to socially engineering the culture around our genders, as is being done on the grand scale at the present time.

I might have called this book *The Abolition of Gender*, which is what those promoting Gender Studies seem to want.

There are, as I have argued, adjustments that need to be made in our intellectual and academic understandings of how we understand gender at the micro level. But not significantly at the macro level.

Gender Studies seeks to *abolish*, to *demolish* gender because it is against *equality*. You may as well try to abolish gravity because *up* and *down* are *unequal* and *oppressive*.

We must understand that gender is a function of nature, of the way that the Universe works. It has archetypal psychological components as well as biological dimensions. To *construe* is not to *construct*, it is to *interpret*, to *understand* something that is not merely of one's own invention, but something greater, something beyond oneself.

As future shock after future shock assaults our civilisation, we will be thrown back onto our roots, our foundations. Logos.

Gender Studies has sought to dismantle how we understand gender in merely social terms, but has failed to understand its purpose and has left a pile of broken components lying around without having any idea of how they should be fit together again to make it work. Indeed, they don't want to put it back together; they want to destroy it.

In doing so it has indeed left the path of wisdom.

This is the war on gender.

APPENDIX A

Letter to *Spare Rib*

I INCLUDE THE COMPLETE TEXT of my letter to *Spare Rib* magazine (late 1987/early 1988), quoted in the article 'Trannies', an interview by the Rev/Rad Feminist Collective with 'Eileen Carter' in the *Revolutionary and Radical Feminist Review* no.18 March 1988. I believe the name *Eileen Carter* to probably be a pseudonym since this is not the name I knew this woman by.

Fear of Transsexuality?

Dear Spare Rib

Not so long ago I was invited to a close friend's twenty-first birthday party. It was to be an all women's day consisting of an outing in the country in the day and a party in the evening. [I don't recall the party]

Eight of us went on the outing in two cars, the weather was marvellous, the company great and the scenery beautiful. I think we all agreed that it had been a wonderful day. There was one woman in the group who[m] I had not met before, but we seemed to strike up quite a spontaneous thing and before the day was over, we made a loose arrangement to meet again sometime.

A couple of weeks later I got round to visiting. We were getting on famously and then after a glass of wine she started steering the conversation to sexual politics and I began to feel I was being cross examined as to my right-on-ness. After a while I felt I had to be honest so I told her that I am trans-sexual [probably *Spare Rib's* hyphenation]. After she had gawped at me like some weird specimen in a zoo, examining me as if I were an object rather than a person, she promptly asked me to leave stating that this was a political act, but that I should not take it personally. She would allow for no discussion whatsoever, and I was turned out onto the street with barely time to finish my glass as if I had committed some vile act against women.

I am aware that trans-sexuality [again probably *SR* hyphenation] is a new and difficult thing to come to terms with for some people but are we to be '**Morally mandated out of existence**' [my emphasis] as Janice Raymond suggests? My trans-sexuality [*SR* hyphen] was never a matter of choice, or of some cheap thrill. It is quite clear that I am perceived as a woman, until occasionally under certain circumstances I feel obliged to explain my position, at which point the knives come out. It is a pity that dogma is more important to some people than personal experience.

Yours

CR Leeds

APPENDIX B

From Hansard

HANSARD 25 MAY 2004 column 1497—1502, which can be found way down on the following page: https://hansard.parliament.uk/commons/2004-05-25/debates/36c03d5e-4aa1-42ea-86of-877bc85d9ca7/OrdersOfTheDay.

Many thanks to the House of Commons Enquiries Service for their assistance in researching this and in providing the URL.

Andrew Selous: I rise to speak briefly to new clause 6, which, as my hon. Friend the Member for Daventry (Mr Boswell) said, had about three minutes' debate at the very end of the Standing Committee proceedings.

First, let me say what the new clause is not about. It is right and proper that transsexual people should use changing and washing facilities appropriate to their acquired gender. That is what should happen, and I am confident that in a vast and overriding number of cases it will happen without difficulty. However, as the measure will give legal recognition, in all cases, to the acquired gender, I want the House to consider, and the Minister to explain, what would happen if someone had a gender recognition certificate but had not undergone sex reassignment surgery and wanted to cause difficulties to the management of the facilities.

Mr Lammy: The hon. Gentleman will know that under the Bill a person would have to be diagnosed with gender dysphoria, to have lived with the condition for two years, to demonstrate that there was some permanence in the condition and to convince the panel that they merited a gender recognition certificate. He is right to suggest that that may not always mean that they had undergone an operation — there could be medical reasons for that — but those are substantial hurdles to overcome and that is the purpose of the Bill.

AS: I am grateful to the Minister for that clarification but, to return briefly to a point raised in debate on new clause 1, I do not know whether he is aware that in the Diane Parry case in south Wales, Diane Parry's physical appearance was very much that of a man. I am concerned about circumstances where someone is legally a man but physically a woman or vice versa, and where there are open changing areas. For example, in football or other sports, teams might change together and there are no cubicles, and in the armed services it is common to find open showers with no cubicle division.

I accept that the possibilities are remote but I want to know what would happen in such circumstances. It is relevant because, as the Minister may be aware, several pub landlords have experienced difficulties in this matter, although they relate to an issue that is separate from my new clause. I simply want to understand what will happen where there are open changing and showering facilities.

Mr Lammy: I do not want to prejudice what I may have to say shortly, but surely the hon. Gentleman is not suggesting that we should legislate to allow a form of prejudice because it may exist in pubs throughout the country.

AS: New Clause 6 does not deal with pubs. It clearly deals with the specific circumstance of complete nudity in open changing areas. The Minister has a slight habit of setting up men-of-straw arguments that differ from the arguments made by those with whom he is debating. I ask him to restrict himself to the circumstances of the new clause

6. I used the pub analogy only because that is happening now, so the scenario that I envisage is not wholly far-fetched.

There is always a very small litigious minority. I accept that the vast majority of transsexual people will want to behave in a discreet and private manner; but, given the Diane Parry case in south Wales, if we are to pass a law of this nature, the Minister needs to explain clearly what will happen to a sports club if parents say, "Right. My children aren't going there anymore." The club could go out of business. He also needs to explain what could happen in the situation that I describe in respect of good order in the armed services, in which I served for 12 years, so I know a little about that. Those are the type of issues that the new clause raises.

Richard Younger-Ross: We debated this issue briefly in Committee. Is the hon. Gentleman aware that most female changing rooms are already divided into cubicles? My background is in architecture, and I cannot think of an instance in all my time in architecture where we have ever built open changing rooms.

AS: The hon. Gentleman is quite right. The public swimming pools that most of us use and where I go to with my family almost entirely have changing rooms with cubicles. That is not a problem. If he reads new clause 6 carefully, he will see the word "open" before the words "showers" and "sports changing areas". He will be aware that hotel sports areas often have open changing areas; football clubs and many other sports clubs have open changing areas; and open showers are very common in the armed services.

The difficulty arises purely in a case where someone is legally a man but has the body of a woman, or vice versa. It may be a small and far-fetched case, but we are entitled to know what would happen for the sake of good order and for another reason as well: the purpose of the Bill is to give transsexual people some rights that are overdue and should rightly be given to them. If the Minister does not deal with the issue that I am raising, there will be resentment and a public backlash that will undo the very work that he is trying to do. He has said time and again that we cannot legislate for other people's concerns on these matters. I am not entirely sure that he is right. It is the function of a Parliament that is considering such matters in the round to ensure that here are reserve powers — I emphasise the word "reserve" — so that public resentment does not build up and undermine the support for the very group that the Bill seeks to help.

Lynne Jones: Does the hon. Gentleman seriously think that a trans-man who has not undergone phalloplasty would go into a male changing room, for example, with a football team and expose himself? That is highly unlikely. I can confirm that there are open women's changing rooms. I went into one just over the road this morning. Quite frankly, the idea that a male-to-female trans-person would be granted a recognition certificate if they did not undergo a penectomy is, again, unthinkable.

AS: If the hon. Lady is fair, she will acknowledge that I said that, hopefully, the circumstances to which my new clause relates would never arise. However, we would be negligent in our duty as legislators if we did not get some guidance from the Minister on what would happen if they did. Perhaps the hon. Lady is not aware that in the south Wales case, Diane Parry had a full beard at the time when he [sic] wanted to join in the ladies' activities. Thus the scenario that I am describing is not wholly far-fetched.

LJ: To be candid, if the hon. Gentleman is suggesting that someone who sports a full beard would have their application for a gender recognition certificate granted, I wonder what world he is living in.

AS: The hon. Lady attacks me for raising the issue, but on several occasions over the years the House has not foreseen potential developments. I fully accept that the vast majority of transsexual people will not want to go down that route, but there is always the litigious minority to deal with. I am keen to avoid public resentment and concern.

Mr Lammy: The hon. Gentleman keeps talking about a litigious minority. I remind him that there are more than 60 million people in this country and only about 5,000 transsexuals, and the Bill contains a number of hurdles. For example, the person concerned must have had gender dysphoria, and as my hon. Friend the Member for Birmingham, Selly Oak (LJ) explained, persons with that condition do not want to be exposed in public in this way. Surely, therefore, the hon. Gentleman's preoccupation with the minority becomes redundant. Has he not argued himself out of the position from which he started?

AS: No, I do not think that I have. Who would have thought that the Churches would be dragged through the courts by people from a very small minority of 5,000 people in a country of 60 million? Yet that has already happened, and other legal cases are in the system. I want the Minister to take the matter seriously. What will happen to a sports club in the scenario that I have described? Is there any protection in the Bill?

Mr Lammy: Let me begin with the remark made by the hon. Member for Daventry (Mr Boswell). The International Olympic Committee announced on Monday last week its policy on the participation of transsexual sportspeople. The policy will apply in the forthcoming Olympic games in Athens. In brief, it allows transsexual sportspeople to compete in their acquired gender, but only if they have legal recognition in the acquired gender and have undergone surgical and hormonal treatment so as to minimise any gender-related advantage. The hon. Gentleman said that we have been waiting a little while for that announcement, but he will understand that, as a consequence of it, new clause 3 is not necessary — although I am grateful for the manner in which he proposed it, as if to move things along. Indeed, the new clause acknowledges that any policy announced by the IOC should supersede the suggestion that it contains.

The Government agree that it is for the IOC to decide the terms on which transsexual sportspeople may compete in the Olympic games. Clause 19 provides UK sporting bodies, including the British Olympic Association, with the scope to restrict the participation of transsexual sports people where that is necessary to maintain competitive parity or for the safety of other competitors. The IOC has been guided by similar consideration, and we believe that the clause provides UK sporting bodies with sufficient scope to use the IOC guidelines.

Mr Boswell: I am grateful to the Minister for updating me. I cannot claim responsibility for single-handedly getting the IOC to get its act together but could he or the Under-Secretary confirm whether there is any possibility, given that transgender people, in addition to the remedial medication to which he referred, typically have to continue with other medication indefinitely, will fall foul of anti-doping codes? Will medication that they are required to take, whether medically or legally, lead to such problems?

Mr Lammy: The IOC prescribes a two-year period for hormonal treatment and so on. The hon. Gentleman has asked an important question to which I do not have an answer off the top of my head, but I shall be happy to deal with it later.

Although the IOC acknowledges that hormonal and other treatments used by transsexual people typically eliminate any competitive advantage that male-to-female transsexual people may have over other women, there may be cases where competitive parity or the safety of other competitors are valid concerns, and the IOC recognises that, as does clause 19. We shall issue guidance to sporting bodies in advance of the implementation of the Bill setting out the legal position and the scope that remains, quite properly, for sporting bodies to make decisions that reflect the needs of their particular sport.

LJ: I am interested that my hon. Friend said that safety grounds might prevent a trans-competitor from competing. Sports bodies already have the power to exclude someone if safety is a factor, and in Committee I queried the need for clause 19. I am pleased to learn that the IOC has made it clear in its ruling that claims, pursued in the House of Lords [should have said 'another place'] that the Bill "has put the entire future of competitive sport in jeopardy" are entirely bogus. The IOC's sensible proposal negates the need for clause 19.

DL: I am grateful to my hon. Friend for putting her views on the record. There were arguments circulating in another place that were deeply unhelpful, but clause 19 makes the position clear. My hon. Friend will accept that there are many sports in which these issues simply do not arise, but there are other contact sports such as rugby and basketball where safety considerations might be pertinent. By definition, the individuals playing those sports come into contact with others, so although the parity test remains, the safety requirement needs to be taken into consideration as well.

In an intervention, I made clear the Government's position on new clause 6, which raises an issue that, even though we had only three minutes to deal with it in Committee, was, I believe, dealt with satisfactorily. Its implication is, unfortunately, that transsexual people are more likely to expose themselves or seek to cause offence than other people who use communal changing or washing facilities.

RY-R: Is not the logic of the new clause on changing facilities that there should be separate changing cubicles in shops, not communal changing areas? Equally, changing rooms at swimming pools would have to have a door saying "Transgender person".

DL: I am grateful for that intervention form the hon. Gentleman, who has drawn the natural conclusion from the debate. Frankly, new clause 6 would warrant the exclusion of transsexual people from changing and washing facilities, and the creation of separate facilities for their use.

AS: If the Minister is fair, he will acknowledge that at the start of my remarks about new clause 6, I said that I hope, expect and believe that the vast majority of transsexual people — if not all of them — will use the facilities appropriate to their acquired gender. I am discussing a reserve power to cover serious difficulties, and we all accept that such circumstances are a remote possibility.

DL: The hon. Gentleman may well approach the issue on the basis of separate-but-equal treatment. But the Government entirely rejects the implication of the new clause that transsexuals might set out to cause offence to others. That is not the Government's experience, and we therefore reject the new clause.

The Government also believe that the separate facilities for minority groups are objectionable, and we urge the House to reject the proposal. For obvious reasons, many hon. Members fought to ensure that separate signs for minorities became a thing of the past in South Africa, and we did not engage in that fight in order to set up such prejudice over here.

Mr Boswell: In view of the Minister's assurance, particularly in relation to new clause 3, I beg to ask leave to withdraw the motion.

APPENDIX C

Gender Diversity, Recognition and Citizenship (Online Summary)

THIS IS THE ONLINE SUMMARY by the Economic and Social Research Council of the research in which I participated for Dr Hines. I am most grateful to the ESRC for permission to reproduce it here.

This summary was written before the Same Sex Couples Act was passed into law in 2013, and was likely taken into consideration for that. As you will see, it does not simply reflect the views of those who have used the GRA 2004 but pushes a particular deconstructionist line. Trans people are used as a means of deconstructing general social values on sex and gender. Thus, the purpose of the research is turned backwards: it is not about how the legislation can be best framed to enable trans people to interface with society, but how society, much the larger of the two populations, can be modified so as to adapt to them.

The full paper remains unpublished. One may question why this is so.[1]

---

1   Dr Hines can be seen explaining her views on Gender Recognition in this video: https://www.youtube.com/watch?v=nMISMRO9IEo&t=616s.

Gender Diversity, Recognition and Citizenship[2]

Lead Research Organisation: University of Leeds

Department Name: Sociology & Social Policy

Description of Outcome

The research indicated that the Gender Recognition Act (GRA) brings a significant challenge to a biological model of gender, which presumes a fixed relationship between sex and gender identity. The legislation also detaches recognition from the requirement of surgical intervention; bringing a more complex framework for understanding gendered embodiment. Moreover, the GRA brings legal recognition that gender identification may shift across the life course. Yet, the extent to which gender identity may be fluidly experienced is limited; for example, the GRA demands that a successful applicant 'intends to continue to live in the acquired gender until death' (Gender Recognition Act, 2004). Thus those who do not firmly and permanently identify and present as male or as female are not covered by the new framework of gendered citizenship. The research suggests, then, that a gender binary model (male/female) remains unchanged by the GRA. (Re: Hines, S. (2009) 'A Pathway to Diversity?: Human Rights, Citizenship and Politics of Transgender', *Contemporary Politics*. 15.1: 87–102)

While the GRA marks a departure from traditional medical discourse and practice whereby genital reassignment surgery was understood as curative, medical perspectives continue to resonate. An applicant must have, or have had, 'gender dysphoria', which is understood as symptomatic of 'gender identity disorder' and remains a listed category in the DSM. Thus, 'transgender' remains medicalised through the legal criterion for gender recognition. The research suggests, then, that there exist both continuities and changes to medical understandings and practices. (Re: Hines, S. (2010) 'Sexing Gender/

---

2   https://gtr.ukri.org/projects?ref=ES%2FF037309%2F1 (2020).

Gendering Sex: Towards an Intersectional Analysis of Transgender' in Y. Taylor, Y., S. Hines and M. Casey (eds.) *Theorising Intersectionality and Sexuality*, Palgrave MacMillan. In Press.)

Significantly, the GRA allows a more nuanced understanding of the relationship between sex, gender and sexuality. Dominant configurations of a 'heterosexual matrix, which assumes correlation between the male or female sexed body, gender identity and sexual desire, are fractured by the law's recognition that these variables may be ambiguous. The research indicates, however, that the demand that existing marriages be annulled means that the GRA fails to fully take account of the complexities of, and between, gender, sexuality and intimacy. Further, while couples may register for a civil partnership after divorce, the law carries a set of assumptions about gender and sexuality, and intimate relationships, which are constructed through a hetero/homo binary; one can be heterosexual (marry) or homosexual (civilly partner). So while the GRA aims to protect the 'right to a family' (ECHR, A.8), the research suggests that it enforces inequality for those who are married or whose sexualities or intimate relationships transgress the homo/hetero binary. (Re: Hines, S. (2009) '(Trans) Forming Gender: Social Change and Transgender Citizenship' in H. Oleksy, et al. *Intimate Citizenship: Gender, Sexuality, Politics*, Routledge.)

The research suggests that the aforementioned complexities impact on trans people's experiences of 'recognition' and variously shape the extent to which they view the GRA as significantly enabling an innovative citizenship framework. While the GRA represents a significant legal moment in the decoupling of sex and gender, the influence of medical discourse and practice, particularly in relation to the evidence based criteria, and the divorce clause, enacts an inconsistent framework of rights and enforces inequalities in the accessing of such rights. (Re: 'Recognising Diversity? Transgender Citizenship and the Gender Recognition Act' in S. Hines and T. Sanger, (eds.) (2010)

Transforming Sociology: Towards a Social Analysis of Gender Diversity, Routledge.)

Exploitation Route: Findings fed into a community-based review of the Gender Recognition Act, which developed recommendations for review of the legislation.

Sectors: Findings fed into a community-based review of the Gender Recognition Act, which developed recommendations for review of the legislation.

Funded Value: £79,553

Funded Period: May 08 — May 10

Funder: ESRC

Project Status: Closed

Project Category: Research Grant

Project Reference: ES/F037309/1

Other References: RES-000-22-2763

Principal Investigator: Sally Hines

Research Subject: Social Policy, Sociology

Research Topic: Social Policy, Sociology

Text of the online summary included by kind permission of the UKRI ESRC Administration

APPENDIX D

Gender Diversity, Recognition and Citizenship: Exploring the Significance and Experiences of the UK Gender Recognition Act (GRA, 2004)

The UK Gender Recognition Act (GRA, 2004)

I AM EXTREMELY GRATEFUL to Professor Sally Hines for granting permission for me to include the entirety of her previously unpublished paper on Gender Diversity, Recognition and Citizenship, which was carried out between 2008 and 2010 and finalised in early 2011.

❧

The Gender Recognition Act (GRA) came into being in the UK in 2004. Before the GRA, Britain was one out of four European countries that failed to legally recognise the acquired gender of transsexual people (Whittle, 2000). The GRA can be contextualised within a post-1997 UK climate in which questions of equality and diversity came to the fore of policy and law. Thus the GRA is one of five recent pieces of UK legislation that address issues of gender and sexual equality. In turn, these legislative shifts map on to a broader equalities and diversity focus within a European context. Representing the civil recognition of gender transition, the Gender Recognition Act (GRA, 2004) enabled transgender people to change their birth certificates and to marry in their acquired gender.

The Project

The project sought to address the impacts and the significance of the GRA by considering how transgender people variously understand and experience this changing policy landscape. Key research questions asked:

1. Why some people view the GRA as significant and register for 'gender recognition', and why others do not.

2. How married people are negotiating the choice between gender recognition and the recognition of their partnerships.

3. The extent to which gender recognition characterises continuities and/or changes to the medicalisation of transgender.

4. The extent to which the GRA moves beyond a binary gender model.

Various qualitative methods were employed to collect data, including textual/policy analysis; 25 in-depth one-to-one interviews; 2 focus group interviews; analysis of virtual materials (online discussion forums).

We recruited participants through transgender support groups, self-help groups and campaigning groups. Some participants were introduced to us through existing participants or word of mouth.

This project was funded by the UK Economic and Social Research Council and took place between May 2008 and May 2010.

Individual Participants

GENDER: 18 participants defined themselves as women or female; 4 participants defined themselves as male or FtM (female to male); 1 participant described themself as non-gendered.

SEXUALITY: 8 participants identified as heterosexual; 4 participants identified as bisexual; 4 participants identified as lesbian; 1 participant identified as gay; 1 participant identified as queer; 1 participant identified as pansexual; 1 participant identified as asexual; 2 participants said that it was 'difficult to say' what their sexuality was; 2 participants were reluctant to talk about their sexuality.

AGE: 2 participants were aged 20–30 yrs; 4 participants were aged 30–40 yrs; 5 participants were aged 40–50 yrs; 8 participants were aged 50–60 yrs; 5 participants were aged 60+; 1 participant did not want to say what age they were.

RELATIONSHIP STATUS: 14 participants were in relationships and/or married/civilly partnered: of these, 6 participants were in relationships with their pre-transition partners and 2 were in civil partnerships; 11 participants were single; 1 participant did not want to talk about relationships.

PARENTING STATUS: 9 participants had children.

Focus Groups and Virtual Discussion Boards

To enable analysis of collective responses to, and experiences of, the Gender Recognition Act, analysis of two wiki discussion boards (anonymous) was carried out over a 6 month period and two focus groups were held. 8 participants took part in the first and 9 in the second. The first focus group took place as part of the Scotland Equality Network and the second was organised by the Scottish Transgender Alliance. Focus group members included transgender activists, community organisers and members of Scotland's broader transgender communities.

Gender Recognition Certificates

12 participants had *successfully applied* for a Gender Recognition Certificate (GRC). 1 participant had applied and received an *Interim Certificate;* 3 participants had *unsuccessfully applied* for a Gender Recognition Certificate; 6 participants were *unable to apply* for a Gender Recognition Certificate due to the application criteria; 3 participants had *chosen not to apply* for a Gender Recognition Certificate even though they met the criteria for application.

Successful Applications: The majority of the 12 participants who had registered, or wished to register, for a gender recognition certificate (GRC) spoke about their decision as being strategically guided.

Interim Certificates: 1 participant had applied for a GRC and had received an interim certificate. This person was married to her pre-transition partner and the interim certificate was given for 6 months whilst she divorced.

Unsuccessful Applications: Reasons for unsuccessful applications were extremely complex and difficult to generalise. However, transitioning outside of a medically approved route of gender transition was linked to unsuccessful applications.

Restricted by Criteria: The participants who wished to register for a GRC yet had not done so fell into three categories: those who were married to their pre-transition partners and did not want to get divorced, those who had not followed a medically approved route of transition, and those who felt that their gender identities were more complex than the recognised male/female gender categories.

Choosing not to Register: Each of the 3 participants who explicitly chose not to register for a GRC described this as a political decision, which was aligned to 'queer' and 'non-assimilationist' politics.

Key Research Findings

Participants overwhelmingly believed that the Gender Recognition Act would not have been possible without the lobbying of government by transgender political campaigning organisation *Press for Change*.

- The majority of participants believed that the Gender Recognition Act was an important law in terms of rights and recognition — a positive move towards citizenship parity.

- There were big differences in attitudes amongst participants as to the overall significance of the GRA.

- The majority of participants felt that the Gender Recognition Act had little impact on their work life.

- The majority of participants felt the Gender Recognition Act had minimal effect on relationships with wider family and friends.

- Participants were divided on whether the GRA had an impact on social and cultural attitudes and understandings of transgender.

- Participants were divided about the ease of the recognition process and on issues around required evidence.

- The majority of participants felt it was correct that the GRA did not demand that an applicant for a GRC had undergone surgery, though it was often highlighted that the continuation of the 'real life test' undermined this.

- Around half of participants believed that medical and psychiatric professionals should not be involved in the process of gender recognition.

- The majority of participants felt that the Gender Recognition Act excluded people whose gender identities fell outside of the categories of male or female.

- The Gender Recognition Act was strongly criticised by the majority of participants for its criteria that people married to their pre-transition partners divorce before being granted a Gender Recognition Certificate.

Key Themes

Transgender Lobbying

When talking about the GRA, the majority of participants were keen to draw attention to the long-time campaigning and lobbying of government by transgender political lobbying organisation *Press for Change*. Though many participants believed that transgender campaigning organisations should have argued more forcefully against the 'divorce clause' and some that they should have lobbied for recognition of non-gendered people, the work of transgender social movements in bringing about legal change was explicit:

> I never—we never—thought this could happen, so there's a massive amount of gratitude to those that have done it."

Citizenship Parity

Many participants talked about the significance of the GRA in terms of extending or protecting their 'rights'. That the Act emerged within a context of European human rights was seen to be important. This was also talked about in terms of 'protection':

> It's a principle, almost to say, 'hey, listen, if you do this you're protected [...] You know there's a framework there that you can move in, to get the test cases. It's all backed up there by the Human Rights Court and you think, 'yeah, wow, this is the way it should be'.

Significance

In the main, the significance of the GRA was discussed in relation to simplifying bureaucracy. In this way, for most of the participants who had successfully applied under the GRA, the significance of the Act was strategic and pragmatic; changes to official documents made everyday life less complicated and smoother on a bureaucratic level:

I guess it's just that it makes everything simpler when all the documents match up.

A minority of participants linked the ability to change their birth certificate to their 'sense of self', seeing this as an important reflection of their gender identity:

For me personally without that legislation my, what I believe is my right to correct an inaccuracy about me, about who I am, my identity, couldn't happen. And yes, you can change your passport, driving licence, any other pieces of documentation, but from my point of view, and I know you don't produce your birth certificate at the drop of a hat, but without that it's a piece of that jigsaw that's incomplete, and would remain incomplete if the Act had never been brought in. And then there's all the rights that go along with that.

Yet for quite a few other participants, the holding of a GRC was not linked at all to self-identity:

Yeah for me it is more of a convenience thing; I don't think it will affect me in terms of my identity. [...] I don't fell in any shape or form that I need a passport or a birth certificate to feel more strongly towards my identity; I just need it for practical reasons.

Work Life

Few participants felt that the GRA had any impact on their work lives. The vast majority felt that both the private and public sector were unaware of the changing law. This view applied equally to work colleagues, human resources and organisational structures:

"I really don't think anyone in my workplace has heard of the GRA. No one has ever mentioned it. No, nothing..."

While some participants talked about hoping that the GRA would be beneficial in relation to future discrimination in the workplace, others were more sceptical:

"You get to work, you get sacked from your job, but no one puts the trans word in the equation. Can you prove it was because you're trans? Well no, the GRA isn't going to help you."

Family and Friends

Participants largely felt that their relationships with family members and close friends had been unaffected by the GRA. Gender transition more broadly was discussed as the factor that strained or deepened familial and friendship bonds, and the GRA was not believed to have affected this either positively or negatively:

My friends are my friends regardless and things with my family have not changed because of that.

Social Attitudes & Acceptance

There was a big division amongst participants around whether the GRA would have a positive impact on cultural attitudes and the social acceptance of transgender. Some participants felt that there would be a 'trickle down' effect, which would enhance trans people's cultural value and lead to a broader change towards social acceptance and greater understanding. Others, however, felt that legal change had little, if no, effect on social attitudes and cultural understanding:

It [the GRA] creates a sense of formality, a sense of acceptance that with time will result in a reduction of prejudice within society as a whole.

A lot of people aren't even aware that the GRA even exists. In fact I guess if you asked the person, man or woman in the street, can you tell me something about GRA? They're not going to be able to. So actually some people seem to be quite surprised that you can do this.

Evidence

There was a big divide amongst participants around the question of the ease of the process and of the evidence required. Not surprisingly, this linked to whether or not the individual had been successful in their application for recognition. Of those that had, most spoke about the application process as being "straightforward" or "easy". These people tended to be people who had transitioned via a medically approved route of care and were several years post-transition:

> Once I knew what I had to do it was ok. My GP had all my records and so it all must have got transferred from him. I didn't have any problems with evidence, no. The whole thing was pretty straightforward really.

For other participants, however, the process was experienced as complicated and frustrating:

> When I first saw the form I thought 'oh no' […] I just hated it. That put me off for ages. I was thinking 'oh, god'…

Several participants had their evidence questioned:

> The major bugbear of mine is providing the diagnosis report. It's a nightmare. I had to be re-diagnosed. Right, I was diagnosed years ago…why do I have to be re-diagnosed? It's crazy. I came across a sticking point […] Even though I've been through surgery, even though I've changed my name for six years, it's perfectly clear what I've done. Which is really stupid, so I asked my GP to check their records and they found an initial diagnosis from X in 2001 and that initial diagnosis did say I had gender dysphoria, which is exactly what the GRP forms requested. I sent a letter back saying 'that's it, that's all I can find you, like it or lump it,' and finally that's been enough.

Some participants spoke out strongly about the medical evidence that was required by the gender recognition panel. Issues around privacy and potential disclosures were often cited as being problematic. One participant refused to supply the required evidence, believing that it broke ethics of confidentiality:

> I felt that the Gender Recognition Act was asking for a level of personal disclosure that was a breach of your medical confidentiality; in terms of the

medical evidence that they were requiring. [...] Because these are highly personal issues, you know, when you go into a counselling session with a gender therapist and you're talking about things to do with your family life, your love life, your sex life, how you felt as a child [...] And I thought, 'no,' that's just wrong, that's inherently wrong. And I thought, ok, I object to that [...] I think this is a breach of medical confidentiality [...] And I thought I'm not willing to do that, I'm going to question this and take it as far as I can.

Other participants had supplied evidence that was rejected and others were not applying because they felt they did not have sufficient evidence. These were people who had not followed a medically approved route of gender transition.

Non-Surgical Criteria

All but one of the participants felt that it was positive that the criteria for a GRC did not involve surgery. It was felt that surgical criteria would have been discriminatory on a number of levels: against people who could not afford private surgery and were on NHS waiting lists; against people who were unable to have surgery due to medical reasons; for people who chose not to have surgery:

I think that's quite important because I've met a couple of trans men who have hepatitis C, they can't take hormones; it doesn't stop them from being trans [...] I mean why should that determine whether you should be a man or a woman or change your birth certificate? So I think that was one of the better parts of it. It's also sort of saying that we don't have any gatekeepers saying if you're allowed to be trans or not. I think the time issue is long enough...that's enough, you don't need to have to prove yourself in any other way. Because who are you proving it to? Who should be judging?

It should never be a requirement. It's down to freedom of choice.

Medical Involvement

Medical involvement in the gender recognition process was a contentious issue. Some participants broadly felt that there had to be some medical involvement to safeguard the process, though even here there was hesitancy:

> It's difficult to know who else you could put in that position... to minimise the chances of mistakes. But then mistakes are rare and you're never going to eradicate them 100% either [...].

Many other participants, however, felt strongly that issues around gender and identity and recognition should not be left in the hands of psychiatry:

> I think it's a very dangerous way of legitimising any piece of legislation that you have to have this array of medical support. You name anything else; you name any other situation that requires similar? You know, so for me it's like, where's the parity in that? Where's equality in that? When you're taking a particular group of people in society and saying in order for you to access and take advantage of this legislation, you've got to have the support, and it is support, not just contact with, but you've got to have the support of the medical profession in order to obtain your legal rights. Point out any piece of legislation that does the same? I'm not unhappy with my gender; it was society that was unhappy with my gender. So having to prove that you need support, treatment, whatever it is to be able to get to that end point... There are far more civilised ways of dealing with it than that.

That 'gender dysphoria' remains a listed mental illness on the Diagnostic and Statistical Medical Guidelines for Practitioners (DSM) was critiqued by many participants, with the involvement of medical practitioners in the gender recognition process being linked to this:

> No psychiatrists should be involved. This is not a mental illness. And in other parts of the world they're enlightened enough not to use mental health professionals any more. We are stuck with being subservient to the American Psychiatric Association and the SM5 which is the psychiatric manual which defines what is a mental illness [...] They see this as some sort of sexual deviancy, right, which has to be dealt with by society and contained. It is absolutely appalling. It is the biggest affront to human rights as far as transgender and transsexual people, because both are tarred

with the same brush, are concerned. It is the fundamental issue. [...] We have to remove this.

Some participants believed that the guiding framework of gender recognition should be separated altogether from a biological model of sex and gender:

> Western society is obsessed with gender and sex. The law should be framed in human rights terms, rather than in a bipolar notion of gender.

Recognition for Non-gendered People

The majority of participants felt that the GRC discriminated against people whose identity was not straightforwardly male or female. Many participants did say that they broadly identified as either male or female and so were not personally affected by having to identify in this way in order to register for recognition. Most of these participants, however, felt that the Act was unfair for those whose gender identities were not binary:

> If people are happy to be not either man or woman, if that is how they perceive themselves to be, then that should be recognised.

Several participants felt that in order to obtain a gender recognition certificate, they had to fit into the categories of male and female when their gender identity was more complex:

> When you have to tick the boxes on a form I would usefully put my tick in the middle and I don't think I want to push the boat, or rock the boat with this...so there are some forms that you don't rock the boat and there are other forms that you think, well, this is a piece of crap anyway and you tick in between the two boxes, create another box called 'other' or whatever. But I don't like the fact that we're always put into these kinds of categories all the time.

One participant explicitly felt that they were unable to apply for a GRC due to identifying as non-gendered. For this person, the GRA had no impact on recognition rights:

> I could only successfully apply for gender recognition if I were to identify within the gendered societal construct and also having been through the relevant statutory procedures and met the criteria as stated within the GRA. The law does not recognise human existence outside the gendered societal structure and I am trying to gain legal recognition as a person of non-gendered identity.

Civil Partnerships and Marriage

Following gender recognition, some participants in same-sex relationships had registered for civil partnerships:

> It meant I was able to enter into a civil partnership, you know, with all the fanfare that that takes, rather than having to hide away and pretend.

One of the key rights brought by the GRA was that, following gender recognition, transgender people were able to marry in their acquired gender. Some participants had taken advantage of this and felt very positively about being able to marry:

> The positives is obviously it's allowed me to get a birth certificate, obviously allowed me to get married, so that side of thing's great.

The situation regarding marriage, however, was very different for participants who remained married to their pre-transition partners. These participants were in a position where they had to choose between their long-standing marriage and gender recognition:

> X [participant's wife] wanted to remain married [...] I feel that I have obligations to X. I mean our relationship is in some ways very similar to how it used to be, in terms of a responsibility relationship. And that is likely to continue because I take that responsibility seriously. [...] The continuation of that relationship has not enabled me to take some of the steps perhaps

that I would have wanted to take to free myself from the past. I'm still fulfilling for X that role as husband; not sexually but in other ways. And I still fulfil the role for my children. And I don't want to take that away from them.

In defence of the divorce clause, Ministers had argued that following divorce and gender recognition, people would be able to register their marriage under the Civil Partnership Act (CPA, 2004). None of the participants in this research project, however, felt that this alleviated discrimination for people in existing marriages. Civil partnerships were not believed to be on an equal footing — either symbolically or legally — to marriage, and participants often said that linking the two pieces of legislation demonstrated a lack of understanding of the complexities between gender and sexuality:

> A civil partnership is not appropriate at all. It's inappropriate for trans people in lots of ways. A civil partnership is not equal to marriage. And it just doesn't…there's no logic to it. I mean why should a lesbian couple, one of which becomes a man, be allowed to then marry, and a heterosexual couple, one of which changes gender, be forbidden marriage? Why? What's the logic? It's completely asymmetrical.

Summary of Research Findings

Overall, participants felt that the UK Gender Recognition Act (GRA) was an important and significant law in terms of transgender equality legislation. The majority of participants had registered, planned to register or wished to register (though were restricted by the criteria) for a Gender Recognition Certificate under the law. A minority of participants actively did not want to register.

The significance of the Act was, in the main, linked pragmatically to the changing of documents and in this way was, largely, discussed strategically rather than as a subjective reflection of gender identity. The GRA was seen to have had little impact on relationships with family or friends or on work life. It was hoped that the Act would have a positive social and cultural impact regarding transgender people, although the link between law and broader societal attitudes was sometimes disputed. Whilst some participants had found the process of recognition straightforward, others had found it a complex and problematic procedure, particularly in relation to the required evidence from GPs and psychiatrists.

That the Act did not require surgery was largely viewed positively, although the continued role of medical practitioners in the gender recognition process was strongly criticised by many participants. The GRA also came under criticism for neglecting the rights of non-gendered people. While a minority of participants felt directly excluded from the new rights brought by the GRA in this respect, a larger group felt that they were inappropriately forced to fit into categories of male or female. In this way, the GRA was critiqued for reproducing a binary gender model. The divorce criteria in the GRA came under much criticism. While a group of participants had benefitted from the Act as they were now able to marry in their acquired gender, participants who remained married to their pre-transition partners spoke angrily about having to choose between marriage to their long-standing partners and gender recognition. While it was felt that civil partnerships worked for transgender people who were in same-sex relationships, linking the Civil Partnership Act and the Gender Recognition Act as the Government had done in defence of the divorce clause showed a lack of understanding of the complex relationship between gender and sexuality.

Overall, the project found that the UK Gender Recognition Act was seen to be an important first step towards greater equality for transgender people; a stepping stone to full citizenship rights:

The GRA is a good start, but there is much more to be done.

Recommendations

Research findings suggest that the following moves are needed to secure that all transgender people obtain the same levels of recognition and protection under the Gender Recognition Act:

- The removal of the divorce clause

- Recognition for non-gendered and multi-gendered people

- The removal of 'gender dysphoria' from the DSM

- A simplified application process and less requirement of medical evidence

- Less involvement of medical practitioners in the legal process of gender recognition

The Researchers

Dr. Sally Hines:

Senior Lecturer in Sociology and Social Policy
School of Sociology and Social Policy
University of Leeds, Leeds, LS2 9JT
Email redacted
Dr. [*****]
Research Fellow
School of Health and Social Care
University of *******
Email redacted

Acknowledgements

We are extremely grateful to all the participants in this study; including the people who took part in the one-to-one interviews and those who participated in the focus groups.

We would like to thank Professor Diane Richardson and Dr Surya Monro who were members of the Advisory Committee and Dr Louis Turner who was a virtual member of the advisory group. We also wish to thank James Morton for his support for the project and for his help with the arrangements for the focus groups. Thanks also to the various other organisations and support groups who publicised our call for participants on their websites.

We wish to thank the Economic and Social Research Council for funding the project (REF: RES-000-22-2763).

Publications

Davy, Z. and Hines, S. (forthcoming) '"The GRA is a good start, but there is much more to be done": The UK Gender Recognition Act'.

Hines, S. (2009) 'A Pathway to Diversity?: Human Rights, Citizenship and Politics of Transgender' *Contemporary Politics*

Hines, S. (2010) 'Queerly Situated: Exploring Constraints and Negotiations of Trans Queer Subjectivities', *Special Issue of Gender, Place and Culture: Towards a Trans Geography.*

Hines, S. (2010) 'Recognising Diversity? Transgender Citizenship and the Gender Recognition Act' in Hines, S and Sanger, T. (eds.) *Transforming Sociology: Towards a Social Analysis of Gender Diversity,* Routledge.

Hines, S. (2011) 'Sexing Gender/Gendering Sex: Towards an Intersectional Analysis of Transgender' in Taylor, Y., Hines, S. and Casey M. (eds.) *Theorising Intersectionality and Sexuality,* Palgrave Macmillan.

Hines, S. (forthcoming, 2012) *Gender Diversity, Recognition and Citizenship: Towards a Politics of Difference,* Palgrave.

APPENDIX E

GRA Consultation Addendum (2009)

THIS IS THE FULL TEXT [with minor redactions of personal data] of the Addendum which I sent to the Research Assistant for Dr Sally Hines' study on the views of transsexuals who had received GRCs about the importance or not of reassignment surgeries in the legal recognition of 'acquired' gender. My views have evolved on some of the finer points, but overall they are still in line with what I present here.

The draft report was amended to take account of the views I expressed below, when having seen the draft I sent it to Dr Hines. However, no explanation was ever given to me about how this important data had been missed out, when I had made a special point of corresponding with the assistant about it and it was noticeable by its difference to the rest of the material included in the survey.

Also, no comment was made in the revised report on my 3000-word Addendum, none of my issues were mentioned, the corrected version merely said 'All but one of the participants felt that it was positive that the criteria for a GRC did not involve surgery.'

Gender Recognition Interview Additional Comments 4 Nov 2009

I should like to add some further comments to my interview for the Gender Recognition research.

When the GRA went through Parliament I recall that in the face of some questioning an assurance was given that for MtF transsexuals it would normally be required that genital corrective surgery had been carried out, or at least was about to be carried out and that a Recognition Certificate would only be granted in the case of exceptions to this in the event that the person had already qualified for surgery but had been turned down by the surgeon on the basis of strong medical reasons, such as haemophilia or other major medical contraindication.

Over the last couple of years I have come across references to more than a handful of cases, and indeed have been on internet groups where there have been MtF transsexuals who have GRCs who have not had or even qualified for, or even desire to have, surgery. There is quite a little backwater debate going on in some trans circles on the net as to whether having a GRA should qualify one to get surgery in the event of applying to a Gender Identity Clinic. (Thus reversing the situation.) Some argue that legal gender recognition in itself, regardless of physical morphology, should remove 'gender dysphoria'! As if a piece of paper could remove a lifelong feeling about one's body. I have even debated online with a person who said they were a woman and 'completely happy' with their 'female penis'. What kind of sophistry is this?

I have mentioned the qualification referred to in paragraph 2 on some internet discussion groups and it has been replied that whether the original proviso was made or not, it could not be enforced on the Gender Recognition Panel. This may be technically correct; however, my own feeling is that there has been, at the least, inconsistency.

I also understand that David Lammy, the MP responsible for steering the GRA through the House of Commons (I watched the Third

Reading debate in its entirety), has since proudly stated that the GRA has detached (or some similar term) gender from physical conditions or qualifiers such as hormones or anatomy.

When I was first interviewed about my views on the GRA, I was reticent concerning my opinions on this matter for various reasons, amongst which were that I was at the time reading some of Judith Butler's works on gender and I wanted to digest what she said.

In my view it is a mistake to entirely detach gender recognition from all physical attributes. As the researcher is doubtless aware, there is now a new debate going on about all this. There are many trans-sexual people who are very unhappy with the now all-pervasive use of the term Transgender under which they are expected to be subsumed.

There is extreme unhappiness in some quarters with the idea that people who conform to a social identity of one gender but have no desire to change their morphology or hormonal status in order to be physically congruent with that should be categorised together with those of us for whom those changes were quintessential to our identities.

Not the least problem with this is whether someone who has male anatomy and hormonal status can be able to participate in sporting events as a woman simply because they wear women's clothes and take on a female social role. Women who take male hormones are disqualified from participating in sporting events on the medical grounds that male hormones affect muscle development, yet the transgender lobbyists claim that to exclude transgender people of male hormonal status but female social role from such sports is discrimination. It is far too large a debate to get into the full depth of argument here about what constitutes male and female, man and woman; however, it is my view and that of many transsexual people that a complete divorce of gender recognition from all physical attributes is a serious mistake.

The GRA refers to 'acquired gender'. In one sense, of course, trans-sexual people have always been of their personally identified gender, but in another it has to be accepted that we at least had the physical sexual characteristics of the sex we did not want to be.

If one 'acquires' a new gender (at least the term used in law), then there must be something that one does to 'acquire' it. To simply say that one always had it is a self-contradiction in the terms as stated by the new law. Self-definition is a part of the process of sex/gender reassignment, but if it were all that is involved, then the whole medical reassignment process would be irrelevant. We are moving from a time when radical feminists argued that transsexual people should not have genital reconstruction because they refused to accept the bodily identification involved, to a time now when some argue that genital reconstruction is not a necessary part of reassignment, indeed that people can be of a particular sex regardless of their morphology or hormonal status.

Try telling that to Kim Petra, the world's youngest fully reassigned transsexual girl. This is playing into the hands of the Blanchards and Baileys of this world who see the whole gender reassignment issue as one of acquired sexual paraphilia and do all that they can towards 'reparative' treatment, otherwise known as aversion therapy, brain-washing, or sexual abuse, psychological torture. There is enough guilt associated with the disgust that a transsexual woman feels towards her unwanted male genitals without trying to persuade her that she has 'only acquired' her feelings about this through social role modelling, and that she should be happy with the way her body is because that has nothing to do with what it means to be a woman.

Again, the same applies to sex hormones and their irreversible effects in puberty. If young transsexual people are conditioned to believe that the hormones which are causing these unwanted and permanent effects are nothing to do with what constitutes being of one sex or another, then they may be persuaded not to engage in preventive hormone-blocking treatment at the time when it will make a difference, and be forced to suffer the consequences, which will likely amount to not being able to successfully pass in their desired sex when they later realise that they cannot avoid how they feel about their sexual characteristics.

In essence I believe that the whole manner in which the GRA is couched is flawed. It should be the Sex Recognition Act, whereby when someone has Sex Reassignment Surgery their new, acquired or corrected sex is recognised. The researcher herself drew attention in a lecture she gave in February 2009 to the fact that before the Ormerod decision of 1970 the correction of the sexual anatomy was considered sufficient to allow legal recognition of the 'acquired' sex.

While Judith Butler has done much good in one aspect of her work in that she has largely been responsible for sweeping away the trans hostile and exclusionary culture of the radical feminists of the eighties (although it still exists in some backwaters), nonetheless I believe she has gone too far in deconstructing gender into no more than a social phenomenon.

The fact remains that female and male exist on the biological level as evidenced by the existence of ova and sperm, which are required for the procreation of life, and that there are (at least external) physical morphologies congruent with these sexes, as well as hormonal status. It may yet not be possible to acquire the reproductive capabilities of the desired sex, but yet may be in some future time with developments in stem cell technologies.

To refer to Rupert Sheldrake's Morphogenetic field theory, there would seem on all the evidence to be two basic morphologies, male and female. Intersexes exist, but are extremely rare. There are variations within those morphologies in terms of reproductive capabilities, but the morphologies were the basis for the first 'gender' or sex reassignments as overseen by Hirschfeld and Benjamin.

As Joan Roughgarden has shown in some depth with her work, of course not all organisms are unambiguously female or male; evolution allows for variation and experimentation, and this is demonstrated in the existence of transsexual people. There is much evidence now that there are sexually dimorphic structures in the brain and that transsexual people exist because of underlying biological causes (Gooren and Zhou, Ramachandran and many others).

It is quite clear that there are different groups of trans people, those for whom their physical morphology is the essence of their gender identity and those for whom it is a matter of social identification but for whom their sexual anatomy is not an issue.

The GRA lumps us all together and falls into the fallacy of conflating sex and gender.

I am involved with a lesbian networking group and have discussed this with quite a number of the women engaged with it. With only one notable exception, they have all agreed that they would feel uncomfortable having transgender 'women' in the group who were clear that they wanted to retain their male sexual anatomy.

The notable exception is someone who is essentially an FtM transsexual but who chose to continue living as female because they are too short and feminine in appearance to pass as male (in their judgement). In such cases there would seem to be personal agendas involved as to ignoring sexual morphologies.

This brings up the issue of whether FtM transsexuals should be required to have lower body reconstructive surgery in the way that I and others believe MtF should. It is argued that genital reconstruction should not be a requirement for either because to require it of MtF would mean that FtM would not qualify since so many fewer of those have the reconstruction.

This is a fallacy. Clearly the genital surgeries are entirely different. The MtF reconstructive surgery is well established and successful, enabling the result to be extremely realistic and with good sexual sensation. The FtM constructive surgery will probably never be truly successful until stem cell research allows for the growing of the required tissue in vitro.

Furthermore, it must be understood that a man can lose his penis through injury or disease and not cease to be a man. What is challenging is that women do not have penises. I may have been born with one, in other words I had male sexual anatomy, but it got in the way of my being able to fully experience myself as female, and so it was necessary for me to get rid of it before I could.

So what we have goes beyond the 'social' construction of gender. There are what Foucault refers to as the 'mysterious essences' of bodily gender, which are not mysterious, but simply endocrinological secretions, sex hormones which are largely responsible for the morphology of sexual somatotypes, and the morphologies themselves which are acquired *in utero* due to hormonal influences. Hormones are also responsible for pheromones which we all emit and which give subliminal clues as to what someone's sex is. If someone is happy to continue giving off male pheromones, can they really be female identified?

Gender theorists usually come from a background in Sociology, but seem to entirely ignore the harder disciplines of Neuropsychology, Endocrinology and the like. The construction of social gender is a very interesting subject but must be overlaid on the substrate of our physical bodies. Even transgenderists who do not wish to have genital reconstruction must acknowledge that physical appearance makes a difference in how well they 'pass'; there is often much competition between trans people of all persuasions about who 'passes' better. Indeed, there are social aspects to 'passing', dress, manner, makeup etc., but physical somatotypes underlie all this. There are psychologists who make convincing cases that there are evolutionarily acquired perceptual recognition patterns which determine how people are perceived as male or female, depending on morphology caused by hormonal developmental influences. Facial feminisation surgeries are now becoming popular with those transsexual women who can afford them as the removal of bone thickening caused by adolescent male hormones, commonly known as 'male markers', facilitates better 'passing' in the desired gender.

It is the case that the argument for not requiring genital surgeries can be traced back to the influence of [******], an FtM man who is a lawyer and who argued that the same criteria should be applied to both directions of reassignment and recognition. This has also been strongly supported by other FtM men, some who have not wished to go through the difficult and unpredictable process of male genital reconstruction. It is my strongly held view that it is inappropriate for an FtM man to recommend or judge what are suitable requirements for MtF women to be recognised as female in terms of surgery or not, since their own circumstances are so diametrically opposite.

He has also been quoted as saying that he was influenced in this decision by the fact that he was assisted in his campaigning in some way by an 'MtF transgender person' who had no wish for genital reconstruction and that he had felt he should reward this person in making it easier for them to acquire female legal recognition.

Such personal favouritism in legal matters is entirely inappropriate and should have had no influence on the matter whatsoever. The very fact that a supposedly eminent lawyer such as [******] could let personal loyalties influence him in this way shows that he is not a suitable person to make recommendations to the government.

The GRA should be a Sex Recognition Act, and there should be objective criteria for what requires 'acquisition' of a particular sex, amounting to hormonal status for both directions and reconstructive requirements appropriate to each sex. If all is required, as appears to be what the GRA amounts to, is to socially reassign, then the law is a laughing stock.

To entirely detach the recognition of what sex someone is from all physical attributes, and to argue that sex is nothing more than a social construction entirely unrelated to reproduction, anatomical morphology and hormonal status debases science into nothing more than a subjective judgement.

To allow non-op MtF transgender people gender recognition certificates on the basis that it is a defence of their rights debases what has been achieved by those of us who have had morphological reconstruction. Now someone who knows that I am transsexual with recognition doesn't automatically have a guarantee that I am morphologically female. It allows for male-bodied people to gain access to lesbian- and women-only space and thus in the long run is counterproductive to the rights of fully reassigned transsexual women, and a possible return to the dark days of trans exclusion from the eighties.

If, as now appears to be the case, gender, or rather sex, is allowed to be an entirely subjective matter, rather than a congruence between mind and body, then anyone can be anything they say, the 'Jeremy Clarkson' postulate as I call it. If physical attributes have nothing to do with sex, and since clothing is largely unisex these days, someone like Jeremy Clarkson can say they are a lesbian and gain access to women's only lesbian space. A logical ad absurdum perhaps, but one that cannot be entirely avoided under the current situation.

I am well aware that my position goes against those held by some gender theorists such as Judith Butler, but in my view her argument verges on sophistry. The strong reliance on psychoanalysis shows the weakness of her position since that school has no basis in objective testing and their postulates are entirely subjective, being as they are completely unfalsifiable. This hypothesis construes gender identity as acquired through experience and identification, rather than as a bodily experience, morphological mapping which is hardwired, as postulated by Ramachandran, who has found supporting evidence, published in the *Journal of Consciousness Studies*, 2008.

We should be working towards a theory of sex and gender which puts sexually dimorphic neural structures at the centre, and congruence of bodily sexual characteristics with them should be the criteria for sex recognition. Social gender characteristics are relevant but must be seen as a thin layer, which overlays and rides on top of much deeper and less mutable structures which are hardwired into our nervous systems. Congruence between all three levels should ideally be sought. To argue that social memes are of more importance than both hardwired neurology and sexual morphology is an attempt to discard the basis on which the whole platform rests.

I am aware that this view is not one which is held by most social gender theorists; however, coming as I do from a background in physiological psychology, I feel it is my duty to ensure that this perspective is included in the research.

The bottom line being that someone who not only has not acquired, but does not even aspire to have the morphology of the desired sex cannot possibly in my view really be considered to be of that sex.

[I have redacted the references to [******] since they are based on private conversations and were originally only intended for Dr Hines and her research assistant.]

APPENDIX F

Radical Transfeminism thread at University College London

June 2015

I INCLUDE BELOW the contents of a webpage which was promoted to subscribers of the CIGS email list on 19 June 2015. Emphasis mine.

Paper abstracts and further details were found at http://london-critical.org/conference. However, the link is no longer active. All names have been redacted. My emphasis throughout.

Conference stream on Radical Transfeminism, London Conference in Critical Thought

Friday 26th/Saturday 27th June [2015]

University College London, anthropology department, 14 Taviton Street, London WC1H 0BW.

Against a backdrop of social gains made by mainstream LGBT movements, the reality of trans* lives (particular for transpersons of colour) continues to be one of material and social struggle, against poverty, deprivation and violence.

While inclusion in existing structures, whether they be social initiatives or current feminisms, is often the focus of the discussion, this stream looks to radicalise the transperspective. This redistribution of emphasis from inclusion in existing centres to the possibility of elaboration from the limits outward, will give the will to create the terrain for alliances, strategies, and politics. We propose to look at points of divergence instead of inclusion, both as means to build practices of solidarity, as well as highlight differences of perspective. By emphasising trans* as an open-ended category without a core, a potential radicalisation of perspective and action, as opposed to erasure, is actualised.

The stream aims to address the social, material and political necessity of transfeminism as a radical and potentially revolutionary sphere of thought and praxis. It will address the importance of a transfeminist critique of the limitations of liberal transgender politics that are being rapidly and unquestioningly taken up across the world. It specifically looks to extend transfeminisms beyond rights discourses, and formulate critiques as evolving practices and theories.

Friday 26 June 9:30–11:00 (room 2/TBC)

1.   The End Times of a Failed Political Myth — openings panel by XXXX XXX XXX XXXXX, XXXXXXX XXXXXX, XXX XXX.

Friday 26 June 13:45–15:15 (room 2/TBC)

2.   Panel: Radical Transfeminist Activism

XXXX XXXXXXXXXXXX — Trans* generational sharing as a form of resistance to normalisation

XXXX XXXXXXXX — I Have No Photo For You — liberal feminism, Germany's Next Top Model and why it doesn't get better

XXXX XXXX — Reclaiming Radical Transfeminism: Time-Travelling Trans* Politics In Neoliberal Times

Respondent: XXXXX XXXXXXXXX

Chair: XXXXX XXX XXX XXXXX

Saturday 27 June 13:30 — 16:30 (Panels will happen with a small break in between) room 6/TBC

3.　　　　Roundtable: Radical Transfeminism in Communities

xxxxx xxxxxxx xxxxx — Sexworker transfeminisms

xxx　xxxxxxxxx — At the margins of margins — the necessity of actual intersectionality and solidarity in transfeminist queer communities

xxxxxx xx xxxxxx & xxxxxx xxxx — The growth and formalisation of radical trans and queer support networks in Brighton, UK

Chair: xxxxxxx xxxxxx

4.　　　　Panel: Theories of Radical Transfeminism

xxxxxxxxx xxxx — Reproducing 'states of injury' on trans* bodies: How does Wendy Brown's concept help to think through the idea of a 'wounded attachment' to the female body in feminism?

xxxxxxx xxxxxxxxxxxxx — Critical Theory, Poststructuralism and the Intersection of Gender and Disability

xxxx xxxxxxxx — The politics of gender variance: a queer materialist critique of identity

Chair: xxx xxxx

GENERAL BIBLIOGRAPHY

HAVE NOT DIRECTEDLY referenced all the works listed below in the text; however, they have all informed my thoughts on this subject and will hopefully do the same for the reader.

Brown, Geoff, *I Want What I Want* (1966), Weidenfeld & Nicholson.

Benjamin, Harry M.D., *The Transsexual Phenomenon* (1966), The Julian Press, Inc., New York.

Fallowell, Duncan & Ashley, April, *April Ashley's Odyssey* (1982), Jonathan Cape, 30 Bedford Square, London WC1.

Jung, Carl Gustav, *Aion* (1959) (second edition, 1991 paperback), Routledge and Kegan Paul, Routledge, 11 New Fetter Lane, London EC4P 4EE.

Jung, C. G., *Psychology and Alchemy* (1968) Collected Works of C. G. Jung, Vol 12, Princeton University Press, Princeton, N.J.

Jung, C. G., *Synchronicity*, (1960) The Collected Works of C. G. Jung, Volume 8 (Book 8), Princeton University Press.

Jorjani, Jason Reza Ph.D., *Prometheus and Atlas* (2016), Arktos, Arktos Media Ltd, London.

Lewis, Clive Staples, *The Abolition of Man* (1943), Oxford University Press.

Lewis, C. S., *Perelandra (Voyage to Venus)* (1943), John Lane (The Bodley Head) Pan Books edition (1983), Cavaye Place, London SW10 9PG.

Morris, Jan., *Conundrum* (1974), Faber & Faber.

Pirsig, Robert M., *Zen and the Art of Motorcycle Maintenance* (1974), The Bodley Head (Corgi 1976).

Raymond, Janice R., *The Transsexual Empire* (1979), Beacon Press, Boston (published in Great Britain by The Women's Press Limited) (1980), a member of the Namara Group, 124 Shoreditch High Street, London E1 6JE).

Sheldrake, R., *The Rebirth of Nature* (1990), Century, an imprint of Random Century Group, 20 Vauxhall Bridge Road, London SW1V 2SA.

Tolkien, J.R.R., *The Fellowship of The Ring* (1954), George Allen & Unwin, Unwin Hyman Ltd., Denmark House, 37–39 Queen Elizabeth Street, London SE1 2QB.

Claire Rae Randall online, https://thewarongender.blogspot.com, https://cosmicclaire.wordpress.com.

OTHER BOOKS PUBLISHED BY ARKTOS

OTHER BOOKS PUBLISHED BY ARKTOS

OTHER BOOKS PUBLISHED BY ARKTOS

OTHER BOOKS PUBLISHED BY ARKTOS

Printed in Great Britain
by Amazon

81117121R00243